RESEARCH IN PARAPSYCHOLOGY 1983

Abstracts and Papers from the
Twenty-sixth Annual Convention of the
Parapsychological Association, 1983

RHEA A. WHITE
and
RICHARD S. BROUGHTON
Editors

The Scarecrow Press, Inc.
Metuchen, N.J., & London
1984

ISBN 0-8108-1695-4
Manufactured in the United States of America
Library of Congress Catalog Card No. 66-28580
Copyright © 1984 by the Parapsychological Association

CONTENTS

Editorial Introduction (Rhea A. White) — vii
Preface: The Twenty-sixth Annual Convention (Richard S. Broughton) — xi

1. Symposium

PSI AND THE NERVOUS SYSTEM (Convener: William G. Roll) — 1

ESP, PK, and Sympathetic Nervous System Activity (William G. Braud) — 1
Brain Hemisphere Specialization and ESP: What Have We Learned? (Richard S. Broughton) — 2
Psi and the Brain (William G. Roll and Elson de A. Montagno) — 4
The Relevance of the Temporal Lobe to Anomalous Subjective Experience (Vernon M. Neppe) — 7
Psi and the Brain Stem (Elson de A. Montagno and William G. Roll) — 10

2. Papers and Research Briefs (RBs), Including Poster Sessions (PSs)

EXPERIMENTAL REPORTS — 14

The Effect of Ganzfeld Stimulation and Feedback in a Clairvoyance Test (RB) (D.J. Bierman, J. Berendsen, C. Koenen, C. Kuipers, J. Louman, and F. Maissan) — 14
Psychokinetic Influence upon Electrodermal Activity (William Braud and Marilyn Schlitz) — 14
Correlated Hemispheric Asymmetry in the Sensory and ESP Processing of Continuous Multiplex Stimuli (Michaeleen Maher) — 18
Psychokinetic Control of Bacterial Mutation (Carroll B. Nash) — 21
Contamination of Free-response ESP Targets: The Greasy Fingers Hypothesis (PS) (John Palmer) — 25
Internal State and Temporal Factors in RNG PK (RB) (John Palmer and Wim Kramer) — 28
A Possible Proximity Effect on Human Physiology:

Similarities to Psi? (RB) (Dean I. Radin and
James L. Collymore) ... 30
Relationships Between Participant Traits and Scores
on Two Computer-controlled RNG-PK Games (RB/PS)
(Ephraim I. Schechter, Charles Honorton, Pat Barker,
and Mario P. Varvoglis) ... 32
Channeling Psi to Critical Observers (RB) (Helmut
Schmidt, Robert Morris, and Luther Rudolph) ... 33
The Role of Noise and the Trait of Absorption in
Ganzfeld ESP Performance: The Application of
Methods Based upon Signal Detection Theory
(Rex G. Stanford and Raymond F. Angelini) ... 35

THEORETICAL, METHODOLOGICAL, AND REVIEW
ARTICLES ... 39

Parapsychology and Radical Dualism (John Beloff) ... 39
Birth and the OBE: An Unhelpful Analogy (RB)
(Susan J. Blackmore) ... 42
Against Historicism (Gerd H. Hövelmann) ... 44
Neal Miller's Rats: A Case Suggestive of the Decline
Effect Outside of the Field of Parapsychology (RB)
(Michael K. McBeath) ... 47
Hypnotic Induction vs. Control Conditions: Illustrating
an Approach to the Evaluation of Replicability in
Parapsychological Data (Ephraim I. Schechter) ... 49
Motivation as the Universal Container: Conceptual
Problems in Parapsychology (Debra H. Weiner) ... 52

SURVEYS ... 57

A Postal Survey of OBEs and Other Experiences (PS)
(Susan J. Blackmore) ... 57
A Survey of Organizations in Parapsychology and
Peripheral Areas (RB/PS) (Laura F. Knipe and
Nancy K. Nybergh) ... 61
A Retrospective Search for Correlates of Belief in
Life-After-Death. I. Icelandic Data (Michael A.
Thalbourne and Erlendur Haraldsson) ... 62
Varieties of Belief in Survival: An Exploratory Study
(RB/PS) (Michael A. Thalbourne and Linda
Williams) ... 66

SPONTANEOUS PSI / FIELD STUDIES ... 68

Characteristics of Purposeful Action in an Apparition
Case (Karlis Osis) ... 68
A Majority-Vote Study of Impressions Relating to a
Criminal Investigation (PS) (William G. Roll and
Roger C. Grimson) ... 72
Spontaneous Precognitive Dreams: A Decline with
Temporal Distance (Nancy Sondow) ... 75

3. Interim Reports

EXPERIMENTAL REPORTS ... 78

Free-Response GESP Performance During Ganzfeld Stimulation (RB/PS) (Lendell Williams Braud, Lawrence Ackles, and Willie Kyles) ... 78
Signal-processing Considerations in Random-number Generator Design and Application (RB/PS) (Robert J. Chevako) ... 80
Independent Confirmation of Infrared Healer Effects (RB) (Bernard Grad and Douglas Dean) ... 81
Differential Micro-PK Effects Among Afro-Brazilian Umbanda Cultists Using Trance-Significant Symbols as Targets (RB) (Patric V. Giesler) ... 83
The Effect of the Presence of an Agent on ESP Performance and of the Isolation of the Target from its Controls on Displacement in a Ganzfeld Clairvoyance Experiment (RB) (Julie Milton) ... 85
A Psychokinesis Experiment with a Random Mechanical Cascade (Roger D. Nelson, Brenda J. Dunne, and Robert G. Jahn) ... 86
Metabolic Types and Psi: A Study of Oxidizer Type and ESP Test Scores (Joyce G. Ruiz) ... 89
A Second Study with the "Psi Ball" RNG-PK Game (RB/PS) (Ephraim I. Schechter, Pat Barker, and Mario P. Varvoglis) ... 93
Field and Stream (RB) (Gertrude R. Schmeidler) ... 94
Superposition of PK Efforts by Man and Dog (RB) (Helmut Schmidt) ... 96
Target Preference as a Modulator of ESP Scores When the Targets Are Cross-Sex or Same-Sex Names (RB) (Kathleen Streber and Gertrude R. Schmeidler) ... 98
Computer-based Long Distance ESP: An Exploratory Examination (RB/PS) (William Tedder) ... 100
The Use of Fantasy in a Children's ESP Experiment (RB) (Rosemarie Pilkington Tornatore) ... 102

QUALITATIVE AND FIELD STUDIES ... 104

Experiments with False Keys that Suggest One More Condition for Excellent Survival Evidence (Arthur S. Berger) ... 104
Selected Static-PK Phenomena Under Exceptional Conditions of Security (William Edward Cox) ... 107
The Happy Princess: Psychological Profile of a Psychic (Joan Healy) ... 111
Thomasville Haunting (RB) (William G. Roll and Barbara Brittain) ... 114

4. Roundtables

THE POLTERGEIST AGENT: FACT OR FICTION?
(Convener: D. Scott Rogo)   117

Psychological Evaluations of Poltergeist Agents:
A Critique (Carlos S. Alvarado)   117
The Psychopathological and the Psychophysiological
Theories of the RSPK Agent (William G. Roll)   118
Pathology and the Poltergeist: Notes on a Proposed
Validation (D. Scott Rogo)   119

THE ROLE OF CONJURORS IN PSYCHICAL RESEARCH AND PARAPSYCHOLOGY (Convener: Marcello Truzzi)   120

(Participants: Loyd Auerbach, Robert E. Cassidy, Milbourne Christopher, Scott Gordon, Jack Malon, James Randi, Anthony Raven)
Summary by Marcello Truzzi

NONLINEAR THINKING IN PARAPSYCHOLOGY
(Convener: Daniel J. Benor)   122

Nonlinear Thinking in Parapsychology (Daniel J. Benor)   122
Acausal World Views and Shamanic Healing Models
(Stanley Krippner)   123
Research Models for Human Sciences (Lawrence LeShan)   125
Linear Research for Any Kind of Thinking (Gertrude R. Schmeidler)   126

5. Invited Addresses

On the Representation of Psi Research to the Community
of Established Science (Robert G. Jahn)   127
Dream, Metaphor, and Psi (Montague Ullman)   138

6. Presidential Address

A Systems Approach to Psi Research Based on Jungian
Typology (Stanley Krippner)   153

Errata   167

Name Index (Emily Williams Cook)   169

Subject Index (Emily Williams Cook)   173

EDITORIAL INTRODUCTION

The first of what may be many changes in RIP format has been instituted with this volume in response to suggestions and criticisms of individual PA members, including Council members. At the PA convention business meeting there was a lively discussion about the purpose and function of RIP. Some members favored abandoning it altogether because its present format does not provide sufficient space to describe essential details, nor are the abstracts refereed. These members argued that at present some papers in RIP make a bad impression on scientists in other fields and on serious students who want to learn about parapsychology. Moreover, many PA convention participants are content to simply publish their abstracts in RIP rather than seek to publish the full papers in the major refereed parapsychological journals. In response to the latter criticism, some favored publishing only brief abstracts in RIP. Other members felt that only the very best work should be presented at the convention and thus be reported in RIP, in order to present our research to others in the best possible light. This was countered by those who felt that the most important function of the convention is to provide a forum for discussion among parapsychologists of their research at all stages.

This discussion is by no means ended. But in the meantime, this year's RIP must go to press. In a first effort to respond to one of the criticisms aired at the convention, in RIP 1983 we are differentiating between papers that represent work that has reached some stage of completion and those studies that are still exploratory or at an early developmental stage. We are doing this by changing the arrangement of abstracts of papers and research briefs (including poster session abstracts). These will be grouped in two categories: Papers and Research Briefs, and Interim Studies. The former will consist of work that has reached a stage of completion, whereas the latter will consist of abstracts of papers and research briefs reporting work that is exploratory or still in progress. We would like to emphasize that this new arrangement is itself decidedly provisional and exploratory, and we welcome constructive criticisms and suggestions from PA members concerning it or in regard to other possible formats.

The new arrangement will supersede the old way of grouping abstracts, which were listed primarily in the same order in which they were given at the convention. In this volume the abstracts in the two new sections will be listed alphabetically under major subject categories by the name of the first author. These broad subject groupings do not reflect the arrangement of the papers as given at the convention, but rather have been devised solely for the purpose of grouping like papers in RIP.

Because of this new arrangement the session chairpersons for papers and research briefs cannot be listed with the abstracts, as was formerly the case. Therefore we would like to acknowledge the services performed by the following persons who chaired paper and research-brief sessions: Stephen Braude, Richard Broughton, Hoyt Edge, Charles Honorton, Robert Morris, Karlis Osis, John Palmer, Diana Robinson, Frank Tribbe, and Rhea White.

I close with an observation to be taken into consideration in the continuing debate about RIP format. The determination concerning the quality of work represented in RIP is the responsibility of the Program Committee, so that discussion of what to include in RIP revolves around what is selected for presentation at the convention. The papers that are chosen have undergone at least a partial refereeing process at the hands of the members of the Program Committee. As for full publication, it is the responsibility of the authors of the best papers to submit them to the field's refereed journals, and also the responsibility of the journal editors of those journals to solicit high-quality convention papers for publication in their journals. (A possible solution to this problem is to have the PA publish a refereed journal to which the full papers submitted for presentation at the PA convention could be submitted as soon as accepted by the Program Committee.) The function of RIP, on the other hand, is to provide a bird's-eye view of what active parapsychologists are investigating and thinking in a given year. What were the topics and activities in which we saw fit to engage during the year prior to the convention? That is what we present at our conventions, and that is what the proceedings of that convention should reflect. Having such a mirror performs a useful function both for those within the field and for those outside. If we don't like the picture we see, we can change it.

That brings us back to the first order of business, which is not so much RIP format as it is the question of what should be presented at our annual convention. Richard Broughton eloquently presented the philosophy of this year's Program Committee in a thoughtful introduction to a session he chaired. Because it also reflects my viewpoint and is relevant to the present discussion, I close by quoting it in full:

> One of the big difficulties I had in chairing the Program Committee was in trying to determine just what is the purpose of our annual convention. The idea which finally seemed to fit is that our convention is nothing more than that opportunity we have to gather with our colleagues and discuss what we have been doing--the one principal time each year which we have to help one another by criticizing weaknesses, suggesting improvements,

taking pride in successes, and learning from failures. One thing our convention is _not_ is a showcase for only our most perfect pieces of research. That function lies elsewhere. Our convention is a meeting put on by parapsychologists for parapsychologists.

In thinking about this, I became sensitive to the possibility that our field, in its zeal to win the approval of some scientists and certain members of the entertainment profession, was running the risk of losing that very aspect of self-help and self-criticism that has contributed to our strength and that has brought us back on track when we seemed to go astray.

I and my committee are of the opinion that preserving that spirit of free and open discussion and debate on controversial topics which has characterized our science throughout its 100-year history will better serve our long-term goals as a science than will any short-term effort to cover over research which may make some of us uncomfortable.

Broughton has performed an important service in pointing out that what is at stake in this discussion is broader than simply the format of _RIP_ or even the choice of what to present at the convention. The answers to these questions implicate our research methodology itself.

                                    Rhea A. White
                                    Editor

PREFACE:
THE TWENTY-SIXTH ANNUAL CONVENTION

The verdant campus of Fairleigh Dickinson University in Madison, New Jersey, was the site of the 1983 convention of the Parapsychological Association. Richard Broughton chaired the Program Committee, which included Gertrude Schmeidler and Michael Thalbourne. Laura Knipe and Donna McCormick handled the arrangements for the affair. Attendance was modest in comparison with recent American conferences with 126 persons participating. Of these 71 were members or associates of the PA.

With four full days of presentations and a smaller than usual number of submissions the Program Committee was able to allot generous amounts of discussion time for papers and briefs. This provided an opportunity to present a program representing a diversity of approaches to psi research and to expose these to discussion and debate by convention participants. Poster sessions, which previously had met with mixed success, were put on a firm footing, thanks to the efforts of the presenters who offered engaging and informative displays of their material.

Rounding out the submitted agenda of the convention were one symposium and three roundtable discussions, one of which provided a high point of the convention when eight prominent members of the magic profession were invited to give their views on the role of conjurors in psi research.

Invited addresses were again a feature of the convention with stimulating talks by Robert Jahn of Princeton University and Montague Ullman. Thomas Budzynki delivered the J. B. Rhine Address, entitled "Clinical Applications of a Brain Lateralization Model." The Presidential Address was given by Stanley Krippner who spoke on "A Systems Approach to Psi Research Based on Jungian Typology."

Several workshops, a mildly satirical revue, and an active social schedule characterized the evening activities, all contributing to a convention which will be remembered for some time to come.

> Richard S. Broughton
> Chairperson
> Program Committee

Part 1: Symposium

PSI AND THE NERVOUS SYSTEM*

ESP, PK, AND SYMPATHETIC NERVOUS SYSTEM ACTIVITY

William G. Braud (Mind Science Foundation)

There is rather good evidence that ESP is facilitated by the presence of <u>decreased</u> sympathetic nervous system activation in the percipient (<u>JASPR,</u> 1981, 1-35). Evidence for this conclusion comes from three sources. First, processes similar to ESP--such as broadened attention, "primary process" ideation, and subliminal perception--are facilitated by low sympathetic arousal. Second, psi-conducive conditions--such as meditation, induced relaxation, Ganzfeld stimulation, and extraversion--are accompanied by reduced sympathetic arousal. Third, of 12 direct studies of the correlation of psi scoring with arousal level, nine studies yielded significantly higher psi scores for low sympathetic arousal conditions; three studies yielded no significant psi-arousal relationship; and no study found higher arousal to facilitate psi.

For PK, on the other hand, the evidence, although extremely sparse, at least suggests that PK effects may be facilitated by <u>increased</u> sympathetic activation of the influencer. The emerging characterization of the poltergeist focal person as one in whom strong emotions are being actively suppressed is not inconsistent with the hypothesis of heightened sympathetic arousal in the PK "agent." During micro-PK metal bending experiments using strain gauges and piezoelectric crystal detectors, Isaacs has reported that bursts of ostensible PK appear to accompany brief, explosive emotional outbursts on the part of his subjects, suggesting the involvement of phasic sympathetic activation. The physical, and ostensibly psychokinetic, manifestations during meetings of such sitter groups as those of Batcheldor and the "Philip" group tended to occur not during quiet, meditative sittings likely to be characterized by sympathetic deactivation, but rather during the more lively, light-hearted, jovial sessions likely to be accompanied by sympathetic

---
*Organized and chaired by William G. Roll (Psychical Research Foundation).

activation. Some physical mediums (Palladino, Rudi Schneider, Kulagina, Parise, and Serios, for example) were often reported to exhibit signs of increased sympathetic activation during the production of their phenomena. The most striking and most consistent effect was a dramatic increase in heart rate.

In better controlled experimental contexts, the facilitation of PK scoring by caffeine (JP, 1945, 32-41) and induced muscle tension (JASPR, 1972, 208-214) is an indirect indication of sympathetic enhancement. Dierkens (in B. Shapin and L. Coly [Eds.], Psi and States of Awareness, 1978, 152-166) reported that an increase in heart rate immediately preceded each successful episode of metal-bending PK in Girard; such tachycardia did not occur when PK attempts failed or were simulated. Hill has reported a similar effect in the PK subject Silvio. Watkins, et al. (RIP 1972, 157-159) reported that during successful anesthetized mouse resuscitation PK attempts, their subjects showed significantly increased heart rate, respiration rate, respiration irregularity, muscle tension, EEG occipital alpha blocking, and decreased pulse amplitude. Houtkooper and DeDiana (EJP, 1977, 68-72) reported heart rate increased and heart rate variability decreased during Matthew Manning's PK attempts.

We might tentatively hypothesize a relationship between PK success and sympathetic activation. However, we should not overlook the possibility that sympathetic arousal and effort itself may be a superstitious ritual with no real PK efficacy. Such a ritual may be a generalization of the usually increased efficacy of increased activation and striving in the realm of conventional effector processes, a form of imitation of other successful PK subjects, or even a way of occupying parts of the brain so that other brain or mental processes can proceed without impediment. Increased activation may simply reflect the increased excitement of attempting to perform PK or of being in the spotlight of others' attention during those attempts. It should be kept in mind that PK has occurred under relatively effortless conditions in which sympathetic activation is unlikely (EJP, 1978, 137-162).

BRAIN HEMISPHERE SPECIALIZATION AND ESP: WHAT HAVE WE LEARNED?

Richard S. Broughton (Institute for Parapsychology, FRNM)

Serious interest in the relationship between the specialized capacities of the brain hemispheres and ESP dates back to the last century when Myers examined graphic automatism (PSPR, 1885, 1-63). For the most part, active experimentation in this area has been underway only since the early 1970s although Broughton (JSPR, 1975, 133-147) has noted that evidence suggesting a special role for the right hemisphere can be found in the literature for several decades.

Two views have characterized the several experimental approaches to ESP and hemisphere specialization reported to date. One position basically holds that the evidence suggests either that the right hemisphere has a special facility for ESP or that ESP information is of a type that favors the right hemisphere. The other position is that there is no reason to expect a right hemisphere advantage for ESP and that psi information is processed in the same way as sensory information. The latter position is tied to a signal transmission model of ESP while the former can additionally be of interest to PK-based theories of ESP because of the observed physical differences between the hemispheres.

Exemplifying the first approach, Braud and Braud (RIP 1974, 17-20) were the first to report work in this area. This experiment provided weak support for a right hemisphere advantage but because there is reason to suspect that the experimental manipulation was not effective this interpretation must be regarded as tentative.

Broughton (JSPR, 1976, 384-399; RIP 1976, 86-88) reported an extended series of experiments which suggested a right hemisphere advantage for ESP; more importantly, it provided evidence that occupying the left hemisphere somehow permitted more successful ESP performance. Furthermore, this finding exhibited a strong gender difference which agreed with findings in cognitive research. Broughton has reported difficulty in replicating this work, however, and the robustness of these findings is yet to be confirmed.

Representing the second position, Maher and her colleagues have reported two experiments (Maher and Schmeidler, JASPR, 1977, 261-271; Maher et al., JASPR, 1979, 167-177) attempting to demonstrate no general hemisphere advantage for ESP. The first experiment provided limited support for their interpretation that the hemispheres process ESP as they would sensory material. This interpretation must be qualified by the fact that the tasks used were arguably less hemisphere specific than they should have been to support the experimental design. Gender differences in the effect conforming to cognitive findings were also noted in the data. The second experiment largely failed to replicate the first, though the authors still claimed some support for their hypothesis.

As for the question posed in the title, the most salient fact to emerge is that it is not easy to conduct careful investigations of hemisphere differences. Two principal views of hemisphere interaction with ESP have evolved and proponents of each have made some clever attempts to support their positions. For a variety of reasons none of the evidence is very compelling so far. Both views merit further investigation.

The decade during which parapsychologists have been working in this area has seen a shift in emphasis for hemisphere specialization research in general. The popular tendency to dichotomize abilities in the hemispheres has given way to a more fruitful search for the ways in which the hemispheres cooperate in the generation of consciousness. My interpretation of the parapsychological evidence is that we are not likely to be successful in trying to determine whether ESP resides in one or both hemispheres, at least not with our present knowledge of psi. We may, however, profitably use current findings regarding the interactions between the hemispheres and the assignment of attentional priorities to help in understanding why we find ESP evidence where we do.

PSI AND THE BRAIN*

William G. Roll[†] and Elson de A. Montagno (Psychical Research
 Foundation)

As knowledge about the brain has accumulated, an increasing number of psychological conditions have been related to brain processes. The same promises to hold true for parapsychological findings. Relating psi to neuronal processes may give us new opportunities to understand and control psi.

The Cortex and Temporal Lobes. Penfield's evocation of memories by electrical stimulation of the cortex of epileptic patients suggests that the temporal lobes may be involved in ESP since ESP responses appear to be limited to the respondent's experiential record (Roll, Int. Jnl. Neuropsychiatry, 1966, 505-521). Specific information, such as foreign language phrasing by cross-correspondence mediums, occurred only in conjunction with the automatist's knowledge of that language (Saltmarsh, Evidence of Personal Survival from Cross-correspondences, 1938). Further, ESP and PK responses seem to follow individual and situational coding functions of the cortex. Subjects tend to respond in accordance with their preferred cognitive styles; e.g., Irwin (JP, 1979, 205-220) found persons who favor visual over verbal response to behave accordingly during ESP. Stanford (JASPR, 1969, 338-351) noted positive correlations between PK scores and the subject's preferred way of relating to the target, either visually or verbally.

The coding processes of the brain also differ situationally. L. E. Rhine (JP, 1954, 93-123) and S. A. Schouten (EJP, 1979, 408-454; EJP, 1981, 9-48) found daytime ESP responses to be predominantly intuitive, and night responses to come as (dream) images.

A pair of structures in the medial temporal lobes, the hippocampi, which control long-term memory, may also be important

---

*This work made possible by the support of Ms. Alta Barnes.

for ESP. Serial learning trials in a person with functioning hippocampi are likely to produce the V or U curves often found in serial ESP tests, while damage to the hippocampi may produce amnesia for new information and disrupt the primacy component of the curve. If ESP is linked to long-term memory we may expect that damage to the hippocampi may affect ESP performance.

Macro-PK effects sometimes seem to reflect sensory input to the cortex or motor activity of the body. In a Swedish RSPK case (Bjerre, Spökerier, 1947) the first RSPK incidents were knocking sounds which mirrored normal knocks on the door that had just startled the agent; in a Russian (Leaf, PSPR, 1896-97, 319-330) and a British (Barrett, On the Threshold of the Unseen, 1918) case, raps kept time, respectively, with singing and piano playing. In our own Olive Hill case (Roll, The Poltergeist, 1972), Roger was observed crossing his legs at the same time a chair next to him turned upside down. Parise (Watkins and Watkins, RIP 1973, 132-134) and Kulagina (Pratt, RIP 1973, 54-57) used forceful gestures to induce movements of objects they were affecting. It appears that cortical instructions to specific muscles may be partially diverted, perhaps in the reticular formation which runs up through the brain stem and controls brain-body interactions.

When the overt activities of the RSPK agent are not reflected in the incidents (which is true most of the time), we can sometimes infer that these reflect the emotions and mentation of the person. For instance, in the Lessing case (Roll, JASPR, 1968, 263-308), the bottles which were loosing their screw caps with explosive sounds seemed suggestive of the images of bombers and rockets Michael saw in the Rorschach cards.

The Limbic System. Consciousness is associated with the brain stem, the core of the limbic system. The system deals with the experience and expression of emotion and with instinctual behaviors which help to preserve the individual and the species. Information flows from the sense organs to the brain stem and then to the cortex, and from the cortex to the brain stem and then to the body.

Above the brain stem and below the cortex lies the hypothalamus. This structure regulates the sympathetic and the parasympathetic autonomic nervous systems. The sympathetic system accelerates the heart and lungs and dominates under stress; the parasympathetic system puts a brake on heart and lung activity and dominates during relaxation. Parasympathetic activation may be ESP conducive and sympathetic activation PK conducive, or at least conducive to macro-PK.

In connection with the former, studies by Rhine (JP, 1954, 93-123) and Schouten (EJP, 1981, 9-48) reveal that 51.5% to 59% of the ESP occurrences from these collections were linked to dream or relaxation states. Schouten suggests that decreased sensory input may facilitate ESP (EJP, 1979, 428). White (JASPR, 1964, 21-56) concludes from her survey of older experimental studies that "complete relaxation" was an essential requirement, and Palmer (in Advances in Parapsychological Research: 3, 1982, 41-82), in a survey of contemporary studies, found that hypnosis--the induction of which usually emphasizes relaxation--has been the most effective technique for enhancing ESP. Braud (JASPR, 1981, 1-35) proposes that ESP deactivates the sympathetic system and shifts brain function to limbic midbrain structures which are more sensitive to psi "signals." Central arousal remains to the extent of attuning psi-sensitive "vehicles," a notion consistent with the evidence: ESP dreams suggest central nervous system arousal and, as Ullman (Proceedings of the PA, 1966, 35-60) puts it, an aspect of "vigilance." In general, ESP activity seems consistent with limbic characteristics; emotionally significant events are more often involved than trivial ones and close relatives and friends more often draw responses than distant ones (Schouten, EJP, 1979, 408-454; EJP, 1981, 9-48).

Contrarily, RSPK may involve sympathetic dominance. RSPK agents are usually awake and active when the incidents occur and may also be aroused, frustrated and tense (Roll, in Wolman Handbook, 1977, 382-411). Experimental studies of macro-PK point in the same direction. Heightened arousal associated with macro physical effects has been observed by such well-known agents as Rudi Schneider (Gregory, Parapsychology Review, 1982, 13-18), Jean-Paul Girard (Dierkens, Psi and States of Awareness, 1978) and Nina Kulagina (Ullman, RIP 1973, 121-125).

We have suggested (this volume 10-13) that RSPK may involve disturbances in the limbic system. A limbic structure, the amygdala, is associated with rage and aggression. Epileptic foci experimentally induced in the amygdalae of rats increases aggressive behavior and its removal in humans makes violent epileptics docile. Could such procedures also impact on a person's capability for PK?

A feature of RSPK which may point to its etiology in brain functions is the juxtapositioning of RSPK effects with medical symptoms. One example is our investigation of Peter (Solfvin and Roll, RIP 1975, 115-120), an epileptic around whom RSPK incidents abated during periods of seizures. Structures exist in the brain stem which determine how brain activities are expressed by the body. In RSPK, neural discharges which usually result in somatic disorders may be diverted within these structures to seek other forms of release.

Of all brain structures, the reticular formation is of special importance because of its role in sustaining consciousness. Neural pathways in this area affect the circadian rhythm. The reticular formation (and other neural structures) may play a key role in dissociative states, and may thereby influence such personality constructs as extraversion, a characteristic linked more closely to ESP than other traits (Kanthamani and Rao, JP, 1972, 198-212). Schmeidler (in Advances in Parapsychological Research: 3, 1982, 83-114) links dissociation with extraversion and proposes that extraversion inhibits the convergence of memory and sensory inputs, thereby enabling the person to respond more freely to the present situation, including environmental psi cues.

In summary, a neurophysiological orientation may increase our understanding and control of psi. This approach holds new implications for research: for example, replication may best be attempted with an eye toward circadian timetables; attention should be paid to factors which reinforce the seemingly different autonomic underpinnings of ESP and PK. Most of all, we need to realize that the human brain is an emotional brain. An especially promising line of research is the exploration of the possible relationship of strong psi to brain anomalies. If medical symptoms can be substituted by psychic interactions, this may point to new therapeutic procedures. Finally, such research may throw light on the survival issue since the psi abilities of persons involved are sometimes expressed as apparent interactions with deceased individuals. We discuss some observations of "mediums" in our second paper in this symposium (this volume, 10-13).

THE RELEVANCE OF THE TEMPORAL LOBE TO ANOMALOUS SUBJECTIVE EXPERIENCE

Vernon M. Neppe (South African Society for Psychical Research)

Despite many attempted psychophysiological correlations of psi, the role of the temporal lobes has been peculiarly neglected other than in South African research. This is surprising as, theoretically, the temporal lobe is the prime integrator of polymodal perceptual input, with the consequence that it could involve the site of integration of psi, be involved in the distortions that so often appear to occur in spontaneous psi, or, in fact, be the origin of the peculiar experiences that are interpreted as psi which would then be regarded purely as a biophysiochemical phenomenon. The temporal lobe is theoretically possibly a better candidate for psi than any other area of the cerebrum, and could be argued to be a potentially more valuable area to focus on than the nondominant cerebral hemisphere. This is so because the research on the latter is somewhat intangible.

The first important work in the area was that of Gordon Nelson in 1970 (Parapsychologica, No. 9, 30-35). He examined 12 trance mediums, finding evidence of anomalous temporal lobe activity in the electroencephalograms (EEGS) of ten. His study was uncontrolled, and his figures may reflect a bias because temporal lobe accentuation on EEG may occur nonspecifically relating to fatigue, hypoglycemia, psychopathology, age, and brain immaturity; and the incidence of such accentuations was 25% (N = 244) in "normal males" evaluated in the same laboratory. Using stricter criteria, five subjects would nevertheless still have temporal lobe foci (Neppe, JASPR, 1983).

Neppe attempted a more definitive clinical study from 1979 onwards (JASPR, 1983). He had informally found that several of his patients with dysfunction of their temporal lobes claimed vivid "psychic" experiences and took advantage of a useful clinical fact: whereas the other lobes of the cerebrum produced signs (i.e., features which must be elicited on examinations), temporal lobe dysfunction involves predominantly symptoms (i.e., data about peculiar subjective experiences elicited on history). On the basis of this, Neppe was able to develop a measuring instrument, "Neppe's Temporal Lobe Questionnaire" (NTLQ). This elicited descriptions of "possible temporal lobe symptoms" (PTLSs) such as olfactory hallucinations as well as more nonspecific symptoms, e.g., depersonalization. Both groups of symptoms are found in temporal lobe dysfunction. To qualify as a "possible temporal lobe symptom" such a feature is required to be elicitable by stimulating areas of the temporal lobe during brain surgery, and also not to occur often clinically in other conditions. The phrase "possible" is used as one cannot prove for certain that such subjective experience derives from the temporal lobe. This clinical research allowed the usage of two comparative groups for which rigid criteria were laid down: one of nonprofessional "psychics" (i.e., Subjective Paranormal Experients) and a second of a "control" group (i.e., Subjective Paranormal Non-Experients) from the same population who denied any subjective paranormal experiences. Results were both statistically and substantively significant despite a small sample (N = 12; 6 per group). The Experients had a mean of 6.2 different PLTSs, the Non-Experients 0.3. Excluding those during altered states of consciousness (e.g., meditation), the means are 6.2 and 0 respectively. The complete absence of PTLSs in the Non-Experients during clear consciousness was fully expected and almost certainly reflects the normal population--one doesn't expect anyone to have any such PTLSs.

These results of 37 different kinds of PTLSs with a range of 2 through 11 per subject in the Experients are truly remarkable. One possibility was that the Experients' SPEs resembled PTLSs. For example, a "chilly feeling with a sense of an apparition" would have been classified as a PTLS--a "thermal hallucination." Eliminating the 17 PTLSs occurring with SPEs (range one to four PTLSs of different kinds per subject), there were still PTLSs occurring (in all Experients) at a significant level. Moreover, one of the Experients happened to have been diagnosed as a Temporal Lobe Epileptic. Even if she were eliminated, results are still statistically significant.

What do these results mean? Briefly, the occurrences together of PTLSs with SPEs may imply anatomicophysiological continuity. Also, the independent existence of PTLSs with SPEs in Experients may imply that they are not artefacts of their SPEs. The susceptibility to such PTLSs may be arising because of the background "trait" of anomalous temporal lobe functioning in

Subjective Paranormal Experients. Their occurrence with SPEs may imply that a momentary "state" of temporal lobe activity sometimes is associated with SPEs. If these results reflect genuine psi experience, then the temporal lobe becomes the prime organ suspect for possible mind-brain interaction. This extreme speculation is not necessarily so. The association may relate to integration of psi experience via pathways in the temporal lobe.

One possible explanation is that some of those PTLSs that appear to be of temporal lobe origin, in fact, have quite different sources. Inter alia, because of this possibility, the most common PTLS found, namely anomalies of smell (i.e., olfactory hallucinations), was examined by extending the sample (N = 17) and examining such a symptom in detail. The author found that the "smell hallucination" that Experients consistently have is perfumy and flowery in quality and experienced as pleasant. These hallucinations are invariably associated with the impression of a "presence" of someone unseen and are sometimes experienced by others present at the same time. Pleasant olfactory hallucinations, in contrast, were found to be (and are also known to be) rare in patients with temporal lobe epilepsy and nonepileptic temporal lobe dysfunction. Instead, the temporal lobe epileptic generally encounters unpleasant, rotting, or burning smells. The author found such smells also occurred commonly in the Subjective Paranormal Experient. A single conclusion for these results is impossible, but an intensive analysis of results in the Experients suggests that it is very difficult to explain them solely on the basis of fraud, temporal lobe firing, common personality and sociocultural features, and that such results could possibly reflect genuine paranormal causes. If it does, it strengthens the possibility that the results found in the Subjective Paranormal Experients may be genuine pointers of their "psi" abilities. Moreover, the occurrence of smell hallucinations similar to those found in temporal lobe disorder may reflect the anomalous (not necessarily abnormal--just different) temporal lobe functioning found in the paragnost.

This raises the possibility that subjects with temporal lobe dysfunction could be useful in screening out genuine paragnosts. Such a study has not yet been undertaken, but Hurst and the author have described two families with ostensible psi abilities and also temporal lobe dysfunctions. Thus, there is also a genetic or at least familial facet that is worthy of further study (Neppe and Hurst, Parapsychological Journal of South Africa, 1981, 35-64).

Finally, déjà-vu research may be relevant as it was for a long time regarded as symptomatic of temporal lobe epilepsy. The author has shown, that, in fact, the "symptom" of déjà vu on its own is nonspecific and actually quite normal and very common. Also, there is a specific quality of the déjà-vu experience in the temporal lobe epileptic. This does not occur in the nonepileptic nor in those with epilepsy not deriving from the temporal lobes. Moreover, the Subjective Paranormal Experient does not have the same kind of déjà-vu experience. Neppe's research has shown that there is a special qualitatively distinct kind of "Subjective Paranormal Déjà Vu" distinct to this group. This implies possibly that the causes of their déjà-vu experiences are quite different. Thus, again here, symptoms having apparent temporal lobe associations may, in fact, be reflecting something different (Neppe, The Psychology of Déjà Vu, Witwatersrand University Press, 1983).

The limited research discussed above should be interpreted cautiously. Nevertheless, it appears that PTLSs are overwhelmingly more common in Subjective Paranormal Experients, and that it is highly probable that these symptoms reflect a pattern of anomalous temporal lobe functioning which is either present all the time or is at certain points accentuated, allowing SPEs to be interpreted as occurring. It appears, too, that the Experient has his or her own special PTLSs, which are different. This may imply slight anatomico-physiological differences, or it may imply that experiencing them is being integrated by the temporal lobe in a different way. Alternatively, the different temporal lobe activity may just be one of several "minus" functions or a reflection of an unusual holographic picture of the paragnost's brain such that the Bergsonian filter or other such critical mechanism is by-passed, allowing SPEs to occur. Replication should, however, involve researchers adequately trained in the application of the NTLQ.

Most important, however, is that these findings neither prove nor disprove the veridicality of the subjects' experiences (Neppe, JASPR, 1983). All their SPEs may have derived endogenously in the brain, or the temporal lobe alone, or with other parts of the brain, allowing the experience of a greater perceptual reality of which most of the population may perceive but a glimpse, or not at all, in their lifetime.

PSI AND THE BRAIN STEM*

Elson de A. Montagno and William G. Roll[†] (Psychical Research Foundation)

In 1971 E.M. met Mrs. L.P., who provided extraordinary evidence of psi gamma during informal interactions. The following years were marked by closer acquaintance with the medium which involved medical care. She used to have edema of her ankles and feet which caused pain and discomfort. Medication for the symptoms did not give her satisfactory relief. Her general state of health was evaluated by physicians who found no organic cause. A cardiologist and expert in psychosomatic medicine opted for the

---

*This research was made possible by the support of Charles and Irma Hooks.

diagnosis of "functional disorder" since he did not find anything wrong with her kidneys or heart.

Mrs. L. P. had alleged healing abilities, and E. M. asked her why she did not manage to heal her own disorder. She replied, "My gift is associated with my suffering."

It seems possible that her complaints were due to water retention caused by a borderline Syndrome of Inadequate Anti-Diuretic Hormone (SIADH). ADH under ordinary conditions is released in larger amounts during stress, thereby causing water retention in the body and also improved memory function. Both processes have survival value since fight or flight situations may not allow for ingestion or elimination of water, and since optimal learning and memory functions are at a premium in such situations.

More recently our interaction with two other psi sensitives has raised the possibility in our minds that ADH may be associated with psi-gamma ability.

S. G., a 31-year-old housewife with two young children, 13 years ago started having discomfort and sharp pain in the hypogastric area. At the time she was pregnant and the problems continued after the delivery. After her delivery, close medical attention revealed water retention of uncertain origin (idiopathic). About that time she became aware of apparent psi sensitivity and attempted to develop this. The water retention became more severe and seemed to parallel her mediumistic development. A psychometry study with S. G. reported at SERPA earlier this year gave significant results (Huegel, Goodrum, and Roll, *JP*, in press).

Relating S. G.'s condition to her apparent psychic sensitivity we speculate that the latter may be related to overproduction of ADH. S. G. has not suffered either from heart or kidney disease, so it seems possible that the water retention is due to conditions in the central nervous system. This interpretation is consistent with S. G.'s claim that she has "an excellent memory."

During a series of mediumistic experiments with A. G., a professional medium, A. G. felt the first sitter to be unresponsive and expressed annoyance. Later that day A. G. complained of pain in her feet. E. M. made an examination and discovered she had edema in her legs, a sign of water retention. A. G. observed that she had not passed water for several hours but denied any history of heart or kidney problems. E. M. therefore prescribed furosemide, 80 mg., a potent diuretic. This relieved her condition but not to the extent expected. E. M. therefore suspected that the cause might be ADH since the secretion is augmented during stress, causing water retention. A. G. has shown evidence of psi gamma in tests we are now preparing for publication. In one of our studies she also produced bending of a fork under direct observation without touching the area where the bend occurred.

Twenty years ago Alain Assailly (International Journal of Parapsychology, 1963, 357-375) made two observations of particular relevance to our discussion, namely, that mediums a) display "a rather exceptional power of memory" (p. 359) and b) often show retention of water. Assailly noted that ADH plays a role in water retention, but at that time the effect of this hormone on memory was unknown.

Assailly observed that the childhood of the mediums he studied was marked by serious emotional shocks in nine out of ten cases (p. 360). Again the fact that ADH is released in larger amounts during stress was unknown at that time. Assailly also observed that all ten of his subjects suffered from epigastric sensitivity and compared this with the epigastric auras of epileptics (p. 365).

The state of neurobiological knowledge at that time did not permit Assailly to connect his observations with the diencephalon and upper brain stem, where the hypothalamus, which produces ADH, is located. It is also of interest that the epigastric region is connected, through the vagus nerve, to the hypothalamus.

Finally, we report some observations of B. B., a 28-year-old woman who has also shown unusual ESP and PK abilities (psi gamma and metal bending without manipulation). She also claims to possess an exceptionally good memory and she has frequent and strong experiences of transcending states. B. B. told us that she has had dizzy spells since childhood; for instance, she could not ride a bicycle. She still occasionally experiences these spells.

B. B. suffered cerebral contusion twice. When she was four years old or so, her brother hit her with a golf club knocking her unconscious. She needed about 40 stitches according to her mother. Between 17 and 18 years of age she received a concussion in an auto accident, losing consciousness from half an hour to one hour.

A neurological examination revealed absence of gag reflex and hyporeaction of plantaris, corneal, and superficial reflexes. Combining these observations it is interesting to observe that cranial nerves 8 (vestibular and coclear) and 9 (glossopharyngeal) feed into the lower brain stem. Damage to nerve 8 may result in dizziness. It is interesting that cranial nerve 8 is adjacent to nerves 9 and 10 (glossopharyngeal and vagus) which are involved in the production of the gag reflex and feed into the same area of the lower brain stem. This leads us to assume that there may be an organic or functional disturbance in that part of her nervous system. Is it possible that the blocks in nervous interactions between B. B.'s higher brain centers and her body contributed to increased psi interactions with her environment?

In comparing S. G.'s and A. G.'s condition with B. B.'s, we notice that for all three unusual conditions may exist in the brain stem. For B. B. the area would appear to be in the lower brain stem (between the pons and the medulla) and in the case of S. G. and A. G. in the upper brain stem (diencephalon).

These observations lead to several questions. For instance, are functional or structural CNS anomalies, such as we have found, more common among sensitives than in the general population? Secondly, do these CNS features play a role in the psi process or do they only facilitate fantasies in the person that he or she is psychic? In this connection it is relevant that the three sensitives all scored high on the Wilson and Barber ICMI scale for the fantasy-prone personality.

We tend to believe that S. G., A. G., and B. B. possess more than the usual share of psi sensitivity and we suspect that this may be related to their unusual CNS characteristics. But a great deal of systematic research with sensitives and control groups is required before the validity of our speculations can be determined.

Part 2: Papers and Research Briefs (RBs), Including Poster Sessions (PSs)

EXPERIMENTAL REPORTS

THE EFFECT OF GANZFELD STIMULATION AND FEEDBACK IN A CLAIRVOYANCE TASK (RB)

D.J. Bierman,[†] J. Berendsen, C. Koenen, C. Kuipers, J. Louman, F. Maissan (University of Amsterdam)

Thirty-two subjects participated in a free-response clairvoyance experiment. Sixteen subjects were tested in the Ganzfeld condition. In the non-Ganzfeld condition the other 16 subjects listened to 40 minutes of relaxing music while giving their impressions of a target picture that was sealed in an envelope which they held in their hands. After the 40 minutes of stimulation the subjects ranked a set of four pictures, among which was a copy of the target. Each subject did two trials on two different days. Feedback was given for only one of the two trials. The results showed scoring percentages of 12.5% in the nonfeedback/non-Ganzfeld condition; 25% in both conditions with feedback; and 43% in the nonfeedback/Ganzfeld condition (MCE = 25%). Targets were pictures of local sites, thus enabling a computerized analytical judging to be performed using 30 descriptors as was previously done in remote viewing studies. Neither the analyses by Sum of Ranks nor the ANOVA based upon the analytically-judged data yielded significant results. A comparison of both methods of analysis shows that the latter is a promising extension of current methodological tools since it enables statistical evaluation of single trials and multivariate methods based upon a known normal distribution of scores.

PSYCHOKINETIC INFLUENCE UPON ELECTRODERMAL ACTIVITY

William Braud[†] and Marilyn Schlitz (Mind Science Foundation)

An experiment was conducted in order to replicate previous successful "bio-PK" experiments (in which biological target systems

are psychokinetically influenced) and in order to determine whether
the presence of need would facilitate the effect. For the purposes
of the present study, need was varied by establishing two groups of
"target persons." Subjects were selected from a pool of persons
who considered themselves to have excessive sympathetic autonomic
arousal and who complained of excessive emotionality, nervousness,
anxiety, living or working under stress, tension headaches, high
blood pressure, ulcers, etc. Degree of autonomic arousal was assessed by recording electrodermal activity (EDA) during a screening session. Subjects who evidenced relatively high EDA constituted the Active group (N = 16); it was assumed that these persons
had a relatively high need to be calmed mentally and physically.
Subjects who evidenced moderate or low EDA constituted the Inactive group (N = 16); it was assumed that these persons had a relatively low need to be calmed. It was the goal of the "PK influencers" to psychically calm the target persons in these two groups.
Our primary hypothesis was that the observed psychic calming effect would be greater for the Active than for the Inactive subjects,
since the factor of need was greater in the former case--not only
for the subjects, but also for the influencers who were aware of
their relatively high autonomic activity and were therefore more
motivated to reduce it.

During the actual experimental sessions, the subjects sat in
a distant room and listened to computer-generated random tones
while watching a display of random colored lights. This audiovis-
ual stimulation was provided to occupy the subjects' attention, to
slightly heighten their alertness and prevent drowsiness, and to suggest a more random mode of cognition (see JASPR, 1980, 297-318)
during the 20-minute session. EDA was monitored by means of
finger electrodes, displayed on a polygraph in the distant influencer's room, and assessed by an analog-to-digital converter inter-
faced with a microcomputer. Subjects were told that psychic calming attempts would be made sometime during the session and were
asked to cooperate with such attempts; subjects were not told, of
course, how many attempts would be made nor their number or
duration.

The subject's EDA was monitored for twenty 30-second
epochs, separated by 30-second intertrial intervals. During each
30-second recording epoch, EDA was sampled at a rate of ten samples per second and averaged by computer. Recording epochs were
signaled to the influencer only by means of a low pitched tone.
Half of the recording epochs were Control (C) periods in which the
influencer attempted not to think about the subject or "allowed" the
subject to be active; half of the epochs were Decrease (D) periods
in which the influencer attempted to psychically calm the subject so
that little EDA would be produced during that 30-second epoch. The
influencer attempted such a psychic influence by relaxing himself or
herself and imagining the subject doing the same, by sending mental
"messages" or feelings of quietude to the subject, and by visualiz-
ing the polygraph pen producing a flat tracing, free of EDA. The
CDDC or DCCD counterbalanced sequence for the 20 epochs was

indicated to the influencer by means of a deck of 20 prearranged cards. Immediate, trial-by-trial, analog feedback was available to the influencers in the form of the polygraph tracing. W. B. and M.S. served as influencers, each for half of the subjects in each condition.

The psi effect for each subject was measured by means of a "percent decrease" score calculated by summing the averaged EDA scores for all 20 recording epochs and dividing this total activity score into the sum of the averaged EDA scores for the ten decrease (i.e., PK influence) epochs. This within-subject, relative score allows comparisons across different experiments and also controls for differences in absolute levels of responding. By chance, the percent decrease score should be 50%; scores consistently below 50%, in this case, indicate the presence of a psi effect. Strict precautions were taken to prevent conventional communications between influencer and subject and to eliminate possible artifacts.

An independent samples t test comparing the two sets of scores confirmed the primary prediction. The percent decrease scores for the Active subjects ($\bar{X}$ = 40.39%) were significantly lower (t = 1.86, 30 df, p = .035, one-tailed) than those for the Inactive subjects ($\bar{X}$ = 50.33%). Single mean t tests were used to test two secondary predictions--that there would be extra-chance scoring in each of the two groups. This prediction was confirmed for the Active subjects condition (t = 2.40, 15 df, p = .014, one-tailed), but not for the Inactive subjects condition (t = 0.09, n.s.).

To determine the likelihood of similar effects actually occurring by chance, parallel analyses were done on the corresponding first (screening) session scores of the two groups, during which session no influence attempts had been made. These first session pseudo percent decrease scores differed neither from one another nor from mean chance expectation.

In order to directly compare the magnitude of the obtained psi effect with the magnitude of a similar effect obtained through nonpsychic means, 16 additional subjects were tested in an autonomic nervous system self-control experiment. The subjects were tested individually by W. B. Electrodermal activity was monitored while, following a five-minute adaptation (which, by the way, had also been included in the psi experiment described above) period, the subject attempted to calm himself or herself as much as possible during ten 30-second Decrease periods, each signaled by a low pitched tone. During ten interspersed (according to the same DCCD or CDDC counterbalanced schedule used in the above experiment) 30-second Control periods, signaled by higher pitched tones, the subject was asked to "be normal"--i.e., not to attempt to increase autonomic activity, but to maintain his or her normal condition. The experimenter made no attempt to influence the subjects psychically. All 16 subjects had relatively active sympathetic nervous systems. Recording and analysis procedures were identical to those described for the above experiment.

Percent decrease scores were calculated as before. These scores reflected degree of autonomic self-control, with a score of 50% indicating no control, and a score of 0% indicating maximal control. In fact, the scores varied from 5.07% to 53.33%, with a mean of 31.33% and a standard deviation of 11.74. Comparison of these 16 percent decrease scores with chance expectation (50%) yielded evidence of highly significant autonomic self-control (single mean $t = 6.16$, 15 df, $p = 3.8 \times 10^{-5}$, one-tailed). Comparison of the 16 self-control scores with the 16 psi-influenced scores for the Active subjects of the psi experiment described above ($\overline{X} = 40.39\%$) yielded an independent samples $t = 1.80$ which, with 30 df, did not reach significance ($t = .08$, two-tailed). Thus, although self-control yielded a stronger effect (an approximately 19% deviation from chance) than did psi influence (an approximately 10% deviation from chance), the effect was not significantly stronger. This suggests that the psi effect was not a negligible one.

Concerning the psi experiment, a number of alternative psi hypotheses should be considered. The first is that the true psi effect may not be upon the subject's physiological activity, but rather upon the selection of the Decrease/Control sequences; sequences might be psychically influenced or selected so as to best match the subjects' ongoing activity to the intended outcome of the study. While such a possibility makes sense in cases in which random sequence selection procedures are used, it would not appear to be very applicable to the present case in which fixed CDDC and DCCD sequences were used.

A second hypothesis is that there was a PK influence, but it was upon the equipment rather than upon the living target system. Such a possibility cannot be ruled out in designs such as this, but could only be eliminated if bio-PK experiments were conducted in which instrumentation was not used at all, but naked eye measurements made instead (as in plant growth or wound healing experiments). We suspect, however, that in these bio-PK experiments, the PK influence is upon the most labile link of the chain of events participating in the recording, and this link would be the activity of the biological target system. Fortunately, this suspicion is not merely speculative. Subjects have spontaneously reported definite physical feelings of activation or quietude during specific periods in experiments and sessions which could be correlated with activity seen in the polygraph records, suggesting that <u>they</u> were responding appropriately and not merely the recording equipment.

A third hypothesis is that a psi effect occurred, but it was a telepathic or clairvoyant effect localized in the subject, rather than a psychokinesis effect localized in the influencer. Such a possibility cannot be ruled out and, indeed, we suspect that such an effect did occur in the present experiment, along with a PK effect.

A fourth hypothesis is that the high scoring for the Active subjects and the lower scoring for the Inactive subjects may be an instance of a preferential or differential effect, or of a psi-mediated experimenter effect. If this is indeed an experimenter effect, it may have been encouraged by the experimenters' knowledge of the group membership of the subjects. This knowledge was unavoidable. We wished to provide the influencer with immediate analog feedback in this experiment, and receiving such feedback allows the polygraph observer to quickly distinguish active and inactive subjects. Therefore, the influencer could not be kept blind regarding the activity condition of the subject.

An alternative explanation for the absence of a psi effect in the Inactive condition is that the psi effects in this study were weaker than usual (perhaps because decrements in EDA are more difficult to produce via bio-PK than increments in EDA?), except in the Active condition in which the weak effect may have been amplified by the need factor.

CORRELATED HEMISPHERIC ASYMMETRY IN THE SENSORY AND ESP PROCESSING OF CONTINUOUS MULTIPLEX STIMULI

Michaeleen Maher (City College of the City University of New York)

It may be naive to regard either of the human cerebral hemispheres as a unified processor that exerts hierarchical control over distinct subclasses of processing. Although speculative models such as this have been proposed for over a century, theoretical closure on the explicit nature and functioning of the hemispheres has remained an elusive goal. However, that processing advantages may be experimentally manipulated by varying the nature of the stimulus input and/or the initial conditions of its entry into the cognitive structure of the organism has been aptly demonstrated by a large body of empirical research. Some robust convergences in these data have led to the assumption that specific psychological functions may be localized (or specialized) in a given hemisphere. It is generally agreed, for example, that the neural resources underlying speech production are specialized in the left hemispheres of nearly all right-handed persons (estimates range as high as 95%). Few researchers, at this juncture, are willing to make similar broad claims for the comprehensive functions of language.

One of the techniques that have been used to study hemispheric responses to different stimuli has been to monitor EEG activity from suitable sites in the left and right hemispheres, and to infer, from the relative pattern of alpha production, which hemisphere has been predominantly occupied with the processing requirements of the stimuli. Because the hemisphere that is producing alpha is not concurrently producing beta (the brain wave pattern associated with cognitive processing), bilateral comparisons of relative alpha production allow us to discern which of the hemispheres has been "busier" processing the stimuli. On a priori grounds, then, the left hemisphere could reasonably be expected to produce relatively less alpha (i.e., exhibit greater engagement) than would the right hemisphere during a task requiring speech production. Using this technique, a number of studies have reported theoretically consistent EEG asymmetries for both overt and covert psychological functions.

Evidence for specialized right hemispheric mediation of human emotional responsivity has steadily been accumulating from research studies employing diverse techniques and methodologies. Some findings suggest that specialized right hemispheric processors may interpret the emotional components of language, including prosody and emotional gesturing. Psychophysiological approaches attempting to use physiological measures as direct indicators of a psi response (i.e., as dependent variables) have successfully utilized stimuli with an emotional component. An advantage of the psychophysiological approach is that it allows us to look at an unconscious psi response and to compare it with subsequent behavioral responding which may or may not reflect psi.

Although laterality research in parapsychology has been scant, the few published studies may be interpreted as indicating that psi processing utilizes specialized hemispheric processors in an orthodox manner. If extrasensory processing of stimuli engages the hemispheres in a way that is homologous to sensory processing of the same stimuli, it should be possible to show patterns of relative hemispheric alpha production during psi processing that are consistent with the patterns exhibited during sensory processing of the same stimuli.

The present experiment was undertaken in an attempt to provide evidence that specialized brain processors are utilized conventionally during psi processing. In addition, the study sought to provide further evidence for unconscious psi responding and to compare such responding with the presence or absence of appropriate behavioral responses in both subjects and judges. The study utilized emotional and nonemotional stimulus sets (videotapes) and predicted that group differences in relative hemispheric processing would be observed, with the emotional stimuli eliciting relatively greater desynchrony in the right hemispheres of males than would the nonemotional stimuli in both the sensory and extrasensory conditions. Females were expected to exhibit the predicted differences in processing to a significantly lesser extent than would males, because of the greater bilaterality of function presumed to characterize the brains of females. It was recognized from the outset that should the emotional and nonemotional stimuli fail to elicit robust group differences in processing, individuals' idiosyncratic laterality patterns for processing the videotapes could be correlated across the sensory and ESP conditions to test the hypothesis of lateralized congruence during the sensory and ESP processing of cognitive material.

Subjects were ten male and ten female adult dextrals who

espoused an open, accepting attitude toward the possibility of ESP success. The experiment took place in a City University EEG laboratory, which was devoted to studying hemispheric asymmetry by means of the alpha monitoring technique described earlier. The procedures used to collect and assess subjects' integrated alpha production (amplitude x time) were the same procedures routinely employed in the laboratory. During the experiment, subjects were isolated in an electrically shielded soundproof room, with electrodes affixed to bilateral temporal-parietal sites (referenced to a common vertex) midway between T_3 and P_3 and T_4 and P_4. A within-subjects design was employed, with each subject having four task conditions. EEG was monitored while subjects attempted to use ESP to perceive the contents of two videotapes, which were played, in random order, in a distant room. After each clairvoyant ESP period, subjects gave mentation reports which were tape recorded for later analysis by outside blind judges. Subsequently, EEG was monitored while subjects watched the videotapes (again randomly sequenced) on a TV monitor.

Both videotapes were the conceptions of artists, who graciously lent tapes to the author for use in the experiment. One tape (for experimental purposes designated the Love Tape), contained a series of interviews with males and females who, often falteringly but sometimes eloquently, discussed their varying attitudes toward love and loving. Introspective reports from viewers indicated that the material incited sympathy, was emotionally compelling, and was often profoundly depressing. A ballad, "I'm in the Mood for Love," weaved plaintively throughout the monologues. The alternate tape (designated the City Tape) was intellectual in its approach and depicted New York City as a giant, automated organism. This tape contained numerous aerial and landscape views of the metropolis, with its pulsing arteries of traffic and miniature figures scurrying in and out of subway exits. Time lapsed cinematography depicted huge architectural structures being swiftly demolished and re-erected, while electron microscopy showed organismic activity on a cellular level. The accompanying soundtrack was electronic or voice automated.

When subjects attempted to match their ESP mentations to the videotapes, results were at chance, with 12 of the 20 subjects (six males and six females) correctly matching their reports to the tapes. One of two outside judges correctly matched 16 of the 20 tandem reports ($Z = 2.46$, corrected for continuity; $p < .014$, two-tailed), while the other judge correctly matched 13 of the 20 reports ($p = ns$). When the ten tandem reports which subjects and both judges correctly matched are contrasted with the three reports which subjects and both judges incorrectly matched, the binomial expansion gives $p < .05$, one-tailed (corrected for continuity), suggesting that chance factors do not account for the consensus difference between correctly judged and incorrectly judged reports.

Noise artifacts rendered the EEG data for one female subject during the sensory viewing of the City Tape not usable, and her EEG data were eliminated from the analysis. Differential alpha produced during the playing of the two videotapes in the sensory and ESP conditions was assessed for the 19 remaining subjects with a repeated measures ANOVA. This showed that subjects produced significantly more overall alpha in the ESP condition than they produced in the sensory condition ($F = 8.41$, $df = 1, 17$, $p = .010$). This nuisance effect may be attributed to the general lack of sensory stimulation during the ESP viewing periods. The ANOVA further determined that males' hemispheres had reacted differently to the videotapes than had females' (sex x tape x hemisphere interaction significant at $F = 4.62$, $df = 1, 17$, $p < .05$). Males as a group exhibited the predicted pattern, showing greater relative right hemispheric participation in processing the Love Tape as opposed to the City Tape, whereas females as a group reversed this tendency and exhibited greater relative right hemispheric participation in processing the City Tape as opposed to the Love Tape.

Individuals' idiosyncratic hemispheric activity differences in processing the videotapes in the sensory condition were then correlated with their differences in the ESP condition. The Pearson $r = .4327$, 17 df, $p < .032$, one-tailed. Separate product-moment correlation coefficients were then derived for 1) the group of subjects whose ESP mentations were correctly matched to the videotapes by all three judges, and 2) all other subjects. One of the subjects whose mentations had received correct consensus judging was the female whose noisy EEG data had been eliminated from the analysis. For the nine remaining subjects in the sample of "best" subjects, $r = .7149$, 7 df, $p < .015$, one-tailed. The correlation coefficient for the group of subjects about whom judges differed or incorrectly matched the mentations was $r = -.1384$ ($p = $ ns). The difference between the two coefficients was significant at $p < .05$, one-tailed.

These data support the hypothesis of congruence in the asymmetrical processing of cognitive information during sensory and extrasensory perception. The evidence for psi processing comes both from the conscious domain of remembered perceptions and from the unconscious domain of lateralized hemispheric activity. Although these converging lines of evidence are encouraging, substantive conclusions must await replication and further brain research on psi.

PSYCHOKINETIC CONTROL OF BACTERIAL MUTATION

Carroll B. Nash (Parapsychology Laboratory, St. Joseph's University)

The purpose of the experiment was to determine whether the mutation rate of the lac-negative strain to the lac-positive strain of the bacterium Escherichia coli, a normal inhabitant of the human large intestine, can be psychokinetically accelerated and/or retarded with subjects not known to be psychically gifted. The lac-negative strain of E. coli is unable to metabolize lactose. The gene determining this characteristic spontaneously mutates to produce the lac-positive strain which metabolizes this sugar. The mutation is reversible so that either strain can arise from the other. The two strains are visibly distinguishable because, in a suitable medium, lac-negative colonies are clear and lac-positive colonies are red. A change in the relative frequencies of the two strains gives an indication of the rate of mutation.

Procedure. The experiment was performed under the supervision of the author by Paul Leary, Louis Petrellis, and Glen Russo with the assistance of John Hemlich. At the time of the experiment, the experimenters were premedical students at St. Joseph's University: Russo was a chemistry major and the other three majored in biology. As determined in advance, 60 subjects were tested, each for one run. The 60 subjects, 20 for each experimenter, were male and female volunteers from the student body and not known to be psychically gifted. The run consisted of the measurement of the relative frequencies of the lac-negative and lac-positive strains of E. coli in samples from the subject's test tubes after an incubation period of 24 hours.

Aseptic technique was used throughout the procedure. After thorough mixing of a stock suspension of E. coli of both strains, equal amounts were transferred by pipet into each of the subject's nine tubes which contained equal amounts of nutrient broth. The nine tubes, each labeled with a number from 1 to 9, were placed in a 3 by 3 arrangement in a rack. As determined by a table of random digits randomly entered once by the author with closed eyes, three of the tubes were selected for promotion of the mutation rate, three for inhibition, and three for controls. The position in the rack and the intended mutation effect of each of the nine tubes had previously been recorded by the author by means of nine circles in a 3 by 3 arrangement on both of two clips of paper with the word top written near the upper edge of each slip to coincide with the upper edge of the rack. In each of the circles for the mutation-promoted tubes was placed a plus (+), for the mutation-inhibited tubes a minus (-), and the circles for the control tubes were left blank. The author placed each of the two slips of paper in a separate opaque envelope, sealed the two envelopes, clipped them together, and randomly shuffled the envelope-pairs. He gave 20 envelope-pairs to each experimenter. The experimenter marked both envelopes of the pair with the same identification, gave one of the envelopes to the subject, and kept the other until the end of the tests, when he opened the 20 envelopes in the presence of the author. The author had no contact with the subjects or the culture tubes during the experiment.

Each subject was shown his or her rack of nine tubes in the laboratory at the beginning of the run. Leary and Petrellis instructed their subjects to open the envelope after the experimenter had gone into a separate part of the laboratory and to try, by wishing during a period the length of which was determined by the subject, to promote the mutation of the bacteria in the "+" tubes from lac-negative to lac-positive and to inhibit the mutation of the bacteria in the "-" tubes from lac-negative to lac-positive. The subject was instructed as to the nature of mutation and as to the color of the colonies of each of the two strains. The correspondence between his or her rack of tubes and the diagram on the slip of paper in his or her envelope was explained to the subject with the aid of a dummy slip. The period utilized by the subjects ranged from 5 to 13 minutes with an average of 10 minutes. The subject took the slip of paper upon leaving the laboratory. Russo treated his subjects similarly except that he observed that they did not handle or manipulate their tubes, did not permit them to open their envelope until after they left the laboratory, and instructed them that their wishing period should extend for the ensuing 24 hours. In all other respects, the experimental procedure was the same for the three experimenters. This permitted a comparison of the effects on the mutant ratio of attempting to influence it 1) during a period of a few minutes while the tubes were observed and 2) during a 24-hour period following the tube viewing. After the subject left the laboratory, the experimenter placed the rack of tubes in an incubator set at 37° C., and the bacteria were grown aerobically for 24 hours. The rack was not looked at or disturbed during the period of incubation.

At the termination of the 24 hours, the experimenter removed his subject's rack from the incubator and, after diluting each of the nine tubes with the same amount of water, transferred a portion from each tube onto a separate plate of MacConkey's agar. MacConkey's medium provides no food source other than lactose and contains a pH indicator which colors E. coli red if it metabolizes this sugar. After supplying the nine plates with the bacteria, the experimenter incubated them for a period of 24 hours. Following this he counted the clear (lac-negative) colonies and red (lac-positive) colonies, which were easily visible in the subject's plates to the naked eye, and recorded their numbers on the record sheet. Dilution of the tubes before sampling widely separated the individual bacteria. After incubation each visible spot represented the progeny of one bacterium. Thus, the color of the spot on the agar was a test of that original bacterium from which it derived.

After the experimenter had completed the tests with his 20 subjects he brought the records and the sealed envelopes to the author. Under the direct observation of the latter, the experimenter opened each envelope in turn and recorded on the record sheets the intended mutation effect in each tube, i.e., "+," "C," or "-."

The mutation rate is the probability of the occurrence of the mutation per generation, i.e., the average number of mutations per cell per generation. As an index of the mutation rate, the mutant ratio of the lac-positive colonies to the total number of colonies on the plate was determined. The subject was taken as the unit of analysis, and the mean mutant ratio of each of his or her three sets of tubes--promoted, control, and inhibited--was determined. For comparison of the results between the subjects, the mean mutant ratio of each of the three sets of tubes for each subject was multiplied by the mean mutant ratio of all tubes for all subjects and divided by the mean mutant ratio of the nine tubes of the subject. This corrected for any differences in the mutant ratio of the stock culture between subjects and for any intersubject differences in the incubation.

Hypotheses. It was hypothesized 1) that the mutant ratio would be greater in the promoted than in the inhibited tubes; 2) that it would be greater in the promoted tubes than in the controls; and 3) that it would be less in the inhibited tubes than in the controls. It was decided in advance to use the subject as the unit of statistical analysis and to use the mean mutant ratio for his or her three tubes for each intended mutation effect. It was also decided in advance to analyze each experimenter's results both separately and combined and to attach primary importance to the latter.

Results. The mean mutant ratio for each intended mutation effect and the t's of the differences between dependent pairs were determined with two-tailed p values. Because of procedural errors consisting of spillage and contamination, results were obtained for only 52 of the 60 subjects.

With Petrellis as the experimenter the t values were significant in the predicted direction for all three differences, i.e., promoted greater than controls, inhibited less than controls, and promoted greater than inhibited. With Russo as the experimenter, only the t value for the mutant ratio being less in the inhibited tubes than in the controls was statistically significant. With Leary as the experimenter, none of the t values were significant although all three were in the predicted directions. With the combined or overall results of the three experimenters the t values were statistically significant for the mutant ratios being greater in the promoted than in the inhibited tubes and for the mutant ratios being less in the inhibited tubes than in the controls. The mutant ratios were also greater in the promoted tubes than in the controls, but not significantly so.

Discussion. The experimental results support the hypotheses that the mutant ratio would be greater in the promoted than in the inhibited tubes and that the mutant ratio would be less in the inhibited tubes than in the controls. However, they fail to support the hypothesis that the mutant ratio would be greater in the promoted tubes than in the controls because, although the difference is in the intended direction, it does not reach statistical significance.

There appears to be some tendency towards a differential effect between the subjects who attempted to affect the mutant ratios during the period they looked at the tubes and the subjects who attempted to do so only during the following 24 hours. The former subjects did better in promoting the mutant ratio in the promoted tubes and the latter did better in inhibiting the mutant ratio in the inhibited tubes.

<u>Conclusions</u>. The results of the experiment are interpreted to suggest that, with subjects not known to be psychically gifted, the rate of bacterial mutation was psychokinetically affected.

CONTAMINATION OF FREE-RESPONSE ESP TARGETS: THE GREASY FINGERS HYPOTHESIS (PS)

John Palmer (University of Utrecht)

A number of free-response (FR) ESP experiments conducted in the 1970s can be criticized on the grounds that the judging sets included the target picture actually handled by the agent. This procedure allows for the possible transmission of subtle cues that may have been "added" (we can assume unwittingly) by the agent. Although the best solution is obviously replication with designs that eliminate this artifact (such studies have been undertaken with no diminution of results), until and unless FR ESP becomes replicable on demand the earlier studies must still be taken into account in evaluating its overall evidential status. Thus the empirical viability of the counter-hypothesis is relevant. A preliminary experiment was conducted to determine to what extent typical volunteer subjects might actually make use of possible handling cues to influence the results of experiments such as those under criticism. The experiment was introduced to subjects as an exploration of the relation between ESP and hypnosis.

<u>Method</u>. The subject sample consisted of 36 agent-percipient pairs, 28 of whom were acquainted with each other prior to the experiment. Fifty-one of the subjects had participated in an earlier hypnosis-ESP experiment conducted by the author (<u>RIP 1982</u>, 55-57).

Two matched pools of targets were used, each containing 40 prints of magazine pictures divided into ten sets of four each. A person not otherwise involved with the experiment prepared a sequence of 36 target designations (set plus picture) based upon a random number table. These were sealed in opaque envelopes numbered 1 to 36 in <u>green</u>. Based on the shuffling of playing cards, two additional binary sequences of length 36 were determined. The first of these indicated from which pool the picture handled by the agent was to be taken for a given session, and the second (which was orthogonal to the first) indicated whether the "contaminated" or the "uncontaminated" set was to be used for the judging. These designations were sealed in two additional batches of opaque envelopes numbered 1 to 36 in <u>red</u> and <u>black</u>, respectively. The three batches of envelopes were then given to J.P., who deposited them in a locked storage room.

The experiment was conducted in a suite of five adjacent rooms designated A through E. The agent was situated in Room A, the percipient in E, and the experimenter, Mr. Arjan Eleveld (A.E.), in C, the door of which was open so that he could monitor the hallway. There was intercom contact between Room C and Rooms A and E, but not directly between A and E.

At the beginning of each session, J.P. went to the storage room (B), determined the target picture from the appropriate green envelope, and retrieved it from the corresponding target set in the pool designated by the contents of the appropriate red envelope. This picture was placed inside a plain manila envelope and deposited on the desk in Room A.

Meanwhile, A.E. explained the experiment to the subjects in Room E and had them decide who was to be percipient. He then showed the agent to Room A. The percipient was seated in a comfortable reclining chair and the agent in a padded straight-back chair next to the desk on which the target envelope had been placed. Room E was kept dark during the test period, whereas Room A was illuminated by a small table lamp.

A.E. next went to Room C and played a taped hypnotic induction, similar to that of Palmer and van der Velden (RIP 1982, 58-61), which could be heard by both subjects. The tape included instructions to the agent and then the percipient. Agents, who had been instructed to open the envelope at the beginning of the session, were told to concentrate on "sending" the picture to the percipient until this became boring. Percipients were instructed to try to clear their minds and to passively await impressions of the target. They had been told to announce orally when they finished receiving impressions. At this point, or after ten minutes, A.E. restarted the tape, which concluded with a short deinduction procedure.

A.E. next phoned J.P., who went immediately to Room A and gave the agent a short questionnaire concerning depth of hypnosis and expectation of success on the ESP task. He then placed the target picture back inside its manila envelope and went to Room B to return the target picture to its set envelope within the contaminated pool. He next took the four pictures out of the appropriate set envelope from either the contaminated or the uncontaminated pool (as determined from the contents of the appropriate black envelope) and placed them inside a manila envelope. He then went to Room C, placed this envelope on top of the sound amplifier, and tapped twice on the intercom to alert A.E. Finally, he returned to Room A to wait with the agent until the judging was completed.

After phoning J.P., A.E. went to Room E to administer the questionnaire to the percipient. Upon hearing J.P.'s tap, he went to Room C to retrieve the judging set before returning to Room E to begin the judging procedure.

Percipients were instructed at the beginning of the judging

that they were to make three sets of ratings (A, B, and C) on a 0 to 30 scale, reflecting the similarity of their impressions to each of the four pictures of the set.

For the A ratings, percipients were instructed not to touch the pictures. They were told to base their ratings solely on their logical assessment of the correspondence between the content of each picture and their impressions during the reception period.

For the B ratings, percipients were told that research suggests that a person's "psychic vibrations" can sometimes be transferred to a target object. They were told to handle the pictures and do anything else with them to try to identify these "vibrations." The rationale was to give subjects who might consciously wish to use artifacts as a basis for their ratings maximal opportunity to do so unobtrusively, while at the same time maximizing the likelihood that they would come into contact with sensory information that might influence their ratings unconsciously and could be rationalized as awareness of "vibrations."

For the C ratings, percipients were asked to rate the pictures on all the information available and their confidence in its value.

A.E. then interviewed the percipients about their judging process, focusing specifically on what "vibrations" were experienced. Finally, the agent was asked to join the percipient, at which time he or she revealed the identity of the target.

Two predictions were made: 1) The C ratings will be significantly different in the contaminated target (CT) and uncontaminated target (UT) conditions, with the larger deviation from MCE in the former; 2) the mean difference between the CT and UT conditions will be greater for the B ratings than for the A ratings, with the B ratings deviating more from MCE than the A ratings in the CT condition.

Because for certain logistical reasons most highly hypnotizable subjects were excluded from this experiment, no "real" ESP effects were predicted or expected.

Results. The ESP scores were Z-scores computed by subtracting the rating assigned to each target from the mean of all four ratings and dividing by the standard deviation. Separate A, B, and C scores were computed for each subject pair. These scores were highly intercorrelated as measured by Spearman correlations (AB: $r = .58$, $p < .005$; AC: $r = .81$, $p < .001$; BC: $r = .77$, $p < .001$.) All p-values in the report are two-tailed.

Neither prediction was confirmed. The mean C scores for the CT and UT conditions were -.02 and -.08, respectively, and did not differ significantly by U test ($z = -.22$). The A-score means for the CT and UT conditions were +.02 and -.00. The corresponding B-score means were -.16 and -.31. A nonparametric test of the interaction, adjusted for main effects, was nonsignificant (chi square = .005, 1 df).

The only significant post-hoc finding was psi-missing among the eight unacquainted pairs. This result was significant at the .01 level, 7 df, for each set of ESP scores (A: M = -.44, t = 3.95; B: M = -.46, t = 4.52; C: M = -.45, t = 5.12), and was equally present in both conditions.

Discussion. There is no evidence from these data that suggests that volunteer research subjects use possible sensory cues from target pictures subjected to normal handling by an agent to produce spurious positive results in FR ESP experiments. This is true in spite of the fact that most of our subjects were "sheep," and several obviously were motivated to prove to their partners, who were often close friends or relatives, that they could communicate psychically with each other.

Most percipients found the B ratings to be awkward or difficult, an observation supported by the high correlations of the B and C ratings with the A ratings. It is evident that the B ratings, although supposed to be made independently of the A ratings, were in fact influenced by them.

Additional studies should be conducted to confirm the generality of these findings with other subject populations, to test the capacity of subjects to utilize sensory cues when explicitly instructed to do so, and to explore possible mechanisms of transmission.

INTERNAL STATE AND TEMPORAL FACTORS IN RNG PK (RB)

John Palmer[†] and Wim Kramer (University of Utrecht)

A random number generator (RNG) PK experiment without on-line feedback was conducted to test predictions based upon five hypotheses inspired by previous research. A focal point was the exploration of an auditory environment of taped 4 Hz drum beats compared to silence preceded by a taped 15-minute progressive relaxation exercise. Pilot testing suggested that the drums promote a passive focus of attention on the PK task, and it thus was hypothesized that they are PK conducive. The second hypothesis was that PK effects would occur following cessation of attempted PK influence ("release of effort") and/or an abrupt change of cognitive state ("startle") induced by a sudden, unexpected onset of the drums. The third hypothesis predicted decline effects both between and within 2.25-minute periods of attempted PK, whereas the fourth hypothesis predicted a change in the sign of the deviation between these two influence periods ("differential effect"). The fifth

Experimental Reports

hypothesis was that more PK would manifest in the experimental series (with subjects attempting influence) than in a matched baseline series with a similar physical setup but with no one attempting influence and only J.P. present.

The subjects were 48 volunteers, most of whom had participated in previous ESP experiments conducted by J.P. The sessions were held on weekday evenings in two adjacent rooms. The subject was seated in a reclining chair in one room, which was illuminated by a small table lamp. The experimenters (J.P. and W.K.) and all equipment were in the other room.

Each session consisted of three "sets" of 2500 trials each, each divided into ten 250-trial "blocks," with trials generated at approximately 18.5 per second. Two of the sets were generated while the subject was attempting PK influence listening to the drums or after the relaxation tape, respectively. The beginning and end of each of these two sets were indicated by tones, in between which subjects were to passively focus on the target number (0 or 1) and wish for its production. These two sets were either Set 1 or Set 3 in the sequence, the order being counterbalanced as described below. Set 2, unknown to the subjects, was generated immediately after Set 1 and constituted the test of the "release of effort" hypothesis.

Sixteen subjects were assigned in random sequence to each of three experimental conditions. In Condition 1, Set 1 was drums and Set 3 was relaxation, while this order was reversed in the other two conditions. In Conditions 1 and 2, the drum set followed a three-minute adaptation period to the drums, while in Condition 3 the drums appeared suddenly and unexpectedly ten seconds after the initial tone. The stimulation during Set 2 was also varied: continuation of the drums in Condition 1, lively music designed to help subjects return to a normal "waking" state in Condition 2, and a continuation of the relaxation exercise in Condition 3.

The target remained the same throughout a session, but was alternated between subjects within conditions.

Five randomicity tests of 100,000 trials each revealed no evidence of RNG bias at either the singlet or doublet levels.

All predictions except No. 4 were based on the absolute values of the critical ratio (ACR) of the set. All p-values are two-tailed. Hypothesis 5 was confirmed, in that the variance of the 144 ACR scores (3 x 48 "subjects") was significantly greater in the experimental series than in the baseline series (F = 1.65, 144,144 df, $p < .005$). However, compared to the theoretical distribution, the variance was significant (low) in the baseline series ($z = -2.39$, $p < .05$), but not in the experimental series ($z = +1.75$), thus suggesting an experimenter psi effect. Post-hoc analyses revealed possible evidence of subject psi in the experimental series when the variance of the block CRs was calculated ($z = +3.23$, $p < .005$). Compared to the expected 5.0%, 6.8% of these CRs were significant

($z = +3.08$, $p < .005$). This effect did not appear in the baseline series.

Subjects' ACR set scores of Set 2 in the experimental series significantly exceeded chance ($z = +2.22$, $p < .05$) and their mean (.97) was significantly greater than that in the baseline series (.64) by U test ($z = +2.30$, $p < .05$), thus confirming the release of effort hypothesis. Evidence for a subject effect in Set 2 was reinforced by a significant PK effect at the level of the block ($t = 2.58$, 47 df, $p < .05$). Several statistical analyses demonstrated that this latter release of effort effect was concentrated in the first half of Set 2, suggesting that it dissipated after approximately one minute.

None of the other hypotheses were supported. Hypotheses 1 and 3 were tested with Condition 3 omitted to maintain proper counterbalancing.

A POSSIBLE PROXIMITY EFFECT ON HUMAN PHYSIOLOGY: SIMILARITIES TO PSI? (RB)

Dean I. Radin[†] (Columbus, Ohio) and James L. Collymore (Piscataway, New Jersey)

Anomalies in a variety of scientific disciplines occasionally show resemblances to parapsychological phenomena. This report describes an example in the field of biomedicine.

Common chemicals have recently joined the list of environmental variables thought to affect health and human performance. One class of chemicals ubiquitous to the environment is food, and a useful source of information on the possible effects of food is nutritional folk wisdom. One claim that has persisted for many years is that refined sugar (sucrose) acts more like a poison than a nutrient in its effects on the human body. As evidence of the debilitating effects of sugar, some have claimed that merely holding a sealed packet of sugar in one's hand will significantly weaken muscular strength. We know of no studies, however, that have tested this opinion under controlled conditions. Since folk wisdom often has a great deal of face validity, we conducted an experiment to test the hypothesis that close proximity to sugar weakens human grip strength.

The experimental procedure was as follows: Two identical, opaque, plastic bottles were prepared. One bottle contained sugar and the other contained sand, both of equal weight. A total of 107 subjects performed six trials each using a hand dynamometer to record grip strength in kilograms (kg). Three consecutive trials measured grip strength in the subject's dominant hand while holding a test bottle in his or her free hand. The other bottle was held during the next three trials. Sugar-sand orders were counterbalanced among subjects; subjects did not know the contents of the bottles before they were tested; and 101 of 107 subjects were unaware of the purpose of the experiment.

In a single-blind experimenter condition, the experimenter knew both the purpose of the experiment and the contents of the bottles. In a double-blind condition, the experimenter knew the purpose but not the contents. And in a "triple-blind" condition, the experimenter knew neither the purpose nor the contents. In chronological order, experimenter one ran one group (27 subjects) in a single-blind condition and a second group (16 subjects) in a double-blind condition. Experimenter two ran a third group (17 subjects) triple-blind; experimenter three ran a fourth group (25 subjects) double-blind; and experimenter four ran a fifth group (22 subjects) double-blind. All four experimenters collected data independently.

An analysis of variance showed that mean grip strength with sugar was significantly less than with sand ($p < .02$, two-tailed) and that the experimenter blindness condition (i.e., group) by substance interaction was nonsignificant ($p < .29$, two-tailed). The interaction term was used to test for a possible experimenter effect--none was indicated. Sugar-sand differences in Groups 1 to 5 were, respectively, -1.5 kg, -2.1 kg, -1.8 kg, -0.3 kg, and 0.2 kg.

A control experiment consisting of 26 subjects in single- and double-blind groups compared grip strength between two identical bottles of sand. The difference in grip strength between control bottles were nonsignificant (0.0 kg, rounded to one decimal point).

This experiment shares four characteristics in common with psi (especially ESP) research. First, the motivations for conducting these studies are similar--they are both attempts to verify anecdotal reports of anomalous human behavior. Second, results from groups 1 through 5 show a trend similar to the so-called decline effect typical of many psi experiments. Third, results of the experiment statistically support the claimed anomalous effect. And fourth, there is a lack of a readily acceptable mechanism to account for the results.

We would not, however, infer from these similarities that a paranormal effect must be responsible. It is possible that an exquisitely sensitive physiological system is the mediating factor. There is growing evidence, for example, that humans can sense electromagnetic and magnetic fields of extremely low frequency and intensity.

We suggest that reports of anomalies in many fields (especially biomedicine) should be collected and studied by parapsychologists. Some unusual sensory phenomena currently presumed to be psi may in fact be subtle, yet normal, perceptual abilities. Investigating the limits of normal senses may help shed light on the little understood (and possibly artificial) distinction between normal and paranormal awareness.

RELATIONSHIPS BETWEEN PARTICIPANT TRAITS AND SCORES ON TWO COMPUTER-CONTROLLED RNG-PK GAMES (RB/PS)

Ephraim I. Schechter, Charles Honorton, Pat Barker and Mario P. Varvoglis (Psychophysical Research Laboratories)

This report deals with relationships between RNG scores on two computer-controlled RNG-PK games and some of the participants' psychological characteristics. The major differences between the games involve the players' task orientation and the feedback they receive about the RNG's output. In Volition, immediate trial-by-trial RNG feedback is presented as an on-line graph of the cumulative deviation from chance. The player's task is to produce high or low RNG values according to "High-aim" or "Low-aim" instructions pseudorandomly determined and displayed at the start of the game. Each game consists of 100 trials of 100 RNG events each. The computer-graphics display shows zones of significance, the developing cumulative deviation line, and a variety of audio/visual rewards for individually strong trial scores. Unknown to the player, a second, "silent" RNG is sampled every time the feedback RNG is sampled, but the results from the silent RNG are not incorporated in the feedback displays.

There is no trial-by-trial RNG feedback in Psi Ball. The explicit task involves hand-eye coordination rather than PK, and players report that attention is focused on the sensorimotor task as the game progresses. A description of the Psi Ball game and experimental design is available elsewhere (RIP 1982, 152-154).

Two general purpose instruments are used to assess participants' psychological characteristics. The Participant Information Form (PIF) is a 55-item questionnaire developed at the Psychophysical Research Laboratories to gather information about attitudes towards psi, related current and past experiences, and demographic information. Five PIF questions are used in this analysis: participants are asked to rate their belief in psi on a seven-point scale, whether they have practiced any form of mental discipline (Y/N), to estimate how often they recall specific dream content (1-7), to estimate how often they lose awareness of surroundings when involved in an activity (1-7), and how competitive they think they are (1-7).

The Myers-Briggs Type Indicator (MBTI) is a forced-choice psychological inventory that yields scores on Jungian conceptual continua of Extraversion/Introversion, Sensing/Intuition, Thinking/Feeling, and Judging/Perceiving. We also use the 34 Absorption Scale items from the Tellegen Differential Personality Questionnaire (DPQ) intermixed with 30 items from other DPQ scales.

Ten participants have completed both Psi Ball and Volition series. Four were in our first Psi Ball pilot study; six were in the second Psi Ball pilot. All of them completed their Psi Ball series before entering the Volition pilot study. Participants complete the PIF and the two inventories before they play any RNG-PK games. Each plays ten five-game Psi Ball sessions, with no more than five sessions on any one lab visit. Five of the sessions (25 games) involve RNG-Contingent Psi Ball and five involve RNG-Noncontingent Psi Ball, in an order individually randomly assigned by the computer program. Each player's Volition series consists of ten games, with no more than five games on any one visit.

The proportions of hits in the Contingent and Noncontingent Psi Ball games are transformed to Z-scores to normalize them. The proportions of hits for the feedback and "silent" RNGs in the Volition game are also transformed to Z-scores. The Z-scores are used to analyze directional deviations in RNG performance; the absolute values of the Z-scores are used to evaluate nondirectional deviations (i.e., variability rather than hitting per se).

Since there are only ten participants (df = 8), Fisher Exact Probability Tests and 2 x 2 contingency tables based on median splits are used to analyze relationships between RNG and psychological-characteristic scores. (The second PIF question is divided on a yes/no basis rather than by a median split.) Most tests are two-tailed. Low MBTI EI scores indicate high extraversion; on the basis of trends in the existing data on extraversion/ESP relationships and the results of the first Psi Ball pilot study (RIP 1982, 152-154) we predicted negative relationships between the MBTI EI scores and the Z-scores from Contingent Psi Ball games and from Volition games. Tests of these relationships are one-tailed.

We also compare Volition Z-scores with Psi Ball Z-scores and Volition absolute Z-scores with Psi Ball absolute Z-scores, using two-tailed Fisher Exact Probability Tests and 2 x 2 contingency tables based on median splits.

There are no significant relationships, nor do there appear to be any meaningful patterns in the data.

CHANNELING PSI TO CRITICAL OBSERVERS   (RB)

Helmut Schmidt[†] (Mind Science Foundation), Robert Morris (Syracuse University), and Luther Rudolph (Syracuse University)

This study is primarily concerned with the existence of psi from the viewpoint of the critical outsider rather than the active experimenter.

The question is this: Supposing that we have an apparently successful psi experimenter, can we channel the test results from

the experimenter to a critical outside observer such as to provide
the observer with firsthand evidence for psi?

Such an arrangement could serve two purposes. First, to
show that experimenter fraud (in some recent experiments the only
alternative to psi) can be ruled out, and second, that psi is robust
enough to survive even under the most rigorously controlled conditions.

In this study, one of us (H.S., at San Antonio, Texas) plays
the role of the experimenter who wants to "get results," and the
others (R.M and L.R., at Syracuse, New York) are the observers
waiting for psi evidence to be presented in indisputable form.

Particularly convenient for strict safety requirements are PK
tests with prerecorded seed numbers (JP, 1981, 87-98). The basic
procedure in the present study is this: First, using a true random
source, H.S. prepares lists of pairs of six-digit random seed numbers. Next, using another electronic random generator, R.M. and
L.R. assign randomly opposite target directions (H)igh or L(ow) to
the two members of each pair. These target directions for each
test run are then communicated to H.S.

Each seed number serves one test run. At the start, the
subject enters the seed into a computer. The computer derives
from the seed a deterministic quasi-random sequence that in turn
determines the feedback display. The most frequently used display
was a pendulum swinging with random amplitude on the computer
screen. The subject's PK goal was to have the pendulum swing
with large (H target) or small (L target) amplitude. One run lasted
typically one minute. At the end, the display showed the average
swing amplitude over the run so that the subject could assess the
success or failure rate numerically.

In this arrangement subjects could do test runs on a small
computer at home whenever they wanted. And H.S. could immediately check the accuracy of the subjects' recording by re-creating
the run, using the same seed number, on his own computer.

We had decided in advance to structure this study into ten
blocks or mini-experiments, and to evaluate the total significance
by appropriately combining the ten Z values or p values of the individual blocks. The number of trials to be made in a block was
specified at the start of this block.

The final evaluation of the results by the observers was
rather simple. Remember that the observers had lists with seed
numbers that they had randomly marked by an H or L indicating
that the subject should try for a high or low score with this seed.
The observers had also received in advance a computer with the
appropriate program so that they could re-create the run and get
the score. The only thing to check was whether there was a tendency for the seeds marked H or L to produce a high or low score
respectively.

The results confirm the existence of psi under these rigorously controlled conditions. In nine of the ten blocks, the scoring went in the desired direction. From the ten individual Z values a total Z value may be obtained by the following equation:

$$Z = (Z1 + Z2 + \ldots + Z10)/SQR(10)$$

This value Z = 2.73 is significant at the 1% level (p = 0.0032, odds against chance 300:1). Another evaluation method, based on the product of the individual p-values, gives a combined p = 0.017.

At this point we will not go into the challenging conceptual questions raised by PK experiments with prerecorded seed numbers. We will not even ask who was responsible for the significant outcome, H.S. and his subjects who made most strenuous efforts to succeed, or the critical observers who through some "super psi" might have made their random generator select favorable target directions. What counts for this study is rather that the existence of some psi effect was established under exceptionally well controlled and fraudproof conditions. The experiment was very formally set up to leave no room for human errors. It was safe against equipment errors like malfunction of either the random generator used by H.S. or the one used by R.M. Fraudulent production of the results would have required the deliberate collusion among at least two of the three authors. Some additional details about the safety features can be found in an earlier report (RIP 1981, 136-138).

THE ROLE OF NOISE AND THE TRAIT OF ABSORPTION IN
GANZFELD ESP PERFORMANCE: THE APPLICATION OF
METHODS BASED UPON SIGNAL DETECTION THEORY

Rex G. Stanford[†] and Raymond F. Angelini (St. John's University)

One major objective of this study was to examine both the cognitive and the extrasensory consequences of using pink noise, as contrasted with silence, during a Ganzfeld session.

Another major objective was to learn whether a correlation exists between the trait of Absorption, as discussed by Tellegen and Atkinson (Journal of Abnormal Psychology, 1974, 268-277), and the cognitive and extrasensory consequences of Ganzfeld stimulation. The Tellegen Absorption Scale measures the inclination "for having episodes of 'total' attention that fully engage ... representational (i.e., perceptual, enactive, imaginative, and ideational) resources" (p. 268, as cited above).

A final, major objective was to have been a preliminary effort to study whether target encodability (the nonpsi probability of a response corresponding to the target type) influences extrasensory sensitivity to the target, but responses corresponding to the low-encodable target type (concrete adjectives) were discovered, at the end of the study, to have occurred with such a low frequency that an extrasensory sensitivity measure based upon them was not feasible. Thus, encodability could not be studied. High-encodable targets corresponded to a response category (concrete nouns) with a sufficiently high probability that a measure of extrasensory sensitivity for such targets could be derived. This constituted the measure of extrasensory response for this study.

One hundred unpaid volunteers, mostly undergraduate or graduate students at St. John's University, were randomly and equally assigned to the noise and silence conditions and were tested by Ray Angelini (R. A.).

The subject, alone in a commercial, acoustically shielded chamber, had half a ping-pong ball over each eye. A 150-watt incandescent bulb with foil-lined reflector and red filter shone onto the subject's face from a distance of six to seven feet while he or she reclined in a recliner chair. Through a headset the subject heard the taped instructions and experimental stimuli (experimenter's voice), as well as the experimenter himself whenever R. A. pressed a button enabling electronic voice communication to the subject. Instructions and experimental stimuli were delivered at approximately 81 dB (as measured by a Realistic sound meter), and the noise (for those in the noise condition), at approximately 77 dB, following the instructions. Subjects had the option of lowering the sound level, but they almost never did this. In the silence condition only intrinsic tape noise (in addition to the experimental stimuli) was delivered through the headset. Subjects' responses were tape recorded for later transcription.

Prior to the session each subject completed a questionnaire which included the 34 Absorption Scale items intermixed with 40 buffer items. It was not scored until after the Ganzfeld session.

Experimental instructions emphasized that the setting would favor ESP and that the experimenter would aid by "sending" a mental message concerning the proper response to give for each word-association stimulus. Brief relaxation instructions were given at the end of the instructions. The announcement that the first word was coming followed about three minutes thereafter. In the noise condition, the noise was gradually introduced at the beginning of this three-minute period. Word association to 87 stimuli (3 initial, buffer words and 84 experimental words) given at 15-second intervals lasted about 22 minutes; total Ganzfeld time (including instructions) was 35 minutes.

Unknown to subjects, approximately one-third of the word-association trials, determined on a one-third probability basis (RAND table), had no targets (blank trials); the remaining trials (two-thirds probability basis) had targets. For each trial with a target the target was either the category "concrete noun" (high encodable) or "concrete adjective" (low encodable) on an equal-probability basis (RAND table). Targets had been prepared by an assistant with no contact with subjects; R.A. did not see the targets until after leaving the chamber and discontinuing electronic voice contact with the subject. The target sheet designated, for each target trial, the target type and an appropriate response example of that type. R.A. focused on sending the example, but was aware, also, of the category (upon which scoring would actually be based). R.A. could hear both stimuli and responses (electronically) and hand-recorded responses (despite the tape record) to allow informal feedback about success at the session's end. The taped responses were later transcribed by an individual blind as to targets. We are grateful to Birgit Stanford for this transcription.

At the end of the word association, Ganzfeld was terminated, and the subject answered a five-item questionnaire concerned with 1) subjective sense of time elapsed during Ganzfeld, 2) liking for the Ganzfeld experience, 3) liking for the specifically auditory aspects of the Ganzfeld experience, 4) degree of relaxation during the word association, and 5) subjective sense of the average time interval between stimulus words.

Each response to each stimulus was categorized (by a person blind to conditions and targets) as either a concrete noun, a concrete adjective, or neither (for the development of ESP data); and each response for which there was no target was also categorized as being a superordinate, synonym, logical coordinate, subordinate, or none of these (for the development of cognitive data). The synonym category contained too few responses to be meaningful; it was not considered further. We are grateful to Amy Raphael, a student in the doctoral program in Clinical Psychology at St. John's, for categorizing responses.

The measure of extrasensory sensitivity was d', a signal-detection-theory measure of the ability to discriminate signal from noise as reflected in how often an appropriate response is given to targets (signals) as contrasted with the same response on blank (noise) trials (J.A. Swets, Science, Dec. 7, 1973, 990-1000).

The cognitive measures (proportions of superordinate, logical coordinate, and subordinate responses given on blank trials) and d' (based on high-encodable, concrete-noun targets and blank trials) were computed for each subject.

The cognitive measures provided no evidence for differential cognitive processes under noise and silence. Subjects' responses were no more divergent with noise than with silence (based on pooled target and blank trials), and none of the content-related cognitive measures showed differences under the two conditions.

Because the noise-silence manipulation did not influence the cognitive measures, the two experimental conditions were pooled for examining the correlation of the three content-related cognitive measures and Absorption. Absorption was not significantly correlated with any of these measures.

We had an a priori interest in whether responses to three (of the five) post-Ganzfeld questionnaire items (Questions 1, 4, and 5) might be related to Absorption, and since answers to these questions were not influenced by the noise-silence manipulation, the two experimental conditions were pooled for examining the correlation of Absorption with each of those questions. Responses to Question 1 (subjective time sense) were not significantly correlated with Absorption. Responses to Question 4 (relaxation during word association) were, as expected, significantly and positively correlated with Absorption; $r = +.190$, 98 df, $p < .03$ one-tailed. Responses to Question 5 (subjective interstimulus interval) were correlated significantly with Absorption; $r = +.232$, 98 df, $p = .02$, two-tailed. (Here no direction was anticipated in advance.)

Question 2 (liking for Ganzfeld experience) was not influenced by the noise-silence manipulation, but the pooled (both conditions) correlation of that item with Absorption was not significant. Question 3 (liking for the auditory background of Ganzfeld) was influenced by the noise-silence manipulation; subjects reported more liking for the silence than for noise (although that finding is difficult to interpret for various reasons, including the question's wording in the two cases). Therefore, correlations between liking for auditory background and Absorption were computed separately for noise and silence. Both correlations were close to zero.

The mean d' (across subjects) for noise was $-.084$ and for silence, $+.049$; $t = 1.88$, 98 df, $p = .063$, two-tailed, a nonsignificant, but strongly suggestive difference. The mean d' for noise was itself suggestive of psi missing; $t = -1.86$, 49 df, $p < .07$, two-tailed. The strongly suggestive difference of d' for noise and silence made it statistically ill-advised to pool the noise and silence conditions for the correlational analyses involving ESP.

Under noise, Absorption correlated significantly with d'; $r = +.286$, 48 df, $p = .04$, two-tailed. Of the five questionnaire items, liking for the noise itself correlated significantly with d'; $r = -.369$, 48 df, $p < .01$, two-tailed, indicating that less favorable responses to the noise were associated with more positive (or less negative) d' scores. Reported relaxation during word association correlated suggestively with d', if a one-tailed test be allowed; $r = +.203$, 48 df, $p < .08$.

For the silence condition none of these correlational analyses reached statistical significance.

Perhaps the noise condition does provide some special element(s) which favor ESP, since all the significant and suggestive extrasensory effects were in that condition. More sensitive methods are needed, however, to measure any cognitive effects peculiar to the noise condition.

THEORETICAL, METHODOLOGICAL, AND REVIEW ARTICLES

PARAPSYCHOLOGY AND RADICAL DUALISM

John Beloff (University of Edinburgh)

The basic question which this paper addresses is whether mind is, to some extent, independent of brain and capable of controlling brain activity or whether all mental activity is to be conceived as no more than a function of brain activity. The first answer is what I am here calling "radical dualism" (the term is less restrictive than the more familiar "Cartesian dualism"); the second answer, which represents the current orthodoxy on the mind-body problem, I shall call "physicalism" (i.e., the doctrine that all phenomena are to be explained as based ultimately on the laws of physics). It is the thesis of this paper that, if psi phenomena exist, then physicalism must be false and radical dualism must be true. If the thesis is correct, then parapsychology affords the only firm empirical grounds for rejecting the orthodox-physicalist position and thereby vindicating the autonomy of mind.

The defense of my thesis will involve two stages. First it will be necessary to show that when we consider what would be involved in a physicalist explanation of psi there is no reason to think that such an explanation is even in principle conceivable and various reasons for thinking it is not. Secondly, granted that no physicalist explanation would work, it will be necessary to show that a mentalistic interpretation of the phenomena, as implied by radical dualism, is required as opposed to other interpretations that invoke some quite different cosmic principle.

The natural starting-point for any physicalist is to consider whether ESP might be explained in principle using a physical communication model. It was often taken for granted that the only real problem in this connection was to propose a feasible form of energy that could act as the carrier of the relevant information. When we come to analyze the situation, however, it transpires that the critical question is how the information might be physically encoded at the target end and physically decoded at the receiving end. It then becomes apparent that, in every physical communication system, the encoding-decoding mechanism is either built in (as with radio or television) or, as with ordinary linguistic discourse, the language or code has first to be learnt by both parties. Now, in the case of the supposed telepathic transmission, it would be plainly nonsensical to imagine that the relevant code might have been genetically preprogrammed in our brains if only because so many of the ideas that would have to be transmitted would concern matters that never existed in a state of nature. But, equally, it would be absurd to suppose that at some stage of our development we quite unwittingly <u>learn</u> the relevant code. How? When? Where? We have only to ask such questions to see that they defy any reasonable answer.

So a physical communication analogy is clearly untenable but perhaps a physicalist solution might still be possible using a different model? Michael Thalbourne has drawn my attention to the fact that, in ESP, what very often gets transmitted is not the idea or concept of the target but some purely formal element or sensuous aspect. In that case, what might conceivably happen is that each time the sender's brain or sensory cortex is appropriately stimulated it sets up some kind of resonance which then duly elicits a corresponding resonance in the brain of the receiver without the necessity for any kind of encoding or decoding. What is involved here, in other words, is some kind of a direct field effect. Such an explanation would take us beyond physics as we now know it, but that is unimportant. The real trouble with any resonance theory is that it offers no solution to the critical question of selectivity. Why should the brain of the receiver resonate only with that of the sender and then only with those brain processes corresponding with the relevant target? Since the extraordinary selectivity of ESP is perhaps even more baffling than its apparent independence of space and time no theory is viable which does not make some contribution towards our understanding of this feature.

In fact, however, the vanguard of the physicalist school now no longer bases itself on any sort of communication model. Thus, Observational Theory, currently the front-runner among advanced theories of psi, takes as its point of departure a certain interpretation of quantum theory. It adopts the assumption that every physical object or system persists in a state of indeterminacy up to the instant at which it is observed. All we can know about the system prior to that instant is the distribution of probabilities of the values that it could assume when it is eventually observed. If, then, an observer had the power to influence that distribution in a desired direction, we would have all that, in principle, we need to account for those non-random effects we identify as a psi phenomenon. Such an observer would constitute a "psi source." The question we now have to consider is whether, granted that such a theory is valid (and it is, of course, highly controversial), would it represent a genuine physicalist explanation of psi phenomena?

To answer this question it should help if we first ask what precisely we are to understand by the key concept "observation"? Does an observation here necessarily imply a conscious awareness? Or, can such an observation be performed by some appropriate recording instrument or by the brain itself without giving rise to a

conscious percept? If consciousness is essential in this context--
and orthodox quantum physicists are still divided on this issue--then
it follows that there exists at least one property of mind, namely
that of conscious perception, which has a power not possessed by
the brain alone, namely the power to produce retroactive PK. And
this directly contradicts the thesis of physicalism. If, on the other
hand, consciousness is not essential, then we simply have no explanation at all as to what it is that makes certain brains at certain
times psi sources. In that case Observational Theory lends no support to the physicalist thesis.

Obviously one must be careful not to be too dogmatic. Physics, after all, is an open-ended activity and may yet generate new
theories of which we have as yet no inkling which could once again
put the physicalist option back into the arena. What one is entitled
to say, as of today, is that nothing that has so far transpired would
lead us to anticipate any such development and that meanwhile we
have every reason to doubt that psi can be explained in terms of
brain activity.

The collapse of physicalism, however, would not suffice to
establish radical dualism unless we could also show that psi phenomena are definitely attributable to the mind. At the present time
there are various models that challenge what has been called the
psychobiological paradigm. Here I have space only to discuss the
two most influential. The one school of thought treats psi phenomena as pure unattached anomalies, trivial hiccups in an otherwise
lawful cosmos on the strength of which no philosophical conclusions
of any kind are warranted, least of all on the mind-body problem.
Its most articulate spokesperson is the English philosopher Antony
Flew, so if we need a label let us call it "Flewism." The other
school of thought uses the term "synchronicity" as its title and is
associated with Carl Jung and, more recently, with the late Arthur
Koestler. It treats psi phenomena as essentially acausal correspondences of a meaningful kind, but not as manifestations of anyone's mental faculties. The question for us is whether there are
any compelling reasons for adopting either of these points of view
in preference to radical dualism? Let us start with the case for
Flewism.

This trades on the fact that psi phenomena are 1) defined in
purely negative terms and 2) behave so capriciously and uncontroll-
ably that they are quite unlike any known mental ability. However,
the fact that the paranormal must, in the first instance, be defined
negatively, i.e., in terms of its inexplicability, does not imply that
particular paranormal phenomena have no positive characteristics,
any more than the fact that a given class of persons may be offi-
cially designated "aliens," implying that they lack citizenship in the
country in which they reside, means that such persons lack any
ethnic affiliations whatsoever! Again, while it is true that psi phenomena are notoriously beyond our conscious control, they are by
no means unique in this respect; the same could be said of our in-
tuitions and sporadic inspirations, not to mention our capacity to

fall asleep and to dream. Moreover, on the positive side, psi phenomena reveal characteristics typical of our mental abilities: for example, we find marked individual differences; performance is highly sensitive to prevailing psychological conditions; and, most important of all, the phenomena invariably display some degree of intelligence and purposefulness, even in routine laboratory tests, which may be considered a rather degenerate case of the psi faculty at work.

Let us turn next to synchronicity theory. This stems from a realization that the kind of causation that would be implied by a causal interpretation of psi phenomena would be quite unlike the mechanical causation with which science has made us familiar and more akin to magic. It therefore seeks to interpret the phenomena in acausal terms as coincidences, but not in the dismissive sense as the skeptic would do, but as indicative of some special principle in nature whereby like attracts like. It is the same general rationale as underlies astrology and other divinatory practices. The weakness of such an acausal interpretation is that it raises many far more intractable problems than it solves. One is forcibly reminded of the extravagant lengths to which some metaphysicians of the seventeenth century were prepared to go to avoid having to acknowledge simple mind-matter interaction as proposed by Descartes. Leibniz, for example, postulated a preestablished harmony such that every act of will would invariably be followed by the appropriate movement of limbs and every stimulation of the sense organs would be followed by the appropriate conscious sensations without any interaction ever having to occur. The irony of this idea is that the preestablished harmony would had to have been imposed on nature in the first instance by some kind of a divine mind. Radical dualism adopts the simpler assumption that the human mind can impose its intentions direct on the physical world.

BIRTH AND THE OBE: AN UNHELPFUL ANALOGY (RB)

Susan J. Blackmore (University of Bristol)

Introduction. An analogy has often been drawn between the OBE (out-of-body experience) and the experience of being born. Superficial resemblances include the experience of rushing down a tunnel which is likened to the passage down the birth canal. Vibrations are compared with those of labor (Honegger, **RIP 1982**, 230-231), and the traditional "silver cord" of astral projection lore has been likened to the umbilical cord. Finally, birth does involve a kind of leaving the body.

The analogy has recently been made an explicit part of a theory of the OBE by Honegger (**RIP 1982**, 230-231). She argues that the OBE is a special kind of lucid dream in which specific features of the experience are attributable to a fetal OBE occurring at the time of birth. The stress of birth triggers the original OBE and this is why OBEs in later life are associated with vibrations, tunnel, cord and out-of-body imagery.

There are phenomenological and physiological similarities between OBEs and lucid dreams, and the same people tend to report both (Blackmore, JASPR, 1982, 301-317). However, there are serious theoretical obstacles to comparing an infant's experience with an adult OBE. Also, cords are known to be rare in OBEs and tunnels occur in many other altered states. Both these phenomena are convincingly explained in other ways (Drab, Anabiosis, 1981, 126-152; Eastman, PSPR, 1962, 287-309).

However, the hypothesis is testable. Babies born by caesarean section often do not experience full labor, do not pass along the birth canal, and do not undergo the sort of stress which Honegger suggests is the trigger for the fetal OBE. Therefore one would expect OBEs and tunnel experiences to be far less common among those born by caesarean section.

A questionnaire was given to people born normally and by caesarean section. It asked about various aspects of dreaming, OBEs, hypnagogic imagery, and tunnel experiences.

Method. A total of 234 people completed a questionnaire. The sample was not random and the figures for incidence cannot be generalized. The questionnaire asked for sex and age and whether respondents were born normally or by caesarean section. There were nine questions about OBEs, lucid dreams, and related experiences.

Results. There were 158 females (68%) and 73 males (32%). Three (1%) did not give their sex. The average age was 35.3 years. A total of 190 respondents (81%) had been born normally and 36 (15%) by caesarean section. Eight persons (3%) did not know how they were born. Those born by caesarean were (predictably) younger. Twenty-nine percent reported having had at least one OBE and of these, 79% had had more than one. One percent claimed to be able to have one at will. Honegger's hypothesis was not supported. There was no relationship between OBEs and type of birth (chi square = 2.6, 1 df, n.s.), nor between tunnel experiences and birth (chi square = 0, 1 df, n.s.). Caesareans were more likely to claim that they could control a pleasant dream (chi square = 8.7, 1 df, $p < .01$) and less likely to report falling dreams (chi square = 7.2, 1 df, $p < .01$).

Sixty-one percent claimed to have lucid dreams, 96% of these claiming more than one. Three percent could have them at will. As expected, the same people reported lucid dreams and OBEs (chi square = 7.1, 1 df, $p < .01$). OBEs and lucid dreams were both associated with having hypnagogic imagery, falling dreams, false awakenings, and the ability to control one's pleasant dreams. The ability to stop unpleasant dreams was less strongly related to the other experiences.

Those reporting hypnagogic imagery were younger than others and lucid dreamers and flying dreamers were more often male. There were no other significant age or sex differences. Altogether 55 chi-square tests were carried out and so some spurious significant results are expected.

Discussion. There are strong associations between many of the experiences. This cannot be taken to infer any causal connection and various interpretations are possible. However, there seems to be a cluster of experiences in which dream control and false awakenings, both strongly associated with each other, are central. These are related to lucid dreams, hypnagogic imagery, and OBEs, and less strongly to type of birth and falling dreams. Having flying dreams and tunnel experiences are unrelated to any other experiences. If confirmed, these findings imply that there is something crucial in the ability to control one's pleasant dreams which aids in having lucid dreams and OBEs.

Honegger's predictions receive no support at all and it is hard to think of other ways of testing her theory. I would conclude that the comparison of the OBE with birth experiences is a superficially appealing analogy but, in terms of prediction, unhelpful.

AGAINST HISTORICISM

Gerd H. Hövelmann (Marburg University)

Because the deductive model of foundation and justification (as advocated by Popper and other philosophers) necessarily runs into several insurmountable difficulties (for instance, with regard to the question of the foundation and justification of this deductive model itself), Kuhn's concept of scientific developments and scientific changes has become most influential in philosophy as well as in many branches of science. Since Kuhn's views are widely known, I need not go into details here. Suffice it to say that, according to Kuhn's historicistic conception, theories and entire scientific branches develop beyond and quite irrespective of any attempt at foundation and justification. The Kuhnian conception which I find quite inadequate has also been accepted by most parapsychologists since it is thought to adequately reflect their own situation vis-à-vis the scientific establishment. So, this conception serves (or may be serving) the following functions (among others) in our field: 1) Kuhn's opinions are believed to be picturing a pathway to future legitimacy; 2) the Kuhnian conception may serve as a welcome excuse for the fact that parapsychology has hitherto failed to gain scientific recognition; 3) this conception seems to dispense with the obligation to advance tightly reasoned propositions, since scientific changes must no longer be regarded a question of foundation and justification but one of social power. Proper justification can thus be viewed as secondary or even unnecessary.

As a consequence of Kuhn's conception, foundation and justification of scientific propositions are replaced by science-sociological and science-historical reflections and by a recourse to factual scientific developments. This is surprising, at first sight, since "foundation" and "justification" traditionally were supposed to mean methodical rather than historical securing of scientific propositions. According to Kuhn's conception which, strictly speaking, is nothing but a highly intelligent excuse for the failure of the deductive model of justification, valid foundation and justification no longer exist in science. Questions as to whether a given theory is a good and sound one are now answered by referring to the fact that--after a "revolutionary" breakthrough that led to a "paradigm switch"--this theory did factually prevail (or fail). A look at philosophy and the sciences suggests that foundation and justification have already been given up to a certain degree in favor of mere analyses of factually existing theories and factually occurring scientific changes which, in turn, seem to gain the character of natural necessities. Even a considerably radicalized version of this Kuhnian opinion is now available in the works of Collins and Pinch.

Now, the Kuhnian conception was only advanced to cope with the problems of the deductive model, and its proponents have lost sight of the fact that there is another model of justification and foundation which does not run into the difficulties with which the deductive one is confronted. This conception is able to provide proper foundation and justification of scientific propositions and, in addition, can provide a legitimizable basis for foundation and justification by way of a recourse to elementary practices of prediction and action.

A science-historically oriented practice in the Kuhnian sense is continuously in danger of becoming a stylish but cheap defense of poor science. If the quality of a theory is not judged by its foundation and justification but rather by the way it has factually superseded competing ones, then a theory can be regarded as a proper one for the mere reason that it superseded rival ones. Consequently, foundation and justification are viewed as mere historical coincidences. Systematic and well-founded argumentation which once had been obligatory in cases where the validity of theories was at issue, comes down to the mere historiography of scientific developments.

Contrary to this Kuhnian conception, I would hold that it is well possible to reconstruct justificatory steps of a theoretical development, instead of merely looking at the results of such a development. Since each form of knowledge necessarily points to a more or less strictly performed methodical and stepwise construction (otherwise we would not at all speak of knowledge!) and since, as a matter of course, questions as to the validity of our propositions are unavoidable, such endeavors to reconstruct justificatory steps of theory-building must primarily aim at a critical judgment of the practical orientations which are at the roots of the development of any scientific knowledge. It becomes possible not only to find out such orientations but also to critically argue against or in favor of them and their expediency. Thus, factual history of theoretical developments can, at least in part, be replaced by a critical foundation and justification of these developments.

Among others, this view implies the following interrelated advantages:

> 1) A very essential part of human work need not be conceived as being ruled by contingent and irrevocable natural necessities.
>
> 2) Historically contingent scientific developments for which one cannot argue <u>systematically</u> need not be conceived as governing the process of science.
>
> 3) Limited contingent parts of theories which may nevertheless exist can be distinguished from well-founded and justified ones.
>
> 4) Faulty developments can be characterized as such. As long as all possible developments of scientific disciplines and theories are taken to be equally valid--as is done, for instance, by Collins and Pinch--such characterization proves impracticable.
>
> 5) Central parts of predominating scientific theories and practices can be substantially criticized and improved by means of appropriate proposals for reorganization.
>
> 6) The Kuhnian as well as the Popperian analytical-descriptive conceptions are totally lacking any <u>normative</u> or <u>prescriptive</u> aspects.

My proposal, however, not only implies that it is possible to criticize scientific orientations, theories, and practices; it also implies that we are able to set norms as to what such orientations, theories, and practices should look like. That means that we can do even more than criticize logical faults or indicate that theories are lacking in falsifiability, etc.

If these arguments prove correct, it may then be concluded that in parapsychology (as in any other discipline) we can learn from our history not only in the sense that we will eventually know how the present situation of the field has come about, but also will know how closely connected it is with our actions as scientists; that is, in a way that will enable us to critically change our own practice where this may turn out to be desirable. Moreover, we will certainly be better able to point out to the critics of the field by means of well-founded arguments not only <u>that</u> they are wrong (if they are wrong), but also <u>why</u> they are wrong (if they are wrong).

As far as I can see, especially in parapsychology there is no reason for dispensing with solid foundation and justification of our practices, our theories, and our argumentation in favor of a conception according to which relatively contingent historical developments are telling us what to do next.

NEAL MILLER'S RATS: A CASE SUGGESTIVE OF THE DECLINE EFFECT OUTSIDE OF THE FIELD OF PARAPSYCHOLOGY (RB)

Michael K. McBeath (Washington University)

      This brief describes a set of experiments performed by the eminent psychologist Neal E. Miller, and his associates, in which repeated highly significant results eventually became nonreplicable. The case is of interest to parapsychologists both because it is suggestive that a kind of decline effect might occur outside of the field of parapsychology and because it sheds light on how other fields of science have reacted to such unsolved declines.

      During the years 1966 to 1972, Miller's group performed numerous experiments in which animals were taught to control visceral responses by means of instrumental learning (or operant conditioning). This work was the precursor to biofeedback. The majority of the experiments involved teaching rats to control their heart rates while temporarily paralyzed with curare. But some experiments were as novel as teaching rats to blush in one ear and not the other. Originally, 11 studies were published of which ten had reported probabilities of less than .001 for at least one of the main effects being observed.

      During this time, apparently, a number of other laboratories were having trouble replicating Miller's work, and by 1972 Miller himself had "joined their ranks." Miller's new assistant, Barry R. Dworkin, was unable to repeat even the simplest of the heart-rate experiments. Dworkin then reviewed the results of the earlier experiments and noticed a pattern of decline over the years. Miller and Dworkin made numerous replication attempts, checking every variable they could think of. Even with the return of Leo V. DiCara, the primary researcher responsible for much of the early work, all replication attempts were unsuccessful. The rats appeared to have a different physiological pattern of response to the curare treatment.

      Meanwhile, the topic remained controversial in the field. In addition to at least three successful replication attempts, there were scathing denials asserting that Miller's earlier work had been proven "impossible." Miller himself originally stood behind his early results, but by the late 1970s he too suggested, "... it is prudent not to rely on any of the experiments...." On August 23, 1976, Leo DiCara died, apparently by suicide. To some his death raised the spectre of fraud. But no public statement has been made by anyone involved with the research even suggesting the possibility of fraud. Miller maintains that a number of researchers in his laboratory were originally able to produce the results.

The case remains unsolved, but Miller and others are now focusing on new areas of research. Miller is quite interested in clinical biofeedback and, among other things, patient fluctuation patterns that could falsely be interpreted as successfully learned outcomes.

This brief does not aim to imply that Miller's set of experiments necessarily involved paranormal phenomena. The primary relevance of Miller's work to parapsychologists is as an example of a certain pattern of nonreplicability that is periodically found when the scientific technique is used.

Miller's case also provides us with an interesting historical perspective on how the scientific community deals with such non-replicable phenomena. The decision of Miller and others to dismiss the early experiments despite highly significant results is an example of the attitude that <u>you cannot have something half right so it must be wrong</u>. The many scientists who choose this attitude will have a tendency to avoid those types of phenomena with unusual, not-yet-understood patterns of occurrence.

Several specific aspects of Miller's experiments are also worthy of note. First, the beginning of the replication failures seems to have coincided with the departure of DiCara and the arrival of Dworkin. It is true that later DiCara was also unable to replicate the experiments, but the coincidence in timing is suggestive of some sort of relationship.

In addition, the new set of physiological responses by the rats to the curare treatment appears to be more adaptive to their self preservation. This may be of interest to parapsychologists because, for example, it is consistent with Sheldrake's theory of formative causation.

Conclusion. Neal Miller's original success with visceral learning remains an enigma, an unsolved case of a decline to nonreplicability. The fact that Miller's results resemble a pattern often reported in parapsychological research suggests that a dramatic decline in results may be characteristic of certain types of scientific phenomena. If this is true we may expect to see periodically cases similar to Miller's in other fields of science.

HYPNOTIC INDUCTION VS. CONTROL CONDITIONS: ILLUSTRATING AN APPROACH TO THE EVALUATION OF REPLICABILITY IN PARAPSYCHOLOGICAL DATA

Ephraim I. Schechter (Psychophysical Research Laboratories)

This paper illustrates some of the processes involved in analyzing research on the conditions that affect psi performance, using studies comparing ESP performance after hypnotic induction with performance in control conditions as an example.

The first step is to ask whether the performance appears to be reliably stronger when the variable is present than when it is absent. The research literature contains 25 comparisons of ESP performance following induction with performance in control conditions. Induction-condition performance was significantly higher than Control-condition performance in seven of the 20 studies for which a simple Induction-vs-Control comparison could be made; the probability of this occurring by chance is only 0.000034 (one-tailed Binomial Test, $p = .05$, $q = .95$). Induction-condition performance was nonsignificantly higher than Control-condition performance in nine of the other 13, and nonsignificantly lower than Control-condition performance in the remaining four. The likelihood that 16 out of 20 comparisons would have stronger performance after induction by chance is 0.006 (one-tailed Binomial Test, $p = q = .5$). The reports of 19 of these 20 studies contain the information needed to compare individual condition performances with mean chance expectation (MCE). Performance after induction is significantly above mean chance expectation (MCE) in nine (48%) of them and nonsignificantly above MCE in another six (32%), whereas performance under control conditions varies widely in direction and strength. This suggests that scoring is facilitated in the Induction condition.

The next step in the analysis is to ask whether this apparent effect could be due to flaws in the experimental designs. There are two levels to this question. First, we can ask whether the effect occurs primarily in studies in which the ESP testing techniques are flawed or potentially flawed, since it could be that these flaws, rather than the experimental variable, are producing the results. If the data survive this test, we can go on to ask whether the effect occurs primarily when some confounding variable is present-- if, for example, the hypnotic induction condition was always tested last, the effect might be due to practice and familiarity with the ESP test and not to the fact of the induction at all.

Nineteen of the 22 forced-choice comparisons were described fully enough to be evaluated for sensory-leakage problems. Comparing the outcomes of those that were protected against sensory leakage with the outcomes of those whose descriptions are either unclear or indicate possible sensory leakage indicates that the proportion of comparisons with greater ESP hitting after induction is no higher when the controls are weak or unclear than when they are strong.

In all of the comparisons, the experimenters knew whether an induction or control test was being given, and it is possible that unintentional scoring errors might have biased the results to favor the induction condition. Fourteen of the forced-choice comparisons contain descriptions of how the scores were checked. Having two or more people independently record and/or check the scores does not appear to interfere with the general pattern. However, six of the eight single-recorder studies with stronger performance after induction produced significant differences, suggesting that this variable should be studied more intensively.

Another potential trouble-spot in forced-choice testing is the method used to randomize the target sets. The randomization method was specified for 19 of the forced-choice comparisons: 15 used hand-shuffled cards and four used random number tables. Two of the studies using random number tables produced higher performance after induction, one produced nonsignificantly lower performance after induction, and in the fourth, which fell into the "Comparison Unclear" category, predicted high-scorers did better after induction than under control conditions whereas predicted low-scorers did worse after induction. Though it's clear that more studies using random number tables to determine the target order are needed, this technique does not seem to have destroyed the apparent effect of induction on ESP performance in the few studies that have been done.

To check on the effects of combinations of design flaws and safeguards, I gave each comparison a "flaw rating" by counting the number of potential procedural problems it had. Where the presence or absence of a problem was unclear I considered that it might have been there and counted it for that study. Then I rated how strongly each comparison supported the idea that ESP hitting is stronger after induction, using a 0 (Induction performance significantly below Control performance) to 3 (Induction performance significantly above Control performance) scale. A rank-order correlation of this "success rating" and the "cumulative flaws" score gave a nonsignificant correlation coefficient of -0.069 with 17 df (t = -0.29, p > .05).

Similar analyses can be done with other aspects of the ESP testing. It might be, for example, that the positive results come primarily from studies in which only a few percipients were tested or in which relatively few trials were used. Low numbers of percipients and trials are not like the variables discussed above-- finding a difference primarily in the studies with few data points would not necessarily lead to a non-psi interpretation, and the use of large numbers of participants and/or trials is not a "control procedure" in the sense that eliminating sensory leakage is. Still, a look at the relationships between the studies' outcomes and the numbers of data points involved may be informative.

The tendency for Induction performance to be stronger than Control performance is not concentrated in the studies with fewer percipients, nor does the direction of the Induction/Control difference appear to be related to the number of trials per condition. When low numbers of percipients and low numbers of trials per condition are included in a "success rating x number of potential design problems" analysis, the correlation between the "potential design problems" score and the "success rating" is not statistically significant (rank-order $r = -.11$, $df = 17$; $t = -.44$, $df = 17$, $p > .05$).

Although more studies are needed before we can be sure about some of the variables, it does not appear from the data so far that the tendency for Induction performance to be stronger than Control performance should be attributed to problems in the design of the ESP tests.

The next step is to ask whether the Induction/Control differences occur primarily when some confounding variable is present. For example, 20 of the 25 comparisons used within-subjects designs and the testing order was described for 16 of the 20. The apparent Induction/Control difference does not appear to be due to order effects in these studies.

Other possible confounding factors might result from aspects of the Induction/Control comparison that have little to do with hypnosis per se. For instance, the ESP differences could be related to the percipients' expectations about induction. However, only two comparisons had the percipients blind to the Induction/Control manipulation, and one of those falls into the "Comparison Unclear" category. Similarly, it is possible that the interpersonal interaction between the experimenter and the percipients and not the fact of induction is what influenced the performances.

Unfortunately, the experimenters knew whether Induction or Control tests were being given in all of the 25 comparisons, so again, no analysis is possible. That is, although it seems that the difference between the ESP performances in the Induction and Control conditions is a reliable effect which occurs more often than would be expected by chance and does not appear to be due to faulty ESP testing or experimental design, it is not clear what it is about the induction experience that is responsible for the difference.

"More research is needed" is a familiar end to a literature review in any field. The frustrations are also familiar. Published descriptions are too often incomplete, and most comparisons cannot use all of the studies. Some studies produce interactions that appear to change the direction of the effect, and cannot be included in any simple way. And even satisfying answers to replicability questions do not mean that we understand the processes involved. A further frustration is the need for more sensitive analyses of the studies' outcomes; the analyses in this paper are too coarse to be statistically satisfying. The use of effect size, a standardized measure of the difference between condition means, would yield more detailed information which could be used in meta-analyses of the relationships between the studies' procedures and their outcomes. However, ten of the 25 reports do not contain either the raw data or the summary statistics from which effect sizes can be computed directly. (Analysis of ways to estimate effect sizes from the more commonly-reported CRds is currently under way, but the most precise measure of effect size comes from group means and variances or from inferential statistics based on means and variances.)

Meanwhile, the analyses that have been possible so far are heartening--it may not be clear how the induction experience affects performance in ESP tests, but the effect does seem reliable, which is a real step towards improving overall replicability.

MOTIVATION AS THE UNIVERSAL CONTAINER: CONCEPTUAL PROBLEMS IN PARAPSYCHOLOGY

Debra H. Weiner (Institute for Parapsychology, FRNM)

Research on nonintentional psi, in which the subject is not aware of the fact that he or she is participating in a psi test, has profound implications for parapsychology. If psi can be used nonintentionally, it is possible that in traditional psi tests the experimenter--not the subject--is the person responsible for significant results. Unless results are consistent over a variety of experimenters, we do not know that a result is not merely a paranormally produced reflection of the experimenter's expectancy. Unfortunately, such consistency is rare in our field; in fact, some have suggested that the psi-based experimenter effect is at the root of this inconsistency. The question "who is 'doing' the psi?" is an important one.

This "source problem" stems from 1) the lack of boundary conditions (for example, distance) that delimit psi functioning and 2) the fact that in nonintentional psi research, the source is _inferred_ from the effect rather than being defined operationally by independent criteria. (Solely for ease of exposition I shall refer to the source in the singular.) If psi were such that it could only be used intentionally, that is, by those who knew they were being tested for psi, we could specify the source on the basis of some behavior: writing guesses, reporting internal imagery, and so on. In an experiment on nonintentional psi, on the other hand, no one--subject, experimenter, assistant--is engaging in such behavior. If the random event generator (REG) is biased we can only infer who the source might be. The source problem arises because the process of inference leads not to just one but to many possible psi sources, with no means to distinguish the real one from the remaining candidates.

This article addresses an issue which has not received much attention in the literature, but which lies at the heart of the problem: the criteria by which these inferences are made. I wish to demonstrate that 1) the source problem is in part a function of unacknowledged ambiguities in these criteria and 2) these criteria have been used to support inappropriate explanations for unexpected outcomes.

The Benefit Rule. Although the observational theories have a rule for determining possible psi sources, I will restrict my attention here to the rule more commonly used in parapsychological writing, which I shall call the benefit rule: any organism which would benefit from a successful psi effect is a possible source for that effect. This rule defines the population of organisms which could be the source of a given effect; it does not necessarily specify the actual source. This is not necessarily a weakness, for circumscribing the set of possible sources is the first step in identifying the actual source.

The benefit rule is assumed in the long-standing tradition emphasizing subject and experimenter motivation in psi success and is implicit in nonintentional-psi studies designed so that a successful outcome on the covert psi test would benefit the subject. It also plays an integral role in discussions of the source problem; for example, Kennedy and Taddonio (JP, 1976, 1-33) employ it in their argument for the psi-based experimenter effect. It is a component of Rao's volitional model (JP, 1978, 276-303; JP, 1979, 101-112), but has received its most sophisticated theoretical treatment in the hands of Stanford. For example, in his earlier model of the psi-mediated instrumental response (JASPR, 1974, 34-57; 321-356), psi is conceptualized as a need-subserving function. In his more recent conformance-behavior model (JASPR, 1978, 197-214), the benefit rule becomes the modus operandi of psi, for the model holds that a random event generator is biased toward the favorable output because it is the favorable output. These are the best, but by no means the only, expressions of the benefit rule in parapsychology.

I wish to address three problems regarding our use of the benefit rule: 1) we have arbitrarily restricted its application; if carried to its logical conclusion, it leads to the untenable situation that nearly any organism can be a possible source for nearly any psi effect. 2) We have not acknowledged the subjectivity of determining whether or not a particular outcome benefits a particular individual. 3) We have made the benefit rule unfalsifiable by using it to explain unexpected, inconsistent, or nonsignificant results.

Who Benefits ... and Why? The psi-based experimenter effect follows logically from the benefit rule; certainly the experimenter benefits from a significant result in a psi test. However, we have no reason to assume that persons outside the laboratory might not also benefit from a successful experimental outcome. Since we know of no physical barriers to psi, we cannot rule out that these other individuals might have caused the REG bias. For example, perhaps there is a high school student who hates mathematics and is motivated to use psi unconsciously to create disturbing statistical anomalies. Certainly we have no evidence that this is the case, but then we have not tried to gather such data. One might argue that the experimenter and subjects are more motivated than this hypothetical person and are therefore more likely to be the psi source. Even if we could prove this, we cannot assume that the most motivated individual is the psi source. Obviously, one can be extremely motivated and still not succeed.

This example is facetious but it illustrates that in the absence of boundary conditions for psi, the benefit rule forces us to consider nonintentional psi effects from any organism living at the moment of the test. It also demonstrates the second point: subjectivity in deciding whether or not a person would benefit from a particular outcome (and therefore be considered a possible source). In some cases, benefit is easy to determine: water is beneficial to a thirsty animal. Unfortunately for the benefit rule, however, survival-related motivators are generally unsuccessful in eliciting psi. When we turn to more abstract motivations, we find some ambiguity in determining whether or not a person would benefit from a given psi event. This ambiguity gives the benefit rule a flexibility which undermines its explanatory power. This point is best illustrated by motivational interpretations for significant below-chance scores, inconsistent findings, and nonsignificant results.

<u>The Omnipotence of Motivation: Benefit as an Unfalsifiable Hypothesis</u>. Psi missing poses a logical problem for the benefit rule because "benefit" is a directional concept. It does not make sense to think that the opposite of a favorable outcome is also favorable. For example, it is ludicrous to say "Since I am poor, I would benefit from obtaining money; therefore, I would benefit from being robbed." We could argue that I derive some <u>other</u> benefit from being robbed--say, that I would change my values about material possessions--but this is an ad hoc explanation. In order to maintain the benefit rule in the case of psi missing, we must invoke ad hoc explanations. Such ad hoc explanations for missing or inconsistent results are not uncommon in parapsychology. For example, in <u>Extrasensory Perception After Sixty Years</u> (1940), significant missing with delayed feedback was interpreted as an expression of subjects' frustration with the lack of encouragement. The authors note that a special subject in another study scored extremely well without ever knowing her scores and explain the inconsistency by presuming that the special subject was highly confident. However, the original report of this study suggests that she had a reluctant, perhaps anxious attitude; thus there is no reason to believe that a difference in motivation existed or that if it did, it was responsible for the inconsistency.

In some cases, motivational interpretations are offered to explain a trend in results when a good argument can be made for why the opposite trend should be expected. For example, the general decline in significance over a line of research has sometimes been attributed to waning experimenter enthusiasm. But wouldn't a parapsychologist feel *very* excited during a replication study, for the experiment is not "just" a pilot but may be the breakthrough? This is not to argue one way or the other, but to demonstrate that with imagination, we can explain *any* result on the basis of benefit or motivation.

Motivational hypotheses have also been invoked to explain why an experiment succeeded in the first place. While clinical impressions of experimenter motivation are extremely valuable, I wonder if they have developed a zeitgeist in which success and failure are interpreted in motivational terms. In my own work I have seen little consistent relationship between motivation and psi success. Perhaps I am not a "psi-conducive" experimenter, with significant results only randomly distributed through my career; however, Carl Sargent, who does enjoy a reputation for success, has made a similar observation (JSPR, 1978, 805-823). These limited impressions do not overthrow a 50-year-old tradition, but they do call for a deeper examination of this tradition and a more circumspect use of motivational interpretations.

Motivation: The Universal Container. In alchemical mythology we read of the "universal solvent," a substance so corrosive that it dissolves all material and therefore cannot be contained. In our current conceptualization of it, psi resembles a universal solvent, for it is not bound by distance, time, difficulty of the task confronting it, nor conscious awareness of its operation by the psi source.

We have assumed that motivation is a container that gives form to psi--determining why it occurs, why it does not, and why it becomes distorted into negative scores. I have tried to show that motivation contains psi only because we have arbitrarily restricted our thinking to certain motivations from certain individuals. I make this argument not because I think we must take into account everyone's obscure motivations, but because an analysis of the nature of these restrictions will bring to light additional assumptions. For example, do we think that the hypothetical math student could not be a psi source because 1) he is too far away from the REG; 2) he probably does not know about the experiment; or 3) gratification of his desire follows too long after the psi test outcome? Perhaps we implicitly believe that there *are* boundary conditions for psi which exclude certain persons as psi sources. While Stanford has addressed a few of these issues, they have not received general discussion. Such discussion would clarify our assumptions about psi.

In this article I have also questioned the usefulness of post hoc motivational interpretations for psi missing and failures to obtain significant results. Saying that subjects miss because of an "unconscious fear of psi" or that an experimenter got null results because he or she did not try hard enough begs the question.

Perhaps our readiness to put forth such explanations keeps us from examining our data more thoroughly and uncovering valuable information.

What I have <u>not</u> done here is resolve the source problem. We can no longer ignore the implications of nonintentional psi, but we do not yet have a viable means to find out who (or what) is causing our results. Creating such means is the challenge facing both those who study psi with traditional scientific methods and those who search for new paradigms.

SURVEYS

A POSTAL SURVEY OF OBEs AND OTHER EXPERIENCES (PS)

Susan J. Blackmore (University of Bristol)

Introduction

Several surveys have provided very varied figures for the incidence of OBEs (out-of-body experiences). Haraldsson et al. (RIP 1976, 182-186) reported that only 8% of Icelanders claimed to have had an OBE, whereas Kohr (JASPR, 1980, 395-411) found 50% among a special population. Other surveys have provided figures in between.

Factors affecting the variation include the wording of the question and the amount of information given (Blackmore, JSPR, 1982, 292-302), the context in which the question is asked, and the population sampled. The survey reported here used a random sample.

Collections of cases provide many descriptions of OBEs, but are necessarily biased in their selection methods. The only survey using random sampling to ask about the nature of the experiences was Palmer's (JASPR, 1979, 221-252). He found that over 100 reported OBEs, over 80% claiming more than one. Most reported seeing their own bodies from "outside" but few traveled anywhere, gained any information by ESP, or appeared as an apparition to someone else.

The proportion of multiple OBEs implies that someone who has had one OBE is more likely to have another, but it is not clear why. Simply variables such as age, sex, and education are not good predictors. Palmer and Kohr both found that OBErs also tend to report mystical experiences, lucid dreams, and dream recall. These are included in the present survey.

It has been suggested that psychological, as opposed to paranormal, models of the OBE predict better imagery skills in OBErs, but this has not been found (Blackmore, JASPR, 1982, 301-317; Irwin, JSPR, 1980, 448-459). Other experiences which may be relevant include hallucinations and body image distortions, both of which are included here.

Method

A total of 593 people were randomly selected from the Electoral Register for the City of Bristol by choosing every 500th name.

In June 1981 a questionnaire, an explanatory letter, and a stamped, addressed envelope were sent out by post. After three weeks a reminder was sent and after a further three weeks another questionnaire, letter, and envelope were sent to those who had still not replied.

The questionnaire included 13 questions about dreams, hallucinations, mystical experiences, psychic experiences and beliefs, and OBEs. There were also two questions on vividness of imagery. For those who had had an OBE (OBErs), 22 additional questions were asked about their experience(s). For each question a number (from two to eight) of possible answers was provided. Some had additional parts to be answered by experients.

The main analysis was by contingency tables with associated chi-square values, pooling cells wherever necessary.

Results

Return Rates. Fourteen people were excluded because they had died or could not be traced, reducing the sample to 579. Seventy respondents (12%) were unwilling or unable to complete the questionnaire. Over half (321, or 55%) returned usable replies. This compares with 51% obtained by Palmer from his townspeople sample and is about the rate expected for a postal survey.

Nevertheless the incidence figures may be artificially inflated if those with experiences were more likely to reply. If so we would expect fewer positive responses in the later mailings. Therefore, for each question the proportion of positive answers in each mailing was compared. For OBEs there were more positive replies in the third mailing. For mystical experiences and body image distortions there were more in the second mailing. Figures for these must therefore be treated with caution. There were no other significant effects.

There were 145 males (45%) and 163 females (51%). Thirteen did not give their sex (4%). Ages ranged from 18 to 87 with a mean of 44.6. Other findings are discussed below by topic.

OBEs. There were 39 respondents (12%) who claimed to have had an OBE. There were no significant age or sex differences between OBErs and non-OBErs.

OBErs were more likely to report lucid dreams (chi square = 10.0, p = .002), flying dreams (chi square = 27.1, p = .00000019), hallucinations (chi square = 15.7, p = .00004), body image distortions (chi square = 5.4, p = .02), and mystical experiences (chi square = 29.7, p = .00000002). They were more likely to have experienced telepathy (chi square = 20.2, p = .000003) and to believe in ESP (chi square = 15.4, p = .0005) and survival (chi square = 8.8, p = .003). Frequency of dream recall was unrelated to OBEs.

A further analysis of mystical experiences showed no significant differences between OBErs and others in the type or circumstances of the mystical experience.

Eighty-five percent of OBErs had had more than one OBE, in line with previous findings. Just 5% (two people) claimed to be able to induce an OBE at will. The most common circumstance for the OBE was "when resting but not asleep" (59%). Other circumstances noted were operations (26%), accidents (18%), drugs or medicines (18%), and "other" (31%); several claimed OBEs during sleep.

The most common length for OBEs was one to five minutes (24%), with many less than one minute. Only 5% claimed experiences longer than five minutes and none longer than 30 minutes.

"Strange sensations before the experience began" were noted by 85%; the most common being unusually vivid imagery and disorientation (28% each). Shaking and vibrations (mentioned by such adepts as Muldoon and Monroe) were only reported by five people (12%). The start of the experience rarely involved tunnels or doorways (8%). Most people just found themselves "out" (67%). At the end few lost consciousness, or experienced tunnels or dark spaces (8% each). Most just found themselves back again.

The state of consciousness during the OBE was usually "like dreaming" (49%) or like being normally awake (44%). The world seen was most often like the normal world (36%) or more vague than normal (24%). Fewer (15%) compared it to a dream or fantasy world. Traveling is often thought essential to an OBE, but less than half (44%) claimed to have traveled away from their body.

Over half (54%) did not see their own physical body. Of those who did most said it looked normal. As for the "other self," most (69%) seemed to be a complete body as usual. Only 24% claimed any connection between the OB self and the body.

Clarity of vision was as usual for 51%, dimmer than usual for 31%, and clearer than normal for 21%. The lighting varied, but mostly (46%) was correct for the actual situation at the time.

Twenty-eight percent said they had seen or heard something they could not have known about beforehand, but most of these (64%) did not check the details. Of those who did, all claimed that they were correct but these claims were not checked.

Most respondents were not sure whether they had enjoyed the experience, did not find it frightening, and were about equally divided as to whether they would like another. Only 10% claimed changes in their life or beliefs. Over half (51%) reported having a little knowledge about OBEs before they had one. The age at which the experience occurred varied between three and 70 years but many were unable to give exact ages.

Dreams. There were 147 people (47%) who reported lucid dreams and nearly all (93%) had had more than one. Five claimed to be able to have them at will. There were no significant sex differences, but experiencers were younger (t = 4.2, 297 df, p = .00004). Lucid dreamers also reported more frequent dream recall (chi square = 30.8, p = .0000009), more vivid dreams (chi square = 16.6, p = .001), more flying dreams (chi square = 15.9, p = .00007), hallucinations (chi square = 12.7, p = .005), and body image distortions (chi square = 6.4, p = .01). They had more often experienced telepathy (chi square = 13.9, p = .003) and believed more in ESP (chi square = 7.2, p = .03), though not in survival. Lucid dreamers reported more vivid imagery on one, but not both, of the imagery questions.

A total of 89 persons (28%) reported flying dreams. There were no sex differences but experiencers were younger (t = 3.9, 168 df, p = .00014). As with lucid dreams, flying dreamers were more likely to report most of the other experiences, except they did not report more vivid dreams or imagery.

Mystical Experiences. Nineteen percent claimed to have had "profound or moving religious or mystical experience," most having had only one experience, taking place during normal waking activity. Most common were a sense of great humility and a oneness with God.

Other Questions. Forty-five percent claimed to have had a waking hallucination and 80% more than one. Telepathy was claimed to have been experienced by 25% and 36% believed that ESP is possible. The main reason given was their own experience. Forty-two percent believed in survival, mostly because of religious beliefs.

Discussion

The details of the OBE are roughly comparable to Palmer's for the questions he asked, but seem to show a less rosy and distinctive picture than Osis' survey. This may be attributable to differences in sampling.

The most important finding is the degree of association between having OBEs and the other experiences asked about. There may be some nonspecific factor, such as age, or social pressures, which predisposes people to answer affirmatively to all the questions. Or there may be some genuine similarity underlying all the experiences. According to psychological models of the OBE, all the experiences involve the creation of an imaginary world which appears real to the experiencer. These models predict the associations found here and the results can be seen as at least circumstantial support for a psychological rather than paranormal account of the OBE.

A SURVEY OF ORGANIZATIONS IN PARAPSYCHOLOGY AND PERIPHERAL AREAS (RB/PS)

Laura F. Knipe[†] and Nancy K. Nybergh (American Society for Psychical Research)

A survey of 241 United States organizations and 180 foreign organizations was taken. Of these, 73 United States organizations responded with 71 still active. Of the 71 active organizations, 64 (90%) are nonprofit and 50 (70%) offer membership. Of the 50 offering membership, 14 (28%) had at least one restriction on their membership (such as an agreeing with the organization's beliefs or requiring professional credentials) and the membership of 36 (72%) organizations was open to the public. At least one periodical is published by 41 (58%) organizations; 49 (69%) hold meetings, 54 (76%) hold lectures, 47 (66%) offer classes, 18 (25%) hold sittings with psychics, and 36 (51%) have other activities, such as seminars or workshops. There are libraries in 49 (69%) organizations with 25 (51%) offering borrowing privileges, although some may lend material only to their members. One chapter or affiliate was claimed by 21 (30%) organizations.

Of the 65 foreign organizations who responded, 63 (97%) are nonprofit, 55 (85%) offer membership with 34 (62%) of these open to the public, and 21 (38%) have at least one restriction. At least one periodical is published by 41 (63%) organizations, 50 (77%) hold meetings, 51 (78%) hold lectures, 25 (38%) offer classes, 28 (43%) hold sittings with psychics, and 18 (27%) offer other activities. There are libraries in 58 (89%) organizations with 36 (62%) offering borrowing privileges, although some may lend only to their members. One chapter or affiliate was claimed by nine (14%) organizations.

For the United States respondents, three (4%) have been established under a year, two (3%) for 1 year, three (4%) for 3 years, four (6%) for 4 years, four (6%) for 5 years, twenty-seven (38%) between 6 to 10 years, ten (14%) between 16 and 20 years, nine (13%) between 21 and 25 years, five (7%) between 26 and 50 years, two (3%) between 51 and 100 years, and none have been established for longer than 100 years. For the foreign organization respondents, three (5%) have been established for less than a year, two (3%) for 1 year, two (3%) for 2 years, five (8%) for 3 years, two (3%) for 4 years, three (5%) for 5 years, ten (15%) between 6 and 10 years, six (9%) between 11 and 15 years, eight (12%) between 16 and 20 years, three (5%) between 21 and 25 years, fourteen (21%) between 26 and 50 years, five (8%) between 51 and 100 years, and one (2%) for over 100 years. Only one (2%) organization did not respond to this question.

A breakdown of the type of organization was almost impossible to do. Many organizations not only have an interest in psychical research, but also seem to be more religiously oriented or interested in UFOs and one organization even had an interest in vampires. This leads the authors to propose that one organization distribute this information about organizations. The authors would like to see the Parapsychological Association act as a clearinghouse for organizations, research, and the work in the field. If the PA were to take on this job, many misconceptions about psychical research might be put to rest. We feel the Parapsychological Association could distribute this information in one major journal composed of contributions by editors from major research centers. This one publication could be sold to other organizations to distribute to their members/subscribers which could help reduce publication costs for all organizations. This one publication would reach others who may be looking for a more scientific approach to psi and/or to skeptics who are skeptics due to the misconceptions about the field in general. This publication could give parapsychology the boost it needs. Most importantly, it would provide a forum for the Parapsychological Association to be able to express its views and the opinions of its members concerning new and established organizations, research, and the work in the field, and include articles on research and theory, book reviews, announcements, and news of research in other fields relating to parapsychology. A Parapsychological Association journal would give parapsychology a unified voice in the scientific community.

A RETROSPECTIVE SEARCH FOR CORRELATES OF BELIEF IN LIFE-AFTER-DEATH. I. ICELANDIC DATA.

Michael A. Thalbourne[†] (Washington University) and Erlendur Haraldsson (University of Iceland)

In virtually every culture and historical period there can be found the belief in some sort of afterlife. The present age is no exception: according to the 1980-81 Gallup Poll, 67% of all persons interviewed in the USA believed in survival of death. But equally, the number of disbelievers is by no means small. In the United States the proportion is 27%, and in nearly every nation skepticism has been on the rise since World War II.

The question we wish to raise is this: What are the variables which determine belief in survival? What causes one person to hold a belief in survival, and another person to reject it? Even granting that the actual content of the survivalists' views is likely to be quite varied--there are many theories as to what is entailed in survival--are there nevertheless any dimensions which distinguish between believer and disbeliever? Previous research indicates that the following variables are associated with belief in an afterlife (hereinafter abbreviated "BA"): 1) There are wide national differences in BA, with Iceland, the USA, and India having approximately 70% believers, whereas Japan has only 18%. 2) There is reasonably good evidence that BA is higher among older age-groups; however, lack of longitudinal data prevents us from knowing whether advancing age is associated with an increase in BA. 3) There is a quite consistent tendency for BA to be more prevalent among women than among men. 4) Believers in survival also tend to believe in psychic phenomena, i.e., to be "sheep" rather than "goats." And 5) British research has suggested that though BA is more common in the upper class than in the working class, this difference is due for the most part to the dimension of political conservatism/radicalism, with conservative voters being the believers.

The authors have a large body of questionnaire- and survey-type data through which we are retrospectively sifting in an attempt to discover or replicate such correlates of BA. For example, we examine the possibility of a relationship between BA and personality factors, since there seems to be more armchair speculation than empirical data on this question.

In this article we confine ourselves to four samples of data collected in Iceland. In these studies, BA was ascertained by using a single question, such as "Do you believe in an afterlife, i.e. that the human soul lives on after the death of the body?" A range of possible responses, numbering either four or five, was then provided, viz. "unthinkable," "unlikely," "possible," "likely," and "certain."

Study I. In a national survey of psychical experiences conducted in Iceland during 1974-75, data were also collected on such items as religiosity, religious experiences, and dream recall in addition to beliefs concerning parapsychological phenomena and Icelandic folklore. The sample consisted of 902 persons (425 males, 477 females), aged between 30 and 70 years, and selected at random from the National Registry.

Results. BA correlated significantly with sex ($r = .25$) and with age group ($r = +.17$), indicating a slight but significant tendency for BA to be stronger among women and older persons. A correlation with education level was nonsignificantly negative.

Correlations were computed between BA and a total of 34 questionnaire items, as well as 11 composite variables constructed out of these and other simple variables. Twenty of the 34 basic correlations were significant and nontrivial (i.e., $r \geq .10$), as were nine of the 11 composite variables. These results may be summarized under three headings: 1) Beliefs: Compared with low BA subjects, those with high BA tend to have stronger belief in the ability to interact with the dead or otherworldly entities, and to have a higher degree of belief in ESP and astrology. 2) Experiences: Believers in an afterlife tend to claim more experiences of a psychic nature, both of a this-world and of an other-world type; they also report more religious or spiritual experiences. 3) Behavior: Afterlife believers tend more frequently to report that they are religious, that they read the Bible and books about psychic phenomena, that they have attended séances and other demonstrations of mediumship, as well as consulted psychics or faith healers; they also explore the meaning of their dreams. Finally, on the three-item Icelandic Sheep-Goat Scale, the differences between the five BA response-categories used were highly significant, indicating a progressive linear increase in Sheep-Goat Scale score as BA increased.

Study II. This sample consisted of 75 male subjects, all First-Year students at the University of Iceland, and on average 22 years of age. All subjects had participated in one or other of two studies conducted to test a possible relationship between ESP scoring level and scores on the Defense Mechanism Test. In addition, subjects were administered Form C of the Cattell Sixteen Personality Factor Questionnaire (16PF). And finally, they completed a short, 15-item questionnaire asking about BA, psychic phenomena, religion, politics, and dream recall.

Results. Because all the subjects were the same regarding sex and educational level, and since exact age was not ascertained, it was not possible to correlate BA with any of the demographic variables. BA could, however, be correlated with the 14 questionnaire items, and indeed ten of these were significant: believers in an afterlife tended to believe in GESP, precognition, and in the supposed ability to see the dead; to read about religion and about psychic phenomena; to report themselves as being religious; to pray; to attend religious gatherings; to engage in dream interpretation; and to vote in student elections.

Of four correlations with the DMT variable, one was significant (rho = +.33, N = 37, 2p = .043), indicating that survival believers were lower in level of preconscious perceptual defensiveness.

Of 29 continuous variables subjected to univariate analysis of variance, comparing the four BA response-categories used, four were significant: the three-item Icelandic Sheep-Goat Scale; a four-item Sheep-Goat Scale; a three-item Religiosity Scale; and the 16PF's Factor Q_{III} (tough vs. tenderminded). Believers thus tended strongly to be sheep and religious, and, to a much smaller extent, tendermindedly emotional. Supplementary t tests suggested that believers might also be lower on Factor M--being more conventional and less Bohemian than disbelievers--and higher on Factor A--being more warm-hearted.

Study III. Form D of an Icelandic translation of the Cattell

16PF was administered in 1978 to 500 people in Reykjavik. Of
these subjects, 113 (76 males, 37 females) were also given a brief
seven-item questionnaire about BA, psychic phenomena, religion and
dreams. Agewise, these subjects ranged from 18 to 45 with a mean
of 23.6 years. All came from various vocational schools which
taught such skills as seamanship, machining, nursing, kindergarten
teaching, waiting and hotel management.

Results. BA did not correlate significantly with either sex
or age. It did, however, correlate significantly with belief in the
supposed gift for seeing the dead, belief in precognition and GESP,
and with reading about religion and about psychic phenomena.

Twenty-two continuous variables were subjected to one-way
ANOVA and to two types of t-test. The results suggested that believers were significantly more likely to be sheep, conscientious
(Factor G), convention (M), conservative (Q_1), group-oriented (Q_2),
subdued (Q_4), and possibly more controlled (Q_3), more extraverted
(Q_I), and less tough-minded (I).

Study IV. This sample consisted of 197 students at the University of Iceland, males outnumbering females by two to one. All
subjects had been administered an Icelandic version of Rotter's
Internal-External Locus of Control Scale. Subjects were also given
a 17-item questionnaire relating, in addition to BA, to religion,
psychic phenomena, and politics.

Results. Exact age was not ascertained for these subjects.
However, belief in an afterlife did correlate significantly with sex
(rho = .24), females having the stronger belief. BA also correlated significantly with 12 of the 16 other items on the questionnaire: Believers in an afterlife tended to score higher on religious
and paranormal belief variables, and are perhaps somewhat less interested in political matters than are disbelievers (though the four
nonsignificant correlations were all with political items). There
was no significant relationship with the Locus of Control Scale.

Discussion. The most obvious and least surprising of the
results was that afterlife believers tend also to believe strongly in
psychic or other anomalous phenomena and are more religious (in a
personal, nonsectarian sense) than are disbelievers. Also, women
tend to believe more than do men, and what little evidence there is
suggests that older persons tend to believe marginally more strongly than younger persons.

The novel findings concern relationships with personality.
Believers tended to be more conservative, group-oriented, and subdued, while disbelievers tended to be more radical, self-sufficient,
and independent. Suggestive results indicated that believers may
also tend to be more conscientious, conventional and self-controlled,
with skeptics being more expedient, unconventional, and lacking in
discipline. These findings make a certain amount of sense: At
least in Iceland and the United States, BA is widely held, with

skeptics in the minority. Those who by personality and disposition tend to orient themselves towards smooth integration with society might thus be expected to be believers, whereas those who tend to be rebelliously individualistic would tend to be disbelievers because they would tend to question widespread opinion. This hypothesis could be tested by comparing the personality characteristics of believers and nonbelievers in environments where belief in an afterlife is in the minority.

VARIETIES OF BELIEF IN SURVIVAL: AN EXPLORATORY STUDY (RB/PS)

Michael A. Thalbourne and Linda Williams (Washington University)

In order to investigate more fully the psychological question of belief in some sort of afterlife, a questionnaire was designed to measure degree of belief in seven possible theories of survival. Our aim was, first, to tabulate the percentages of belief and disbelief accorded each theory; second, to examine the intercorrelations among the seven theories; and third, to search for correlations between these theories and a number of demographic variables.

A Belief-in-Afterlife Survey was constructed in which were contained seven variations on the theme of survival. These were in order: 1) the theory of "extinction," or "non-survival" of the conscious personality; 2) the theory of survival for a limited period after death, where the consciousness persists for a time but then itself "dies" and ceases to exist--what we may call "death-after-death"; 3) the theory of reincarnation (on Earth); 4) reincarnation on another planet; 5) the theory of the Resurrection of the Dead; 6) the immortality hypothesis; and 7) the "selective survival" hypothesis, that the consciousness of some people is extinguished at death but that for others it continues.

Each of the seven theories was presented as a statement with five alternative responses being allowed (viz. "completely disagree," "disagree," "uncertain," "agree," and "completely agree").

The two-page survey was administered to people attending a lecture given by the first author during a Regional Gathering of the high intelligence club, MENSA, in St. Louis, Missouri. (There does not seem to be any evidence that high-intelligence persons differ systematically in afterlife-belief from persons of lower intelligence, and it was thus assumed that no bias would be introduced on that account.) A total of 52 questionnaires were returned. Of the subjects, 19 were male, 26 were female, and 7 gave no information; mean age was 39.5 years, s.d. was 12.2, and the range was 18 to 72. We also asked the subject's marital status, their religion of upbringing and their present religious affiliation, but the sample size was too small to be able to calculate meaningful inferential statistics with these variables.

For ease of interpretation, "completely agree" responses were pooled with "agree" (and similarly for the two responses expressing disagreement), resulting in three response-categories: agree, uncertain, disagree. The most commonly endorsed particular theory was found to be the extinction hypothesis (27%). However, 62% of the sample disagreed with this hypothesis, thereby implying their belief in some sort of (unspecified) afterlife. Taken as a straightforward "Do you believe in life-after-death?" question, this item yielded figures remarkably close to those recently obtained for a national sample by George Gallup (Adventures in Immortality, 1982)--namely, 27% disbelief, 67% belief, and 6% no opinion. This suggests that despite the small sample and the high intelligence of its members the subjects may nevertheless for our purposes be reasonably representative of the U.S. population as a whole.

As is to be expected if the questionnaire is functioning in a valid and self-consistent way, belief in extinction was found to be negatively correlated with belief in five out of six theories of survival, four of these being significant (viz. belief in immortality, resurrection, and the two reincarnation types; the nonsignificant association was with belief in selective survival). A significantly positive correlation was found between extinction and the Death-after-Death item. This is perhaps due to the latter's incorporation of the extinction notion.

Inspection of the rest of the correlation matrix suggested that two independent belief systems were operating--the first containing belief in immortality (without rebirth) and the Resurrection of the Dead; the other belief cluster centering on belief in reincarnation (on Earth or another planet) plus selective survival. It is noteworthy that these clusters correspond so closely to, on the one hand, the Western, Christian tradition, and on the other hand, the Eastern, Buddhist-Hindu tradition.

There was no indication that any survival hypothesis was related to age. As regards the sex variable, however, the males were found to be significantly more likely to believe in the extinction hypothesis (rho = .28, N = 45, p = .030, one-tailed). The only other specific survival theory correlating significantly with sex was the immortality hypothesis (rho = .40, N = 45, p = .004, one-tailed), with women believing in immortality to a greater extent than do men.

These encouraging results suggest that there is promise in this more differentiated approach to the belief-in-afterlife question.

SPONTANEOUS PSI / FIELD STUDIES

CHARACTERISTICS OF PURPOSEFUL ACTION IN AN APPARITION CASE

Karlis Osis (American Society for Psychical Research)

Apparition experiences (AEs) possess a bewildering, sometimes contradictory, variety of qualities. In near-death experiences apparitions evoke peace and fascination; in other contexts they evoke fear and depression. Apparitions rarely say or otherwise communicate anything; some use this to justify categorizing all apparitions as images void of consciousness. Apparitions make much more sense if we postulate specific interpretations for the different kinds of AEs. This present case depicts one type of AE: the appearer seems to have its own purpose and the experients responded positively to it.

This case involves the apparition of a middle-aged, married businessman, Leslie,* father of four children, one of whom died 18 months before the airplane crash resulting in Leslie's death. This case came to my attention in early 1983. Three experients and six witnesses were interviewed over the telephone and through written correspondence. On March 18, 1983, the research team (Osis, Donna McCormick, and a psi practitioner) visited the ostensible appearer's widow and his mother, Marge; the following questionnaires were then administered to Marge: Thurstone's "Closure Speed Test"; Sheehan's revised version of Betts' "Questionnaire upon Mental Imagery"; a slightly modified (by Osis and McCormick) version of the absorption scale of Tellegen's "Differential Personality Questionnaire"; and Osis' "Questionnaire on Psychic Experiences" (see Osis and McCormick, RIP 1981, 120-123, for further information on questionnaires).

In 1982, Leslie was alone piloting a private airplane across the southern United States. After the second refueling, Leslie reached an altitude of 3,000 feet, apparently lost control of the craft, and at 11:30 p.m. (EST) crashed; his family was notified several hours later.

---

*Fictitious names are used and dates and places deleted to ensure the privacy of those concerned.

The family feared Leslie's death would be a dangerous shock to his mother, Marge, who was in her late fifties and had severe health problems. A relative, Vivian, phoned her own mother, Constance, to inform her of Leslie's death. Constance, knowing of Marge's health problems, was concerned that the news would adversely affect her and wanted to help. She tried to summon Leslie's surviving spirit by concentrating on his photograph and requesting him to soothe Marge's anguish by appearing to her. Knowing Marge was an ardent disbeliever in afterlife, Constance implored Leslie to give his mother a sign to convince her it was actually him. The suggested sign was of Leslie holding his recently deceased ($1\frac{1}{2}$ year old) son by the hand. Constance repeated this plea once or twice the next day; no one except her husband knew what she was doing.

Two nights after Constance's first request to Leslie, Marge was awakened by a disturbance in her room and saw someone at the foot of her bed:

> There he was, Leslie, with the baby, and he was holding the baby's hand.... I was wide awake then. They were content; they were happy that they found each other, that they were together now. And they were letting me know that it is so; I got that feeling.... They were solid. There was like grayness around, like a gray cloud around them.... The room was dark ... but I didn't need light to see them. There is alot of traffic around my area.... Not one sound then, all was excluded at that moment, everything, as though the world had stood still. And there was nobody but us three in the world. I got a peaceful feeling, everything around was completely serene. I felt them as if they were breathing my life into me. He was giving my life back to me. And it's the most lasting feeling: I will never, never forget this.... It never happened before and never happened since. They were just there, I believe, to give me peace of mind. It really helped. I have not gotten over it [the grief] yet, but it made me able to live through very hard times without killing myself, because I was very despondent.

She said the experience lasted about 15 seconds, but its effects were still felt.

Leslie's favorite niece, Jennifer, witnessed a similar apparition a few hours before and 100 miles away from Marge. Six-year-old Jennifer already knew of her uncle's death, but not of Marge's experience until two days later at the funeral (when Marge also heard of hers). Jennifer's mother remembered the experience well; her father's memory was vague.

Jennifer described: "I was up and awake when I saw like a cloud in my room and there was Leslie and Rusty [his son] holding hands.... They looked just regular [life-like].... It looked almost exactly like him [Leslie]." When asked how they disappeared, Jennifer said, "I stopped thinking about them and they went away." Jennifer consistently stated she was awake and her eyes open. Her feeling about the event: "Part of it was happy and part of it was sad." She said, and her mother confirmed, that she felt close to Leslie when he was alive. This was Jennifer's only AE. No tests were administered to Jennifer because she and her family are now living in California.

Although each AE was observed by a single individual, they reported the event within hours to at least one other person; neither knew of the other's experience until after her own. Therefore, each experience was independently witnessed. The temporal proximity, and the independence of and detailed similarity to Marge's AE, seem to increase the importance and validity of Jennifer's vision.

The following are results of the tests administered to Marge:

1. <u>Questionnaire upon Mental Imagery</u>: the highest extreme for vividness of imagery was checked on all items;

2. <u>Absorption Scale of the DPQ</u>: tendency to become absorbed was in the upper range for two thirds of the items;

3. <u>Closure Speed Test</u>: below average ability (compared with other apparition experients) to perceive objects from fragmented and poorly structured gestalts;

4. <u>Questionnaire on Psychic Experiences</u>: moderate belief in afterlife; claims some personal ESP.

How does Marge's description of the apparition fit with these test findings? The exclusion of traffic noises and reduction in clarity of visual surrounds fit with above average ability to become absorbed. She described shadow-like apparitions, lacking detailed features; this fits her low scores on the closure speed test but is contrary to her high vividness of imagery scores, which might suggest perceptual rather than fantasy processes.

Interviewees showed no motives for perpetrating a hoax or grossly distorting their narratives. I learned of the case through a questionnaire routinely sent to new A.S.P.R. members, which Constance had completed; she first described two precognitive experiences, then reported the case in an enclosed letter. Leslie's mother and widow were initially reluctant to respond to our inquiry. No one seemed eager to impress the investigator. The AE seemed to conflict with Marge's preapparition belief system. The descriptions of events were reasonably consistent.

Traditionally, two competing hypotheses are used to interpret AE cases: 1) <u>survival hypothesis,</u> which assumes the active participation of a deceased agent--in this case, Leslie; 2) <u>super-</u>

ESP hypothesis, which assumes the AE is ESP-based and generated exclusively by living individuals, i.e., Constance, Marge, and Jennifer. The survival hypothesis seems to accommodate the facts in this case, but requires the assumption that Leslie complied with Constance's request and appeared to the experients with his dead son. The super-ESP hypothesis is more difficult to apply.

The super-ESP hypothesis assumes Constance unintentionally sent a telepathic message to Marge and Jennifer (despite being unaware of the latter's existence). Hours later, the experients had hallucinations depicting the way Constance requested Leslie to appear. This resulted in attitude changes and emotional reorientation for Marge. The super-ESP hypothesis must account for: 1) the time lag between message being sent and received; 2) ostensible telepathy between individuals whose existences were unknown to each other; 3) the creation of identical images in percipients' minds and at different times; 4) the penetration of Marge's passionate disbelief in survival. It is perhaps most difficult to understand how Constance, a distant relative, could telepathically induce an experience that would have such a tremendous impact on Marge's life. Successfully sending a telepathic message to a completely unknown person 100 miles away has no clear precedent, so perhaps we must interpret Jennifer's AE as a precognition of later hearing about Marge's experience, a seemingly remote possibility in the absence of close emotional ties between Marge and Jennifer. Transmission of the complete image, which then resulted in the only AE Jennifer ever had, would also be required.

An interpretation applying the survival hypothesis does not encounter such difficulties. A time lag is implicit in responding to a request. Appearing first to a believer--presumably an easier task--then later to a disbeliever in a relaxed, post-sleep state, is also understandable. The impact of the AE on Marge closely resembles that of some near-death experiences, which evoke emotions of love, contentment, and peace. According to Marge, the experience certainly renewed her inner strength and will to live.

One case alone cannot decide the survival issue. Different scholars will interpret the data differently according to their own belief systems. The manifest characteristics of this case certainly do not support the notion that apparitions are images void of consciousness; something much more powerful and purposeful seems to be indicated.

A MAJORITY-VOTE STUDY OF IMPRESSIONS RELATING TO A CRIMINAL INVESTIGATION (PS)

William G. Roll (Psychical Research Foundation) and Roger C. Grimson* (University of North Carolina)

Introduction. In 1981, at the request of the Special Task Force investigating the 27 child murders in Atlanta, Georgia, the Psychical Research Foundation (PRF) undertook an analysis of more than 2,000 supposedly psychical reports received by the police in connection with the crimes. These impressions, offered by persons in Atlanta and around the U.S., were compiled on a computer printout from which the PRF analysis was made. Though the statements offered little enlightenment as to the presence or absence of psi, there were some suggestive patterns.

The period studied was January 1, 1981, to June 1, 1981, and all comments received during that time related primarily to the deaths of the 11 (later 12) children during that year. On June 21, 1981, Wayne B. Williams was arrested and later convicted of two of the murders. Since the data analyzed by the PRF were received by the police prior to Williams' involvement in the case, it could not have been influenced by news coverage. Williams, a black male who earned his living as a free-lance photographer, was linked to the crimes on the following evidence: dog hairs and carpet and blanket fibers from his home matched those found on several victims; blood taken from his car matched the blood type of one of the children; and his car was stopped by the police after he had crossed a bridge over a river where a splash was heard and a murdered child was later found.

Procedure and Methods. Our data were first culled to eliminate contentless comments and to consolidate reports by the same person containing the same information. A total of 580 reports remained for analysis. These were divided into two segments: material from persons claiming to be psychic and material from those not making such claims. For each segment, an analysis was made of the characteristics of the supposed criminal and of the conditions relating to the murder. Impressions of the murderer's name were then analyzed without the psychic-nonpsychic distinction. Information on the printout was first coded for keypunch/computer use, with care taken to minimize the subjectivity involved in building structured codes from unstructured materials. The data were statistically analyzed using the chi-square method for determining departures from chance.

Characteristics of Criminal and Crime. Of the 580 reports, 146 percipients were classifed as psychic, 434 were not. Both

---
*Grimson is now at the State University of New York at Stony Brook.

psychics and others overwhelmingly had the impression the killer was male (p. < .001). The total sample significantly judged the murderer to be black (p < .01), though values for the psychic group alone were not significant. In fact, the only significant difference found between the psychic and nonpsychic groups concerned the murderer's motivation: psychics believed sex was the key motive; others felt revenge was primary. Williams' motivation has not been satisfactorily verified, though a witness during the trial said Williams had asked him if he was homosexual.

Impressions relating to the murderer's activities most often saw him as "driving or riding" in connection with the crimes. A car was significantly singled out as the vehicle in use (p < .01), rather than a van or truck. Nine percipients specifically said the murderer used a green car (which Williams drove), though there was no significant difference between this statement and claims that the car was black, white, or blue. Twelve persons said the car was "old" (Williams drove a 1970 model).

In commenting about the criminal's occupation and apparel, the sample showed an orientation toward a person in uniform, military or police; the difference between this impression and the others was significant at the .01 level both for psychics and the total sample. The impression that the killer may have been a school teacher was second in frequency. Williams' conditions did not support these impressions.

The murderer's psychological makeup was most often described by callers as "emotionally disturbed" or "schizophrenic," references to the former outnumbering the latter. The difference between the two impressions was significant at the .01 level, though only nonpsychics used the "emotionally disturbed" description. The few psychics who commented used the term "schizophrenic" or described the criminal as a religious fanatic.

The percipients described the physical environs associated with the crimes as urban, with roads or highways seen as important. This is consistent with the location of the crimes in the city of Atlanta. Private homes were the types of buildings most often described as being relevant to the crimes (significantly, at the p < .001 level) both by psychics and others. One difference between the two groups was in the place percipients "saw" the murderer. Psychics saw him at the murder scene; others saw him at home.

Finally, eight percipients said that a dog was somehow connected with the murders (three psychics, five nonpsychics). It will be recalled that Williams was partly linked to the crimes by the hairs from his German shepherd.

<u>Name Impressions</u>. The letter most frequently cited as part of the murderer's name was the letter "J." (Sixty percent of the initials given included a "J.") When full names were given, "J" was also the most common beginning letter. (Thirty-two percipients

gave names like Joseph, Johnson, Jones, and so on. "John" and
"James" were the most frequent first names.) There seems to be
no connection between Williams and the initial "J." Analyzing the
first two letters most often combined, we find that "JO" is most
frequent, with 15 mentions versus 14 for "WI." "JA" was mentioned 11 times and "JE" three.

In an analysis of the number of appearances of names with
the first three letters the same, the combination "WIL" was used
most commonly by a wide margin (e.g., WIL 16, JIM 3, CAL 3).

Discussion. The person typified by the reports was a black
male in military or police uniform who might have been a police
officer or a school teacher. He was emotionally disturbed and his
motivation was sex or revenge. He drove an old car of green,
black, white or blue color. An urban area and a home were important, and were either the killer's home, the scene of the crime,
or both. A dog was somehow connected with the murderer, as
were "JO," "JA," and "WIL."

A comparison of these impressions with what we have been
able to verify with Williams himself reveals, in summary, nine
possible "hits": he is black, male, drove a green car which was
older than average, lived in urban Atlanta, his home and his car
were linked to the murders, a dog played a role in the case, and
his name begins with WIL.

Can any of these similarities be ascribed to psi? It seems
clear that simple logic could lead to many of the items. For instance, only persons who were seen as trustworthy, such as black
policemen or teachers or people in uniform would have been considered able to approach the children without arousing suspicion.
The killer almost had to be male. Cars might be seen as the
most likely way of luring the children away and later disposing of
the bodies, so it is not surprising that cars and driving should
come to mind. We do not know what the predominant car colors
in the Atlanta area are; if green is not common it could be more
significant that this color was mentioned frequently. It is of somewhat more interest than an "old" car was emphasized, though the
definition of "old" is subjective. It may also be of interest that a
home was emphasized and that this was the key location at which
some of the convicting evidence was found. The mention of a dog
is of interest since it relates to a more specific piece of evidence.
Finally, we found it of interest that the letters "WIL" appeared in
the reports as often as they did.

SPONTANEOUS PRECOGNITIVE DREAMS: A DECLINE WITH TEMPORAL DISTANCE

Nancy Sondow (City College of the City University of New York)

In this report I will present some observations on what I have judged to be spontaneous precognitive dreams. During a 50-month period (March 1979 through April 1983) in which I wrote down 943 dreams, 96 (about 10%) meet the criteria suggested by Dunne (1927) that at least two unusual elements that do not usually occur together appear in both dream and later real events. Since some dreams labeled precognitive by this criteria correspond to events occurring over more than one day, the 96 dreams yield 123 days with precognized events, ranging from less than one day to 478 days after the dream.

There is a strikingly steep fall-off of events with increasing time after the dream. Over half of the correspondences occur within one day of the dream. Some dreams contain "keys" indicating to whom the future events will occur. Events of dreams with "keys" occur throughout the range and show a similar fall-off. A Pearson correlation between log incidence of events per day (+3) and log distance in time from dream (+1) yields a coefficient $r = -.9972$, which closely replicates Orme's analysis (1974) of spontaneous precognitions from four sources in the literature.

There are two arguments against a precognitive interpretation of such data. The coincidence interpretation, which argues that one will eventually find coincidental correspondences to many dreams if one looks through a long enough time span, predicts that more dreams at the beginning of the sample will eventually be labeled precognitive, and holds that the percentage of such correspondences will increase with increasing time spans examined. The memory-artifact interpretation predicts a fall-off in correspondences with increasing time spans, since one is less likely to notice a correspondence as the memory of the dream decays over time. Although these arguments predict opposite effects, both could combine to produce the observed data.

Against these arguments for a non-psi interpretation are the quality of the correspondences, many of which exceed the criteria and include elements that occur only once in the dream sample, and the subjective feeling of déjà vu that often accompanied the later events. A test of the memory-artifact hypothesis would be to compare a period where dreams are written but not reread and never studied for correspondences to a period where dreams are reread every day so there is no forgetting. If the fall-off is an artifact of memory decay, it should be strongest in the former, and disappear in the latter. Two such periods that occurred accidentally in my data do not support the memory-artifact argument. A three-month period of overlearned dreams produced 23 events with a fall-off with a similar slope to that of the full 50 months, with the correlation of log incidence per day and log distance in time yielding r = -.9969. The five-month period of untyped dreams produced 14 events showing a weaker fall-off rather than a stronger one. This should be replicated as a planned experiment.

Tart (1982) found a significant difference favoring real-time over precognitive information rate in a survey of significant psi-hitting forced-choice studies, and a significant (post-hoc) difference in the precognitive data favoring temporal distance of five minutes or less over longer intervals, suggesting information was better perceived through a shorter time. The memory-artifact argument does not explain this finding, although one might argue a psychological interpretation.

There is thus converging evidence from both experimental and spontaneous data suggesting there may be a nonartifactual fall-off of precognitive information over time. However, in the spontaneous material, although the frequency decreases with time, the accuracy of detail does not. Farther in the future there are fewer cases, but they are not more fuzzy or indistinct. Any model of time that accounts for the fall-off should also account for the clarity of the more distant events.

A possible model that would produce a fall-off of frequency but not of accuracy would be to envision future time as a branching tree rather than a straight line, with decision points leading to different possible future paths. If one assumes different futures are equally likely to be precognized before a decision point is reached, then events precognized that manifest on the branch of the single time path that actualizes through the time tree as choices are made will fall off as a power of the number of possible branches at each decision point, yet a few very distant events will eventually actualize on the time path with the same clarity as the more numerous ones closer in time before potential futures diverged.

To test precognition experimentally, one should use altered states procedures and selected subjects. However, if, as this model suggests, the fall-off is due to branching decisions, it might be irrelevant to vary only the time between impression and target generation when the target is always determined by a single decision.

A first naive approach to testing the model might be to vary the number of branching sequentially-dependent decisions toward target generation, where each branch might lead to mutually-exclusive kinds of target pools. Ideally, targets should exist only in the future. For instance, future newspaper articles might be specified by decisions concerning which newspaper, which page, etc. However, PK always looms as a problem in experimental approaches to precognition, especially if PK is independent of complexity.

The pattern in the present data, in Orme's data, in my accidental periods of studied and unstudied dreams, and in Tart's analyses converge to suggest a nonartifactual fall-off in number of precognized events as the time from the precognition increases. I have suggested an experimental approach to test the memory-artifact interpretation in spontaneous material and hope that others will examine the phenomenon in their own dreams without emotional resistance preventing the recognition of the relationship between dreams and future events. If the phenomenon is ubiquitous, and the fall-off nonartifactual, I hope my speculative (and simplistic) model of time may, at least, stimulate further thought.

Part 3: Interim Reports

EXPERIMENTAL REPORTS

FREE-RESPONSE GESP PERFORMANCE DURING GANZFELD STIMULATION (RB/PS)

Lendell Williams Braud, Lawrence Ackles, and Willie Kyles
(Texas Southern University)

Ganzfeld stimulation has proven to be one of the most psiconducive techniques. The present study explored psi reception during Ganzfeld stimulation, with a target pool of 20 pictures chosen from our best pictures. Previous research by Braud and Duke (RIP 1979, 74-77) and Sondow, Braud, and Barker (RIP 1981, 82-85) has demonstrated that target qualities are important in psi performance. Braud and Duke developed a Target Evaluation Rating (TER) to measure specific target qualities. Targets were rated on 25 qualities that were grouped into three main dimensions: general qualities, altered states qualities, and emotional qualities. The authors felt that good ESP targets contained a high degree of some of the qualities described as intense, interesting, dynamic, natural, trippy, spacey, flight-floating, fantasy, and positive emotion. The authors predicted that psi-hitting was associated with these target qualities. Several studies confirmed this prediction. The present study employed 20 pictures that possessed high ratings on the TER. In addition, some of these pictures had been used three or more times as a target and were associated with good psi performance. Five target packs were constructed and duplicate pictures were used to eliminate any possibility of sensory cueing. The targets were selected via a table of random numbers by a Texas Southern University (TSU) faculty member not involved in the experiment.

Ten subjects were tested in the experiment (seven females and three males). Subjects included students enrolled at TSU or friends of the experimenters. The subject population included seven black and three white subjects. A 14-minute relaxation tape followed by a 31-minute Ganzfeld stimulation period was employed. Our standard 16-item questionnaire was used to assess other variables, such as belief in ESP, state of consciousness, mood of the subject, attitude toward the experimenter, and introversion-extraversion.

Experimental Reports

The subject was tested in a reclining position, with head elevated. The first experimenter prepared the subject for Ganzfeld stimulation by taping half ping-pong balls encircled with cotton over the subject's eyes and adjusting the lamp so that it was positioned approximately 12 inches above the eyes. A cantilevered lamp was modified to fit into a metal base, thereby becoming free-standing. The lamp contained a 60-watt incandescent bulb surrounded by a 22-watt fluorescent bulb. Both bulbs were turned on and the lamp was adjusted for the subject's comfort. A microphone was hung from the lamp, the signal amplified and sent to a speaker in each of the experimenters' rooms. In this way the subject's mentation could be heard by each of the two experimenters. No communication system was provided from either experimenter to the subject. The 45-minute tape, containing the relaxation instructions and auditory Ganzfeld stimulation ("white" noise), was presented to the subject through stereo headphones.

After preparing the subject for the Ganzfeld stimulation, the first experimenter retired to an adjacent closed cubicle and prepared to record the subject's mentation that he received over the speaker system. The first experimenter had a set of duplicate picture packs. He received information concerning the correct pack (for later judging) from a card inside an envelope left outside his door. The first experimenter was instructed not to obtain the envelope nor select the pack until he had finished recording the subject's mentation. This occurred at the end of the session, but before he unhooked the subject from the Ganzfeld apparatus.

The second experimenter entered a distant (locked) target room after greeting the subject and listened to the relaxation procedure and the subject's mentation over the speaker system. After the first ten minutes of the session, he opened an opaque envelope that contained two other opaque envelopes marked "first experimenter" and "second experimenter." He delivered the unopened envelope marked "first experimenter" to a table outside the closed cubicle of the first experimenter. He returned immediately to the target room and opened the envelope marked "second experimenter" and selected the correct target pack and correct target listed on the card inside the envelope. Viewing the target briefly, he put it aside and did not begin "serious" sending until about five minutes into the Ganzfeld stimulation period. During the sending period, he traced the target, drew it on paper, silently acted it out (if appropriate) and, in general, involved as many senses as possible in his transmission. Since the second experimenter (sender) was able to hear the subject's mentation he was encouraged to use silent "<u>psychic cheering</u>" when the subject mentioned target relevant information. Of course, there was no <u>sensory</u> communication possible from the agent (second experimenter) to the subject.

At the termination of the psi impression period, the subject was unhooked from the Ganzfeld apparatus by the first experimenter and led into the adjacent cubicle, whereupon the door was closed. The subject drew any images that he had experienced and then completed the remaining items on the 16-item questionnaire. The target pack was opened and the first experimenter reviewed the mentation notes with the subject. The subject was asked to note all mentation responses that corresponded to any of the four pictures. The subject rank-ordered the four pictures (1-4), giving a rank of 1 to the picture most similar to his psi impressions and a rank of 4 to the picture that was least similar. The subject also ranked the pictures (1-4) on how well he liked them as pictures. After judging was completed, the agent brought in the correct target so that performance feedback could be provided to the subject. The TSU faculty member that generated the targets retained a duplicate master list for verification at the end of the entire experiment.

Four pictures were used during judging by the subject. A ranking of 1 for the target picture is a direct hit with an associated probability of .25. There were six direct hits for the ten subjects (MCE for direct hits = 2.5). The predicted psi-hitting was significant ($Z = 2.19$) with a $p < .015$, one-tailed (corrected for continuity).

The present study was designed to investigate the effectiveness of the Ganzfeld technique with good targets and therefore no other formal analyses were planned. However, additional information is provided for the reader's interest. Rankings of 1 and 2 for the target picture can be combined to yield the number of hits. There were eight hits for the ten subjects and only one direct miss (rank of 4). In general, there were no differences between the psi-hitting (N = 8) and psi-missing (N = 2) subjects on the 16-item questionnaire. However, it is interesting to note that although there were only two subjects in the psi-missing group, both subjects were introverts and both rated their mood as very depressed for the day they participated in the experiment. No introverted and depressed subjects were found among the psi-hitters. I think that this points to the importance of the interaction between trait and state variables. In addition, the psi-hitting subjects liked their targets better than the psi-missing subjects.

SIGNAL-PROCESSING CONSIDERATIONS IN RANDOM-NUMBER GENERATOR DESIGN AND APPLICATION (RB/PS)

Robert J. Chevako (Syracuse University)

This report considers the design, testing, and application of random number generators (RNGs) from a signal processing point of view. The act of extracting data bits from an available data stream is viewed as a sampling process, for instance; and the effects of controlling (or ignoring) various design parameters in the RNG circuitry are discussed. The interaction of a nonuniform noise power spectral density and a sampling frequency in the vicinity of a frequency maximum may combine to provide an instrumental source of nonrandomness in standard RNG operation which may be of statistical significance. The concerns expressed here are most applicable to electronic-noise RNGs operating at high data rates, and with computer sampling of sizable amounts of data.

The matching of data streams from such RNGs and from other generators using a pseudorandom sequence is also considered, again primarily under conditions of fast sampling of large amounts of data. The major goal is to insure the appropriate matching of properties among different RNGs if they are to be used in comparison experiments.

INDEPENDENT CONFIRMATION OF INFRARED HEALER EFFECTS (RB)

Bernard Grad (McGill University) and Douglas Dean[†] (Princeton, NJ)

At last year's PA convention Douglas Dean (RIP 1982, 100-101) presented evidence of a healer effect using infrared (IR) and ultraviolet (UV) spectrophotometers. Dean found that using two-ounce bottles filled with distilled water held by healers gave larger bands at the 2.7 micron IR frequencies than control bottles that were not held. The size of these larger bands decreased slowly on the days following the experiment.

Confirmation Instrument. Grad at McGill University, Montreal, had available to him one of the new computer-operated IR spectrophotometers in the Otto Maas Chemistry Department. Dr. Butler, head of the department, gave permission to use it. It is a Nicolet 7000 machine. It scans the whole IR region in a second so that 100 scans take less than two minutes. The computer averages the 100 scans so that noise is averaged out leaving a pure IR band if there is one. In addition, there was available an MIR unit with germanium plate (multiple internal reflection cell), which is essential for this research. The IR light is reflected in and out of the water 25 times. This enables the 2.7 band to be separated from (and so becomes measurable) the 3.0 OH Band. The operator and computer programmer of the Nicolet 7000 was Ishmael Ashraf, a graduate student in the department. He was blind even as to the purpose of this research.

Grad Band at 7.9 microns with Saline. Grad (IJP, 1964, 473-498) had used saline in his original work and he used it again on the Nicolet. In the first study six charts were obtained, two for control saline not held, and four plastic packets of saline held by healers. Grad's big healer effect using saline occurred at 7.9 microns whereas Dean found it using distilled water at 2.7. Dean's charts did not go as far as 7.9 microns. Packet #1 was held for 7 1/2 minutes; #2, #3, and #4 for more than one hour; and #5 and #6 were control saline not held. The control IR ratio values are low and the four healer-treated values are high. The 7 1/2-minute treatment value of 0.053 is small compared with the hours-long treated salines which are up at 0.121-0.130. These IR ratio values are about a third more than Dean got for distilled water, but that may be due to the longer time of holding (Dean's longest holding time was 30 minutes).

Dean Band at 2.7 microns with Saline. In Grad's charts for saline the 2.7 band is very small (particularly the control values), so the error is large. But again it shows an effect similar to the 7.9 band Grad obtained with saline as above and also as Dean obtained with distilled water. The two controls are low (averaging 0.008) and the four healer-held values are high (averaging 0.019).

Control Band at 6.2 microns with Saline. For a control check the same measurements were done at 6.2 microns where a prominent band occurred. All six charts, control not-held and healer-held alike, showed similar IR ratios averaging 0.032. This band does not show any healer treatment effect at all, whereas the 7.9 band especially, and to some extent the 2.7 band, do.

Grad Band at 7.9 microns with Distilled Water. On February 23 and March 8, 1983, Grad asked one of the healers, George Ille, to hold an eight-ounce bottle of distilled water for 27 minutes. On March 14, three measurements, one a repeat, were done of the healer-treated waters and another of control distilled water not held. The healer-treated IR ratios were 0.49 and 0.47 for the March 8 bottle, six days from holding, and 0.29 for the February 25 bottle, 19 days from holding; whereas the control was 0.047. Thus the healer-treated water six days after holding showed ten times the intensity of the 7.9 micron band as did the control water; the healer-treated water 19 days from holding was but six times as large. This follows the pattern Dean found of slow decrease in intensity with days following. However, the absorbency decreases instead of increasing as found each time before. The reason is not known at present. Further research is needed.

Dean Band at 2.7 microns with Distilled Water. In this experiment this 2.7 micron band is again small and subject to error. There is considerable noise, including vertical lines somewhat out of place. However the healer-treated IR ratios were all two to three times higher than the control water not held. The absorbency increases as is usual. However, here the 19-day-old treated water had a higher IR ratio than the six-day-old samples contrary to what was found before. This needs to be checked.

Control Band at 6.2 microns with Distilled Water. The control band at 6.2 microns was again checked and again there is no healer treatment effect. The control and healer bottles give IR ratios which are quite similar, averaging 0.37.

Summary. Grad independently of Dean attempted to confirm Dean's results with healers which suggested that healer-held bottles of distilled water gave higher IR ratios at 2.7 microns than control bottles not held. In the first study using saline, four healer-treated values at 7.9 microns were three times higher on average than two controls. In the second study using distilled water three healer-treated values were six to ten times higher at 7.9 microns than the control. In total, seven healer-treated IR values were all higher and three controls were all lower in the same direction found by Dean.

DIFFERENTIAL MICRO-PK EFFECTS AMONG AFRO-BRAZILIAN UMBANDA CULTISTS USING TRANCE-SIGNIFICANT SYMBOLS AS TARGETS (RB)*

Patric V. Giesler (John F. Kennedy University)

The healing practices of shamanic groups have recently been of particular interest to parapsychologists and anthropologists alike. I would like to report on a study of the ostensible PK abilities of the Afro-Brazilian Umbanda practitioners, who are well known in Brazil for their healing sessions. The adherents of Umbanda and those who consult them claim that the "entity" possessing the shaman or medium during the healing rituals has the ability or power to influence human organisms in such a way as to enact a cure. I hypothesized that the Umbandistas (adherents of the cult) employed a mixture of PK and various forms of suggestion in their healing ceremonies and that their PK abilities had been developed in the Umbanda.

A Schmidt REG (Random Event Generator) designed for PK testing in the field setting (compliments of Dr. Helmut Schmidt) was used in an experiment to investigate the acclaimed healing abilities (assuming a PK aspect and assuming a micro-macro PK continuum) of Umbandistas. There were two parts of the PK task. In one part the subject attempted to light one of two protruding light bulbs on the REG as often as possible during 20 trials. The subject held a micro-switch button in the hand which she would press at the moment she wished to initiate a trial. The results of each run were recorded automatically in the REG. The second part proceeded in the same fashion, except that a small plastic statue of an important Umbanda deity of the subject's choosing was utilized as the target. The figure was placed behind the light bulb used as a target in the first part. Thus there were two target types, with

---

*I would like to thank the Parapsychology Foundation for its generous funding of my research with the Afro-Brazilian cults of which this study was a part.

and without the deity symbol, 20 trials for each condition. Task order was counterbalanced, and target bulb was reversed for each new subject. Ten Umbanda cultists and ten noncultists, all of São Paulo, served as subjects.

Before the experiment it was predicted that 1) Umbandistas would demonstrate PK on the REG test ($p < .05$, positive). 2) Umbandistas would demonstrate PK with the deity target alone (positive mean, $p < .05$); 3) Umbandistas would score significantly higher with deity statue than without it (positive direction, $p < .05$); and 4) the Umbanda group would score higher than the noncultist controls ($p < .05$). As a secondary research objective, Winkelman's maturation, education, and psi hypothesis was tested: that years of formal schooling inhibit the development of psi abilities. It was predicted that the PK scores would correlate negatively with education and that the correlation would be maintained independent of age ($p < .05$).

The overall number of hits for both Umbanda and control groups did not deviate significantly from MCE. The overall number of hits for the Umbanda group alone did deviate from MCE with marginal significance ($Z = 1.65$, $p = .05$, one-tailed). The significant Z value may indicate PK in the data, but nothing may be inferred about Umbanda subject performance in general from a Z test. Neither the overall mean PK score (21.7) for Umbanda nor the mean Umbanda PK score (11.3) for the with deity condition was significant by t test, and thus hypotheses (1) and (2) were not supported. Umbanda subjects did perform better with the deity statue as a target than without it as predicted in hypothesis (3), but the difference was not significant ($t = 1.489$, 9 df, $p = = .085$, one tailed). Neither mean (11.3 with; 10.4 without deity target) was independently significant. Umbandistas did perform better than noncultist subjects as predicted in hypothesis (4), but the difference was not significant. Finally, Winkelman's hypothesis was not supported in the overall data (PK did not correlate negatively with education). However, an analysis of the cult and noncult groups separately yielded a nearly significant positive correlation between noncult PK scores and education, contradicting Winkelman's hypothesis ($r = .6271$, 8 df, $p = .052$, two-tailed). The coefficient was maintained when age was controlled for in a partial correlation analysis ($r = .6120$), indicating that maturation (represented by age) contributed little or nothing to the PK-education relationship for noncultists. For cult subjects the tendency was reversed as the PK-age correlation was the highest and negative; this correlation was maintained to some degree when education was partialled out. But neither of these cult PK-education and PK-age correlations was significant.

THE EFFECT OF THE PRESENCE OF AN AGENT ON ESP PERFORMANCE AND OF THE ISOLATION OF THE TARGET FROM ITS CONTROLS ON DISPLACEMENT IN A GANZFELD CLAIRVOYANCE EXPERIMENT (RB)

Julie Milton (Edinburgh University)

Many cases of apparent displacement--the misdirection of a subject's ESP to some experimental material other than the target --are given in the free-response literature in the form of anecdotal cases on individual trials or post-hoc statistical analyses usually performed to investigate psi-missing. However, Child and Levi (JASPR, 1980, 171-181) give examples of remarkable correspondences between mentation transcripts and control pictures selected some time after the trials to be used by independent judges, quite as striking as those experimental cases put forward as evidence of displacement: Post-hoc analyses may simply reflect random fluctuations in correspondence between mentation reports and nontarget pictures in the target set.

Given the unreliability of the evidence concerning displacement, it was decided that a study manipulating variables which may lead to displacement, with displacement as a dependent variable, would be of value. A common theme of explanations proposed for displacement involves the agent as a beacon guiding the subject's ESP (Tyrrell, PSPR, 1947, 65-120; Stanford and Neylon, RIP 1974, 89-93; Rogo, Research Letter, 1979, 40-54).

The working hypothesis in this study was that the agent's attention guides the subject's ESP. Thus, better performance would be expected if an agent was with a target than if he was not; in addition, if the nontarget pictures in the target set were with the agent as well as the target, all pictures in the target set should be available to the subject's ESP, giving chance-level scoring overall due to a combination of equiprobable psi-hitting and displacement to controls.

To test this hypothesis, a within-subjects design was used in a Ganzfeld clairvoyance study with three conditions. In the first condition, an agent remained with the target isolated from the nontargets in its set during the Ganzfeld period; in the second condition, there was no agent and the isolated target was left in the agent's room; in the third condition, the agent remained with all four pictures in the target set.

Twelve subjects took part. Each subject had the same agent on all three trials, and with one exception, agents were all subjects in the study. Subjects knew that the experiment involved a clairvoyance procedure, but did not know the purpose of the experiment. On any trial, neither experimenter (J.M.) nor subject knew which condition was operating, and the agent did not know the outcome of the trials until the end of the experiment.

After setting the subject at ease in the laboratory, the experimenter took the agent to her office and returned to the laboratory. In three separate envelopes, the agent received instructions for the trial, the number of the target set, and the code identifying the target within the set. The condition, set, and target were predetermined by an independent randomizer using random digit tables. The target pool consisted of 22 sets of four pictures of at least moderate complexity. In the first condition, the agent took a sealed envelope containing the target picture to a room three floors below the laboratory and attempted to concentrate on it for the duration of the Ganzfeld period. In the second, the agent left the envelope containing the target in the room and left the building before the Ganzfeld period began. In the third, the agent took the entire target set to the room and attempted to concentrate on the target, with the other three pictures out of sight behind. The agent never saw any of the pictures, targets or controls; they always remained in the sealed envelopes. After each trial, the agent completed a questionnaire measuring mood, motivation, concentration, and boredom, and left the building.

Meanwhile, in the laboratory the subject relaxed on a reclining chair with halved ping-pong balls taped over his or her eyes, illuminated by a red desk lamp, wearing headphones over which he or she listened to a tape of pink noise. The experimenter, in an adjacent cubicle, noted down the subject's mentation. At the end of the 30-minute Ganzfeld session the experimenter retrieved from the office a duplicate judging set specified by the set number left by the agent. The subject completed a questionnaire concerning his or her preference for and familiarity with the pictures in the set, and then ranked and rated each picture on the basis of its correspondence to the mentation transcript. The experimenter retrieved the target from the agent's room and showed it to the subject.

In addition to the main predictions, the relationship between the subject's picture preferences and the agent's state and performance and displacement will be investigated.

A PSYCHOKINESIS EXPERIMENT WITH A RANDOM MECHANICAL CASCADE*

Roger D. Nelson,[†] Brenda J. Dunne, and Robert G. Jahn (Princeton Engineering Anomalies Research)

Introduction. The Random Mechanical Cascade (RMC)

---

*This work was supported in part by grants from The McDonnell Foundation (Psychophysical Research Laboratories), The John E. Fetzer Foundation, Inc., and the Ohrstrom Foundation.

experiment described herein was developed to explore the hypothesis that human consciousness, interacting with a macroscopic mechanical system in a sensitive, carefully controlled experiment, may effect a measurable change in the behavior of that system. This study was motivated by the growing body of research with microscopic-scale random event generators (REGs) using electronic or radioactive decay noise sources, which suggests that human consciousness can produce psychokinetic effects on the behavior of such microscopic random systems. (See Dunne, Jahn, and Nelson, RIP 1981, 50-51; Jahn, Proc. IEEE, 1982, 136-170; Nelson, Dunne, and Jahn, RIP 1981, 47-50; RIP 1982, 152-178; and B.B. Wolman, Ed., Handbook of Parapsychology, 1977.)

It seems important to ascertain whether similar effects could be produced on a more macroscopic scale. In an effort to explore this, we have adapted a mechanical Gaussian distribution analogue device, frequently featured in large science museums, which allows a large number of balls to drop through an array of elastic pins into a set of collecting bins to demonstrate the development of a quasi-normal distribution. Suitably modified and instrumented, this statistical demonstration device has become a viable experiment for assessment of the interaction of consciousness with a macroscopic random mechanical system.

Experimental Equipment and Procedure. Our Random Mechancial Cascade experiment is implemented with a machine roughly 10' x 6' in size, which employs 9,000 polystyrene balls 3/4" in diameter, cascading through a quincunx array of 330 3/4" nylon pins on $2\frac{1}{4}$" centers. A conveyor transports the balls from a plenum at the bottom to a funnel at the top, from which they drop into the matrix of pins. The balls bounce in complex stochastic paths through the matrix, colliding elastically with pins and other balls, accumulating finally in the 19 parallel, vertical collecting bins arranged across the bottom. The front of the pin chamber and of the collecting bins below it are clear Plexiglas so that both the active cascade of balls and their disposition into the developing distribution of bin populations are visible as feedback to the operator.

Each collecting bin is equipped with an optoelectronic counter at its entrance. These 19 counters are scanned on-line by a microprocessor which transmits in real time the ordered accumulation of counts in each bin to LED displays at the bottom of the bins, and to a TERAK computer where the ordered sequence of ball drops is registered on disk as a file of 9,000 characters, A through S, representing the bins 1 through 19 respectively. Each file is associated with indexing information including file number, instruction, operator, date, time, humidity and temperature within the pin cavity, and various experimental parameters. A logbook is maintained with the indicated index information; a photograph of each completed run distribution, including the bin totals displayed on the LEDs; the bin totals as registered by the computer, with summary information including total populations right and left of the tenth bin, a right-left ratio, and the distribution mean; and any appropriate comments.

Data are collected in sets of three runs, including a baseline, an effort to distort the distribution to the right (greater frequency of counts in high-numbered bins), and a left-directed effort. This "tripolar" experimental format is important in mitigating biasing effects of physical changes in the operation of the machine.

Each run takes about 12 minutes and most operators sit facing the maching on a couch about eight feet away. Optional experimental parameters include choice of lighted versus blank LED displays, and of volitional versus random assignment of direction of effort. As in our other experiments, operators freely develop their own strategies and schedule their own sessions, subject to the requirement to perform sets of three runs. Operators are encouraged to generate large data bases, divided into series of 20 sets of runs wherein experimental parameters are not varied, and over which some informal general strategy may be maintained.

Statistical Treatment. Although a sophisticated model of the path of one ball might be developed using Markov chain techniques, the complex of collisions is so fine grained that the conceptually simpler binary model which fits the REG experiment may serve also in representing the RMC. In particular, as runs accumulate, the envelope of the 19 bin populations closely approaches a Gaussian curve.

Using bin units as the statistical variable, the distribution mean of baseline runs is found empirically to be approximately 10.03 (the center bin) with a standard deviation of about 3.24 bins. Given a binary model with unit probabilities $p = q = .5$, and $\sigma = \sqrt{\nu pq}$, the expected number, ν, of "binary equivalent events" can be estimated for the path of one ball: i.e., $\nu = 4\sigma^2$ or about 40 effective binary decisions. Thus in the RMC experiment, a "trial" may be considered to be the 40 "binary equivalent samples" in a single ball's path into one of the 19 bins, i.e., into the frequency of count distribution. Since there are 9,000 such "trials" in a run, the statistical power of each run is considerable, comprising approximately 360,000 binary equivalent bits. The expected mean of repeated runs is that of the distribution, 10.03, with a standard deviation of .035.

The series length of 20 runs is arbitrary, but provides a data base which in most series is sufficient to distinguish trends from stochastic variation. The stability of the parameter estimates for the distribution is apparent in a small standard error for estimates of the mean. For a series of 20 runs, the standard error is .0078, yielding a 95% confidence interval around the grand baseline mean of $10.019 < \mu < 10.049$. It is clear that persistent small changes in the mean of the experimental runs cumulate rapidly to significant deviations from expected values.

Experimental Results. Eleven people are currently engaged in formal series with the RMC device. Of the 11 operators, six have completed one or more full series, and five of these generated at least one data set whose mean differed significantly from the expected value. Of the 48 comparisons which could be made in 24 completed series, 11 showed significant deviations. Analysis of volitional versus random assignment of instruction showed no difference; comparison of full versus partial feedback indicated a transient effect of this variable. Separating data according to time of day suggested that for some operators this variable was a strong predictor.

Discussion. One of the most intriguing features of the data thus far assembled in the RMC experiment is the appearance of individual "signatures" in the results generated by the various operators, wherein each person's output in a given condition progressively acquires a distinctive character.

Signatures like these also appeared in the REG experiment, and most interestingly, there appears to be some correspondence between each operator's signatures in the two experiments. These similarities of yield in experiments based on distinctly different physical systems provide encouraging confirmation of the viability of both experiments, and suggest important criteria for development of a general theoretical model of this class of psi phenomena.

Summary. At this point in the evolution of the RMC experiment, it has proven to be a statistically powerful and operationally attractive system. By its tremendous effective bit rate, it generates enough information in each run to provide data bases sufficiently large for the examination of experimental variables in a short time, matching or surpassing even the contemporary REG experiment, which itself is a very efficient design for assessing small putative effects. Of equal importance, the machine is intrinsically interesting, a delight to most operators, and it therefore provides motivation and a center of focus which readily elicits directed attention. In short, it appears to be an excellent vehicle for examining the interaction of human consciousness with a macroscopic random mechanical system. Thus, it takes a useful place beside the electronic REG in a growing array of physical devices potentially vulnerable to conscious operator influence in studies of engineering anomalies.

METABOLIC TYPES AND PSI: A STUDY OF OXIDIZER TYPE AND ESP TEST SCORES

Joyce G. Ruiz (John F. Kennedy University)

Few studies associating biochemical characteristics and psi behavior are reported in parapsychological literature aside from the effects of drugs. Yet, it seems very likely that some relationship exists.

Although it has been difficult to quantify the extent of behavior which can be directly attributed to biochemistry, recent research and clinical findings in psychobiology, nutrition, orthomolecular psychiatry, and holistic health medicine indicate that relationships do exist and that the biochemical condition of the body plays a basic and a dynamic role in behavior and experience. Psychological states, physiology, nervous system activity, emotions, mood, personality, and experience can be directly influenced by biochemical conditions of the body. These same variables are thought to influence psi behavior and experience also. Investigation has indicated some of these variables seem to have associations with psi. The proposition that biochemical conditions of the body which are present in all psi experiments can directly or indirectly influence psi behavior is the basis of the present study.

Examination of individual previously reported studies of psi research findings related to biochemical conditions does not indicate unequivocally a relationship between psi behavior and specific biochemical conditions. However, taken collectively, the finding emerges that individuals and groups who demonstrated psi ability, some exceptionally, all had biochemical dysfunctions or changes. These dysfunctions or changes can 1) all be related to endocrine hormonal changes and 2) all affect intermediary metabolism and glucose homeostasis. Because glucose is the only energy source for the brain and continuous supplies are required, imbalances or changes could be expected to affect any of its processes, including psi, which is believed to be mediated by the brain. Thus, endocrine abnormalities, metabolic imbalances, and glucose homeostasis may have some effect on psi behavior.

The present study was conducted to explore the relationship between endocrine-metabolic imbalances and psi ability to determine if there are biochemical metabolic types that are psi conducive and to determine if temporary shifts in metabolic type affects psi ability. The study is designed to compare ESP test scores of four different oxidizer types that differ in their intermediary metabolite balance and glucose production patterns: slow (SO), normal (NO), fast (FO) and variable (VO) in three conditions of metabolic activity: passive (before breakfast), active (after a meal), and retiring (before bed). It is also designed to compare psi scores of the VO between shift and nonshift sessions. A session where a change from the previous session's oxidizer type occurs is a shift session. It is designed to compare psi scores between the imbalance-prone and balance-prone groups. Subjects reporting certain endocrine or metabolic imbalances are imbalance-prone.

There were four hypotheses:

1) The FO and VO types will demonstrate more psi ability on ESP tests than SO or NO types.

2) The active condition will demonstrate more psi ability on ESP tests than passive or retiring conditions.

3) The VO type will demonstrate more psi ability on ESP tests in shift than nonshift sessions.

4) The imbalance-prone group will demonstrate more psi ability in ESP tests than the balance-prone group.

Groups selected to demonstrate more psi ability were chosen because they had unstable and inconsistent energy production patterns or endocrine-metabolic imbalances.

Forty-seven female subjects between the ages of 18 and 70 years were selected from 70 unpaid volunteer participants on the basis of completion of all experimental tasks.

Seventy research packets were assembled prior to the experiment. Each packet contained an odor test kit and sets of 15 printed response sheets for the odor test, the ESP test, the mood inventory, and the food diary. A general questionnaire and two envelopes were included.

ESP target sets were prepared prior to the experiment, placed in separate envelopes, sealed and numbered in order of preparation. Each set contained 15 target sheets with four runs of 25 trials each (1,500 trials total). ESP symbols were used as targets and target order was determined from a table of random numbers. Target assignment was made prior to the experiment by a person otherwise unassociated with the experiment.

The odor test kits were assembled according to Watson's (Personality Strength and Psycho-Chemical Energy, 1979) directions. The odor test identifies the four different oxidizer types from the results of a standardized forced choice test comparing scores on two successive odor reports of the same six food substances using a numerical scale.

At an initial meeting each participant was given a description of the experiment, completed a general questionnaire, and received instruction in test procedure. Each participant was given a research packet to take home. All tests were performed at the participant's own convenience within the guidelines of the experiment.

For five consecutive days each participant took a 100-trial forced-choice ESP test before breakfast, after a meal, and before bed. The ESP task was to correctly guess the preselected targets. Standardized odor tests were taken following each ESP test. Each participant also completed a mood inventory after 50 trials of each ESP test session and kept a daily food diary. Session date and time were recorded on each response sheet. Participants returned ESP test response sheets in sealed envelopes separate from other materials. These were held on file until the experiment had been completed and subjects assigned to groups.

Results of the odor test identified 3 SO, 13 NO, 9 FO, and

22 VO; the 23 unassigned participants had incomplete tests. VO scores were evaluated for temporal changes noting test sessions where change from previous type was indicated and VOs were assigned to shift or nonshift session groups. General questionnaire responses were tabulated for reported endocrine-metabolic abnormalities and subjects assigned to imbalance-prone or balance-prone groups.

ESP tests were scored by two independent scorers and results checked for accuracy. Each subject's psi score was the correct number of responses from 1,500 trials for the oxidizer condition and 500 trials for the metabolic activity condition.

The 3 X 3 ANOVA (repeated measures on one factor using unweighted means solution for unequal cells) performed on oxidizer type and metabolic activity condition indicated a significant main effect on oxidizer type ($F_{2, 41}$ = 5.52, $p < .01$). Results of a Neuman-Keuls test performed on oxidizer means revealed NO psi scores were significantly less than FOs or VOs both individually and together ($p < .01$), and VO psi scores were significantly less than FO ($p < .05$). The SO group was too small to be included in ANOVA. NO psi scores were significantly below chance (single mean t: t_{12} = 5.34, $p < .001$, two-tailed). Results indicate significant psi-missing was demonstrated by NOs and the NOs showed more psi ability than FOs or VOs. Thus, Hypotheses 1 and 2 were unconfirmed.

These results suggest that psi may be enhanced by the relatively balanced and consistent metabolic state characteristic of the NO rather than the relatively unbalanced or changing metabolic state of the other oxidizer types as was proposed.

Psi scoring was not differentiated by metabolic activity conditions, but the retiring condition had significant below chance scoring (single mean t: t_{46} = 2.67, $p < .02$, two-tailed). This unexpected result is consistent with the NO's psi-missing and balanced metabolic state because the retiring condition approaches a relatively more stable state. Decreased metabolic activity and physical energy combined with a "letting go" at the end of the day may have created a more relaxed physical and mental state. Although finding no significant difference between conditions weakens any suggestions made, results support the findings that relaxation enhances psi ability (Braud and Braud, JASPR, 1973, 26-46).

No significant differences were found between VO shift and nonshift sessions. Hypothesis 3 was not supported. All subjects reported two or more imbalance-prone conditions and were assigned to the same group. Thus, Hypothesis 4 could not be tested.

The number of shift sessions for all subjects was greater than expected; this meant oxidizer type was more likely a trait than a state. Results of post-hoc analyses failed to provide evidence for significant relationships between psi scoring and state. Additional tests for metabolic type could be included in future studies to define more precisely the influence of metabolic state versus trait.

Post hoc analyses using single mean t tests also showed significant below chance scoring for small groups reporting premenstrual breast enlargement (t_{23} = 2.22, $p < .05$), regular medication use (t_{33} = 2.33, $p < .05$), poor taste or smell discrimination (t_3 = 4.75, $p < .02$) and low pain tolerance (t_4 = 6.58, $p < .01$); all tests were two-tailed. These significant results could all be statistical fluctuations, but may be helpful in forming hypotheses for further research.

Results of this study indicated a statistically significant relationship between psi ability and metabolic type: NO type demonstrated psi-missing and more psi ability than the FO and VO types. The results suggest further study in this same area could be fruitful.

Further investigation of what and how biochemical conditions influence the operation and manifestation of psi behavior could reveal some of the more functional aspects of psi, uncover specific characteristics and provide an understanding of psi through its interaction with known physical processes.

A SECOND STUDY WITH THE "PSI BALL" RNG-PK GAME (RB/PS)

Ephraim I. Schechter, Pat Barker, and Mario P. Varvoglis
(Psychophysical Research Laboratories)

At the 1982 SPR/PA conference we reported the results of the first pilot study with a computer-controlled video game ("Psi Ball") involving a random number generator (RNG) PK task (RIP 1982, 152-153). Pilot #2 involves several changes from the Pilot #1 procedures. 1) Eleven-event RNG samples are taken, and the game-difficulty in Contingent games is increased if there are fewer than six hits. This keeps the rate of difficulty-increase in chance-level Contingent games the same as in Noncontingent games. 2) At the end of each five-game session, the player indicates whether and how strongly he or she thinks the session's games were Contingent or Noncontingent. A Wilcoxon signed-ranks test is used to evaluate the difference between the ratings in the two conditions. 3) Because of the low degrees of freedom (number of players = 10), 2 x 2 median-split contingency tables and Fisher Exact Probability Tests are used to evaluate relationships between game scores and psychological inventory scores. 4) To check on the likelihood that significant game-score x inventory-score relationships would occur simply because there are a large number of analyses, players' psychological inventory scores are randomly assigned to Control (no player involved) data sets; contingency tables and Fisher Exact Probability Tests are used to evaluate the relationships.

As in Pilot #1, four sets of ten million RNG events each are gathered as a check on the RNG's general performance; Z-scores and Komolgorov-Smirnoff analyses of chi-square distributions indicate no significant departures from chance performance.

On the basis of Pilot #1 results, we predicted no significant differences in Z-scores or absolute Z-scores between conditions and no significant deviations from mean chance expectancy in any condition. We also predicted that the mean game lengths would be the same in the two conditions and that players would be unable to distinguish Contingent from Noncontingent games, i.e., that there would be no significant differences between the mean numbers of RNG samples per session or between the game-type ratings for the two conditions. All of these predictions are confirmed.

The RNG Z-scores are positively and significantly correlated with the mean number of RNG trials per session in the Contingent games (Pearson $r = .207$, df = 248, $t = 3.328$, $p = .001$ two-tailed) in Pilot #2. (A similar result in Pilot #1 [$r = .177$, df = 248, $t = 2.833$, $p = .005$] had originally been discarded because Contingent game length in Pilot #1 was artificially inflated, but the similarity between the Pilot #1 and #2 data suggests that it may be meaningful.) This is the only aspect of the data suggesting psi. RNG performance (Z-scores and absolute Z-scores) was not significantly related to any of the other measures, including the psychological inventory scores. On the basis of the Pilot #1 results, we had predicted a significant negative relationship between Myers-Briggs Type Indicator Extraversion/Introversion scores and Contingent-condition Z-scores; this prediction was not confirmed.

The results of two pilot studies suggest that if the current version of Psi Ball is eliciting any psi at all, it is too weak an effect to be useful for process-oriented research with small samples.

FIELD AND STREAM (RB)

Gertrude R. Schmeidler (City College of the City University of
   New York)

When the field of ESP targets is irregular, does the stream of consciousness change? With many targets of one type, like a hillock in a field, will ESP responses eddy around that type? This experiment compares ESP responses to such multiple background targets and to single targets, all embedded in a design which manipulates speed of ESP calling and categorizes subjects by personal tempo.

Inquiry into global versus specific target effects was introduced by Child and Kelly (JP, 1973, 278-297). Their gifted subject's responses were significantly related to target frequency, thus showing quantitatively what many argue from qualitative evidence: that ESP, like perception, can respond globally to the general impression or Gestalt of stimuli.

Method. Thirty subjects were tested: adult volunteers, chiefly students. Experimenters were a graduate student, Hazon Na, and myself. Another series of 30 subjects is planned.

Target and response sheets were pages of 12 "clocks" (circles with 12 tick marks around the edge). Target clocks had one hand pointing to a tick, were wrapped in aluminum foil, and put in a manila envelope. A response sheet was stapled above.

Target pages had four clocks showing the same hour. The hour used repeatedly rotated for 12 pages. Choices of the 495 possible positionings were determined randomly without replacement. The eight other clocks showed different hours, randomly selected for each page without replacement. Target envelopes were assigned randomly.

The personality measure was Messer's Matching Familiar Figures Test (MFFT). It is widely used and well validated. It shows a line drawing of a familiar figure. The page below shows eight similar figures, seven differing in some detail, one matching. After practice, subjects try to match 12 figures. Scores are median time of first responses, and total errors before correct responses. Each group provides its own norms. Medians divide subjects into Impulsives (fast time, many errors); Reflectives (slow time, few errors); Fast Accurates; Slow Inaccurates.

A short introduction described the ESP procedure. It included a concrete example of random target selection, prefaced by, "This is not exactly how the targets were chosen, but...." The experimenter recorded time for the first page. With appropriate explanations, subjects then filled out one page as fast as possible, another page slowly (time for each response set at one-sixth total time for the first page). A short questionnaire followed, then the MFFT and another short test. Targets were then opened and viewed.

ESP scores are the number of hours between target and response.

Results. By current norms, subjects are five Reflectives, seven Slow Inaccurates, ten Impulsives, four Fast Accurates, and four fast subjects with median errors.

Pooling all subjects, both total ESP scores and scores for repeated targets were insignificantly better than chance for the first page and insignificantly worse for the fast and slow pages. Differences between pages were insignificant (although Impulsives had significantly worse scores on the fast page than on the first [$t = 2.47$, 9 df, $p < .05$, two-tailed]).

To examine global responding, we score the eight responses to nonrepeated targets against the hour of the repeated target. For the first page these totals were insignificantly worse than chance; for the slow page, insignificantly better. However for the fast page they show significant psi-hitting (t = 2.36, 29 df, p < .05, two-tailed) and are significantly better than scores on the true targets (t = 2.68, 29 df, p < .02, two-tailed).

MFFT categories show this effect related to personality. Impulsives scored significantly well on repeated targets (t = 2.33, 9 df, p < .05, two-tailed) and better than on the true targets (t = 3.30, 9 df, p < .01, two-tailed). Further, all fast MFFT subjects pooled had highly significant psi-hitting for global responding (t = 3.59, 17 df, p < .005, two-tailed), significantly better than on true targets (t = 3.50, 17 df, p < .005, two-tailed). In contrast, slow responders to the MFFT had global means near chance expectation, significantly worse than fast MFFT responders (t_{diff} = 2.65, 28 df, p < .02, two-tailed).

Discussion. If the replication series yields data similar to these, they will support two theses. One is that situational demand interacts with personality type to influence ESP responses. (On the fast page but not the other pages, the MFFT's fast responders had significantly different ESP scores from the MFFT's slow responders.)

The other thesis is that ESP may, without a person's awareness, respond to a predominant feature in a field, even though that feature differs from the desired target. The data imply that those who are temperamentally hasty may, during rapid ESP responding, be wrong on specifics but right on an underlying theme.

SUPERPOSITION OF PK EFFORTS BY MAN AND DOG (RB)

Helmut Schmidt (Mind Science Foundation)

One of the most interesting questions raised by PK experiments with prerecorded targets is what happens when two subjects make subsequent PK efforts at the same prerecorded target sequence. My initial paper (JASPR, 1967, 267) gave some suggestive evidence that repeated efforts on the same target could strengthen the effect. A number of authors have also studied questions related to the superposition of PK efforts.

Experimental work in this direction is particularly challenging because different theoretical models make different predictions on the superposition effect. One of the first models (JASPR, 1975, 301) implies a very specific superposition, independent of the time sequence of the PK efforts. A more recent model, on the other

Experimental Reports

hand, suggests that the first effort, even when made by a subject without "PK abilities" could inhibit or reduce the success of any subsequent PK effort (Foundations of Physics, 1982, 865).

This led to the following pilot study in which a (supposedly "nonpsychic") dog, a seven-year-old miniature dachshund, much attached to the experimenter, acted as first observer.

The experiment used prerecorded seed numbers (JP, 1981, 87) with randomly assigned target directions, H(igh) or L(ow). Entered into a computer, a seed number served as source for a sequence of quasi-random binary decisions that determined the course of a test run and the final score. For the human subject, feedback was provided by a pendulum swinging on a computer screen with randomly fluctuating amplitude. The subject could choose as aim high or low pendulum amplitude, and the computer could internally adjust the display form so as to make the chosen target consistent with the prespecified score direction (H or L). To let the dog "observe" the outcome of a run, an automatic dispenser of M&M's (chocolates) provided a reward whenever the final score was on the prespecified side of the expectation value of 500. In addition, the dog received continuous feedback in the form of a tone that measured the cumulative score such that a high end frequency of the tone implied a reward. But we do not know whether the dog cared about the tone or could associate high frequencies with impending rewards.

The required random seed numbers were generated by a computer with attached Geiger counter and printed out 20 seed numbers per page. The seeds for the trials with the human subject alone were supplied by 11 pages (1A, 2A, ... 11A). For these runs, which formed part of another experiment, the target assignments were made by R. Morris and L. Rudolph (see this volume, 33-35). The same sequences of target assignments were used for 11 pages with seed numbers (1B, ... 11B). These seeds served first in a dog run and then in a run with the human subject. In half of the trials of the B-pages, dog and man were motivated to make a PK effort in the same direction (whenever the dog got an M&M the human subject would be successful, i.e., score in the desired direction). But in the other half of the trials, the dog feedback was inverted so that the dog was rewarded when the human subject failed.

Thus tests were done under four conditions: 1) with the human subject alone; 2) with man and dog working together; 3) with the dog working against the human subject. In these tests the human subject was kept blind with regard to the conditions, so he never knew whether he was working alone or whether the dog had made a previous effort in one or the other direction. After completion of the runs (1), (2), (3), a last series (4) was made with the dog alone.

The chance score in a trial is 500, with a variance of 123. The average deviation per trial from this chance score and the corresponding Z-values under the four conditions are as follows:

(1) man alone: aver. dev = 17.8, Z = 2.2

(2) man+dog: "   = 13.2, Z = 1.1

(3) man-dog: "   = 3.6, Z = 0.3

(4) dog alone: "   = 25.8, Z = 2.3

Here positive deviations indicate success for the human subject in the first three conditions and success for the dog in the last case.

The results are not significant, but suggestive in the direction that the previous attempt by the dog might reduce the human subject's later success rate and that even the dog might add some PK effect of its own. Further experiments are planned.

TARGET PREFERENCE AS A MODULATOR OF ESP SCORES WHEN THE TARGETS ARE CROSS-SEX OR SAME-SEX NAMES (RB)

Kathleen Streber and Gertrude R. Schmeidler[†] (City College of the City University of New York)

Sargent (EJP, 1977, 36-59) used novel binary ESP targets: pairs of male and female names. He presented to mixed groups of men and women a list of 32 pairs of male names and 32 pairs of female names. In two groups where males predominated, cross-sex names had higher ESP scores than same-sex, and in one group where females predominated, same-sex names had higher scores than cross-sex. He hypothesized significantly different ESP scores for cross-sex and same-sex names. He did not examine liking for individual names.

To replicate and extend his approach, we administered similar targets, using names familiar to Americans. After ESP testing, subjects rated each name on a five-point scale (strongly like, mildly liked, neutral, mildly disliked, strongly disliked).

Subjects were 15 male musicians and 15 female graduate students in psychology. K.S., a female, tested them individually except for one male pair tested together and one female pair tested together.

Half the target sheets listed male names first, half female. Targets within each pair were selected randomly by coin flips, separately for each page, and encircled. Target pages were wrapped in aluminum foil and put into manila envelopes. A response sheet with the same placement of male and female names was stapled above. Envelopes were assigned randomly. Another page listed separately the 128 names for ratings of liking.

Experimental Reports

Data had two independent scorings. Computations used each subject's deviation as the unit.

We expected a significant difference between cross-sex and same-sex scores, higher scores for liked names, and an interaction between these.

Results. With liking disregarded, Sargent's hypothesis had no overall support. ESP scores were insignificantly above chance for all cross-sex names, all same-sex names, all male names, all female names, all males, all females, and all scores.

To examine liking, our major division was between pairs with equal ratings on the five-point scale and pairs with different ratings. This immediately helped clarify the data. Subjects showed significant psi-hitting for pairs with equal ratings (t = 2.17, 29 df, p < .05, two-tailed); chance scores for the others.

Pairs with equal ratings were divided into four sets: strongly liked plus mildly liked, neutral, mildly disliked plus strongly disliked, total. Each of the four had six listings: males, females, all subjects, for cross-sex names and for same-sex. Two of these 24 categories showed psi-hitting: all subjects, same-sex liked names (t = 2.13, 29 df, p < .05, two-tailed) and its mirror image, all subjects cross-sex disliked names (t = 2.23, 24 df, p < .05, two-tailed). Cross-sex versus same-sex differences were significant for two of 12 comparisons: females, disliked names (t = 2.36, 13 df, p < .05, two-tailed) and all subjects, disliked names (t = 2.09, 24 df, p < .05, two-tailed).

Pairs with different levels of liking were divided into three sets: those where the ESP choice was the preferred name, where it was the nonpreferred, and total. As above, there were six subject groups for each set. Of the 18 categories, two had significant scores, both for psi-missing: females same-sex, with nonpreferred name the ESP choice (t = 2.30, 14 df, p < .05, two-tailed) and females, all female names (t = 2.27, 14 df, p < .05, two-tailed). Cross-sex versus same-sex differences were significant for two of nine comparisons: females, choice of nonpreferred name (t = 2.22, 14 df, p < .05, two-tailed) and females, all names (t = 2.16, 14 df, p < .05, two-tailed).

Only one of 12 comparisons showed a significant difference between liked and disliked names: higher scores for liked names when there was equal liking within the pair, all subjects (t = 2.21, 29 df, p < .05, two-tailed).

Discussion. When corrected for selection, none of our expectations are clearly confirmed. It should be noted, however, that the four significant differences between cross-sex and same-sex names all showed higher ESP scores for cross-sex. It might be committing a Type II error to claim that our expectations were clearly disconfirmed.

A major methodological shortcoming was omission of information about sexual attitudes. If, for example, some subjects were homosexual, or some were recently hurt by unhappy love affairs, their cross-sex scores should obviously be examined separately from those of persons happily in love.

Two tentative conclusions are suggested. 1) Further work with targets connoting sex should examine subjects' general attitudes as well as their feelings about specific targets. 2) An ESP choice between items which arouse similar feelings may offer a freer opportunity for psi, and thus be more psi-conducive, than a choice between targets which arouse different feelings. With different feelings, the cross-currents of affect may obscure or interfere with psi processing.

COMPUTER-BASED LONG DISTANCE ESP: AN EXPLORATORY EXAMINATION (RB/PS)

William Tedder (Parapsychology Information Network)

An exploratory study was conducted with unselected subjects who were involved in an ESP experiment in which they were separated from the targets by several miles. Individuals who had the necessary computer equipment for accessing the Parapsychology Information Network had the opportunity to run a program that tested for either clairvoyant or precognitive abilities. The Network is menu driven and by pressing a specific selection, the user could access an ESP number game. The experiment spanned an approximate three-month period and the length of the study was time-based since it was unknown as to the number of people who would access the game and the number of trials that would be requested. Therefore, an a priori decision was made as to the day on which the experiment would end and the data would be collected and analyzed.

Examination of fairly unique experimental conditions provided the basis for the study. People were able to access the game at any time and from any location. The computer automatically maintained a record of all calls and the user's subsequent activity while on the system. Information from this daily log indicated that most participants called from an approximate radius of 1 to 30 miles from Denver; however, some individuals called from as far away as New York City, Virginia, and Florida. The daily log also indicated that the ESP program was run at different times, during normal waking hours and sometimes as late as 2:00 or 3:00 a.m.

Another point of interest was the psychological conditions under which people participated. Although these conditions were not directly observable, it was hypothesized that accessibility to the program at the user's convenience and from a location of their choice would produce a psi-conducive atmosphere.

Experimental Reports

The ESP program was run on a TRS-80 Model III microcomputer; the hardware random number generator that was utilized in the experiment was developed by Randy Stahla of Symtek DSA. The basis of the 32-bit RNG is the MM5837 digital white noise generator made by National Semiconductor. Randomization tests with the RNG provided no significant biases.

The ESP program could be accessed by anyone who had a computer screen width of 40 columns or greater. People had the option of playing identical versions of the game (for computers with 40-63 columns or for those with 64 columns or more). Instructions that were provided were identical for either version. People were provided with the choice of testing for either clairvoyant or precognitive abilities. Although they could request from 1 to 60 trials, they were informed that a minimum of 50 trials during a run was required for valid statistical feedback.

Two displays could be requested: one in which the numbers 1 through 5 were normal sized or one in which a larger display was utilized. The smaller display allowed people to complete the session within a shorter period of time if they desired, or they could utilize the larger display for concentration purposes.

For each trial, participants were requested to make a selection (between 1 and 5) that they believed corresponded to the computer's choice. They received continuous feedback as to the number of trials, hits, misses, and chance expectation. When they matched the computer's choice, the word "HIT" would be displayed on the screen. At the end of each session, the person received feedback as to the odds against chance, probability against chance, standard deviation, and a brief explanation of the three statistical measures utilized. A chart was also provided that displayed a trial-by-trial summary of their choices and the computer's selections.

During the experiment, the game was accessed 53 times by 41 people, with no one participating more than three times. For the clairvoyant portion, 912 trials were completed which produced a total of 161 hits (MCE = 182.4, CR = -1.77, $p < .08$). For the precognitive portion, 629 trials were completed, resulting in 124 hits (MCE = 125.8, CR = .18, p = ns). Overall, 1,541 trials were recorded, resulting in 285 hits (MCE = 308.2) and a CR of -1.48, which was nonsignificant.

The psi-conducive hypothesis was not supported in this preliminary study and the suggestive negative results in the clairvoyant portion are somewhat disconcerting. The inferred presence of conducive conditions for the participants did not produce the desired results. Further studies will be conducted in the investigation of mass testing for psi abilities.

THE USE OF FANTASY IN A CHILDREN'S ESP EXPERIMENT (RB)

Rosemarie Pilkington Tornatore (Saybrook Institute)

Psychological resistance to and disbelief in psi have been posited by some parapsychologists as causes of poor scoring on ESP tests. Batcheldor (Psychoenergetic Systems, 1979, 77-93), e.g., theorized that one means of overcoming resistance and disbelief may be the creation of illusions. Involving children in fantasy has seemed to contribute to high scoring (e.g., Anderson & Gregory, JP, 1959, 149-177; Louwerens, JP, 1960, 75-93). It might follow that the creation of illusions in children through involvement in fantasy could result in a temporary reduction of psychological resistance and disbelief in their own psi abilities. This study addressed the question, Is involvement in fantasy an effective means of facilitating the elicitation of ESP in children?

The subjects were second-graders whom I taught and with whom I had established good rapport. The experiment was conducted in April-June 1983, with the assistance of J.M., their science teacher. Two groups were formed, each consisting of six pairs of children and matched as to sex, age, and intelligence.

The target pool consisted of 144 magazine pictures. These and duplicate slides made from them were divided into 36 sets of four and numbered (1, 2, 3, 4). The four-slide sets were placed in small opaque envelopes numbered 1 to 36. The corresponding originals were placed in large opaque envelopes labeled with the same numbers.

The control group subjects were told that they were going to play an "ESP game" in which one child in a room with J.M. would view a projected slide and try to "send" the picture to his or her partner who would be with me in a nearby room. In the other room I would guide the "receiver" in a relaxation exercise instructing the subject to picture a blank screen and allow thoughts or images to come. When ready I signaled J.M. by buzzing twice on an intercom.

Meanwhile, J.M. had opened a sealed envelope (prepared by Charles Honorton at the Psychophysical Research Laboratories) containing two lists of five random numbers. The first, 1 to 36, to determine which pack of slides to open, and the second, 1 to 4, to select the actual target from among the four slides. She recorded the top numerals on her control sheet and then inserted the slide into the projector. At my signal she would project the slide for 60 seconds then replace it in its proper envelope and order, and set up the next slide according to the second pair of random numbers.

After more than 60 seconds had elapsed after my signal, I opened my sealed envelope containing a copy of only the first list

(1-36), then the envelope indicated by the top numeral. I spread out the four pictures contained in it, asking the subject to rank them (1-4) as to which picture he or she thought was being sent. After each trial the receiver was also asked whether or not mental contact had been made (ranking of 1-4). In addition, both J. M. and I ranked (1-5) our evaluation of the children's enthusiasm and involvement in the task, our own enthusiasm, and our feeling toward each child.

This procedure was followed until five trials were completed. The children then reversed roles for five more trials for a total of 60 trials per group.

The same procedure was followed with the second group except that they were first reintroduced to the fantasy of E.T. They heard a tape of the music and story, viewed and colored pictures from it, etc. An addition to the story was read placing E.T. back on his planet and providing a scenario for the two to communicate mentally. J.M. and I were now "interstellar communication helpers" while the sender and receiver became "E.T." and "Elliott" respectively, switching roles after five trials each.

Both the direct hit and sum-of-ranks techniques were used with an appropriate correction--based on the Bonferroni inequality --for multiple analysis. Because two tests were used, the significance level was adjusted from $p = .05$ to $p = .025$ (i.e., 05/2). Comparison of the two groups was made using the Mann-Whitney U Test.

The fantasy group's sum-of-ranks was 141, nine less (lower score = higher ESP) than the MCE of 150 ($Z = .98$, $p \leq .164$) while the control group scored 148 ($Z = .17$, $p \leq .433$). The difference, while in the predicted direction, was not significant ($p \leq .3431$).

In the experimental group higher scoring was associated with more positive experimenter attitudes towards the subjects (rho = -.375, $p \leq .2284$), supporting previous findings (e.g., Anderson & White, JP, 1957, 81-97). This was not true for the control group. In the control group psi scores were positively correlated with the subject's evaluation of whether or not psi was taking place (rho = .333, $p \leq .2889$).

It must be noted that the groups were much too small for accurate statistical evaluation. Especially in searching for correlations, the number of subjects becomes crucial because unless the relationship is extremely strong a small sample will not reach significance. In addition, the need to reverse roles, time limitations, pressures, and difficult conditions resulted in my not being able to create the fantasy setting I had intended and probably contributed to lower-than-expected scores. The experiment should be repeated at a more leisurely pace, allowing longer mentation periods, and with larger groups.

QUALITATIVE AND FIELD STUDIES

EXPERIMENTS WITH FALSE KEYS THAT SUGGEST ONE MORE
CONDITION FOR EXCELLENT SURVIVAL EVIDENCE

Arthur S. Berger (Survival Research Foundation)

Since the early days of psychical research, people have made antemortem plans or pacts to communicate specific information after death as a signal of postmortem survival and identity. These postmortem experiments are highly regarded as providing prima facie evidence of survival and identity if they meet five conditions: 1) The information to be communicated must not be known to any living person except the planner. 2) The information must not be left in any recorded form. 3) The experiment must produce a definitive result. 4) The experiment must permit repeated trials. 5) The information must be verifiable.

Not only the founders of the Society for Psychical Research but also modern day parapsychologists believe it to be highly desirable that many persons undertake to make such antemortem pacts in order to supply strong survival evidence (Myers, Human Personality and Its Survival of Bodily Death, 1903, vol. 2; Thouless, PSPR, 1948, 253-263). To encourage multiple replications of such pacts and postmortem experiments with the aim of accumulating over the years a mass of data which may yield significant results for survival research, the Survival Research Foundation (SRF) is conducting a large-scale, international, long-term program (Berger, JP, in press; Theta, 1982, 82-84).

Because the old sealed-envelope experiment did not meet all five conditions, four new experiments were created to replace it. Thouless, the "father" of this type of test (Berger, RIP 1982, 306-315) designed the first (PSPR, 1948, 253-263) in which a message is enciphered in letters with a verbal key by using a random key letter series and an established method of encipherment such as the Vigenère letter square. Another cipher test, devised by Frank C. Tribbe in conjunction with Clarissa Mulders, is based on a key quotation from a standard reference work. A private code is then created on the basis of which a message is enciphered in letters (Journal of Religion and Psychical Research, 1980, 44-46). A third cipher test has been developed by the author (Learning Tests for Survival, 1982) in which a key dictionary entry is randomly selected and a code created by numbering every letter in the entry and what follows it for an indeterminate length. By the use of this code a message is created and enciphered in numbers. Ian Stevenson has designed a test using a combination padlock (JASPR, 1968, 246-254). The lock is set to a combination of three pairs of digits to be remembered by means of a verbal key which, according to a formula, can be converted into the right combination.

The new experiments fulfill all five conditions and are meant to provide prima facie evidence of survival and identity. Repeated trials can be made. The outcomes cannot be debated. The verbal keys are not revealed to anyone or written down. Every experiment is designed to permit verification. To combat the argument that there might have been paranormal cognition of the minds of the planners while they were alive, all experiments require that psychics make a number of attempts through ESP to acquire the verbal keys of the planners during their lifetimes. Failure of these attempts will suggest that the secret key has remained secret. Communicators are to supply keys after death whose correctness can be checked by researchers. If the keys make sense out of coded letters or numbers or permit locks to be opened, they are correct. It is the receipt of these keys which no one else could have known which is taken to be prima facie evidence that the persons who enciphered the letters or numbers or set the locks have survived death and identified themselves.

The basic premises of all the experiments are 1) that deceased persons may continue to exist and can communicate with the living and 2) that without the keys known to the deceased communicators alone the test messages they left cannot be deciphered and the test locks they left cannot be opened.

This article deals with the second premise stated above. In order to improve the design and methodology of the SRF program, the author asked this question: Could a key, other than the one used by and known to a communicator alone, be discovered that would allow an enciphered message to be read or a lock to be opened? To answer this question three messages were enciphered by the author according to the methods of encipherment of the Thouless, Tribbe, and Berger experiments. Based on the Thouless experiment and the Vigenère letter square, the message CBDAGDL was prepared. The Tribbe experiment, based on a quotation, was used to encipher the message CTCVO QIOIU RMBLM DO. Under the Berger experiment an entry as a verbal key was picked at random from an unabridged dictionary. The resulting enciphered message was: 132, 140, 249, 24, 159, 73, 49, 236, 200, 68, 11, 32, 271, 198, 300, 288, 17, 123, 7, 225, 278, 9, 121, 251, 129, 215, 146, 309. All enciphered messages were sent to Professor X who said he would see if he could discover keys for them. Along with the test messages were sent full instructions explaining the methods of enciphering the messages. The verbal keys used by the author to encipher the messages, however, were kept secret, the reasoning being that if the premise above was correct Professor X would not be able to decipher the messages without the keys. X's task was to find any key that would render the enciphered messages plausible.

Although X did not find the actual key used by the author in the Thouless experiment, he produced several keys which made sense out of the message enciphered under it. Thus, three of his keys allowed the message to be read as "Believe," "I Live On," and "Rejoice." X would not state the deciphering procedures he followed, but the author deduces that X's keys were the result of inventing the words, aligning their letters with the ciphers in the message and then using the Vigenère square to create key letter series which, in turn, produced verbal keys.

X did not find the key used by the author in the Tribbe experiment, either. He produced a key, however, which not only made the message enciphered under this test plausible but converted it into "O Love the Human Race," which was the author's original message. It is deduced that X's key was the result of X's being able to note the frequency with which the same letters appeared in the enciphered message and thus being able to arrive at the original message and eventually a workable verbal key.

X did not produce a key for the message enciphered under the Berger experiment. It has remained unbroken.

The combination lock test was not made the subject of experiment with X because, on the face of it, it appears that, if a lock is set to a combination of six digits, the combination, according to a given formula, can be translated into a number of verbal keys which will permit the lock to be opened.

The experiments with X suggest that false keys can be produced for the Thouless and Tribbe tests. The lock test seems exposed also to the production of such keys. Although they would not be the keys which antemortem planners had kept secret, used and intended to communicate after death, all would appear to be correct because they would make readable the messages enciphered by planners or would open the locks they left. The possibility of multiple keys raises serious questions: If keys are received after the deaths of planners, are they the planners' keys? Did the planners in fact communicate?

In recognition of the problem of false keys, the SRF's program has been designed to offer three solutions: 1) Safekeeping by researchers of all test messages and locks to ensure that no one will be able to concentrate on them, as did X, in a deliberate and methodical effort to find verbal keys for them. 2) Double-checking or double-enciphering which requires antemortem planners to take the first (or last) word of the verbal key used to encipher a message or set a lock under one system and to use it again to encipher a second back-up message under a different system. A false key should not work with two tests. 3) Antemortem planners are to prepare their messages carefully so that they are longer and more complex than the messages submitted to X, which may have been too short and too simple.

With his postmortem experiment which inspired Tribbe, Berger and Stevenson to design their experiments, "Thouless has given survival researchers the opportunity to make a major advance in the experimental investigation of the survival question" (Berger, RIP 1982, 306-315). These postmortem experiments can provide excellent evidence of postmortem survival and identity if they fulfill the five stipulated conditions and one more which the experiments conducted here suggest: Researchers must adopt safeguards to be sure that the information verified by them could have come only from the deceased persons from whom they purport to come.

SELECTED STATIC-PK PHENOMENA UNDER EXCEPTIONAL CONDITIONS OF SECURITY

William Edward Cox (Rolla, Missouri)

Introduction. In 1979, at Rolla, Missouri, there began an extended series of filmed records of widely assorted physical effects upon stable systems. These occurred under lock and seal, and to all appearances were paranormally produced. Later, to confirm the nature and security of such evidence, I employed a disinterested locksmith.

Under an inverted aquarium tank I would place objects upon microswitches, arranged to trigger an 8 mm. motion picture camera which would capture any internal RSPK disturbances caused by the responsible agency.

Most of the claimed paranormal effects in which I have been involved were at the Rolla residence of Dr. and Mrs. John Thomas Richards, early members of what has been known for some 20 years as the Society for Research on Rapport and Telekinesis ("SORRAT"). Their custom always had been to solicit paranormal phenomena, from raps to levitation, by appealing to discarnate intelligences by name, in the manner followed by the late Prof. John G. Neihardt, an authority on American Indians. I objectively would follow the same policy myself, on occasion, when referring to the agency, regardless of my holding no personal belief concerning the survival question, or other settled convictions concerning the phenomena.

The term "mini-lab" (ML) will be used in referring to the apparatus. It was coined, and this equipment was suggested, by J. B. Rhine, whose personal interest in the source of these Missouri phenomena preceded my own. Considering the controversy which naturally might be caused by such extreme claims, only the locksmith's very select portion of the apparently parapsychophysical effects at Rolla (which numbered well into the hundreds) will be described.

There appear to be few precedents for in-progress filming of reputed physical phenomena. Other novelties included these: 1) The apparently inexplicable effects were produced at exceptionally arbitrary times in the Richards' home, including various forms of "matter-through-matter." 2) Bright lights and the camera were no hindrance. 3) The traditional mental effort of a sensitive at the actual site has not appeared necessary, nor was I able to catch ML phenomena in action.

Accordingly, the question of fraudulently animated films has arisen, despite the apparent adequacy of equipment security. My employing a locksmith was partly out of respect to those who might otherwise deem my own routine precautions as having been deficient.

Construction of the Mini-Labs. Two aquarium tanks of 10-gal. and 5.5-gal. size were used. They were secured to wooden platforms which extended approximately 10 cm. beyond the front and sides of the tanks. Except when I periodically would rearrange their target objects, these MLs were kept locked and sealed, tightly mounted on the platforms with the normally open side face-down. When in use, encircling heavy-duty steel straps secured them, plus the lock and special seal(s). (I should add that for all of my own experiments, though not the locksmith's, a special string was tied, in addition to the lock and parallel with it. This was synthetic, varicolored, and was purchased by me in Europe in order to preclude matching it here. Whenever I locked up the ML I would tie a bit of this string and with a match melt the ends together. Richards had no access to any remnant of it, which I always would take away along with my key. In addition, I often taped onto this string a white tape bearing a private Notary Seal imprint. These constituted what I called the "seal.")

The Locksmith's Failure. I employed the proprietor of Abel Lock & Key Co., of Rolla, Mr. R. Henson, in May 1981 to lock securely the larger ML for a special test under the best safeguards available. He asked if I were a magician (true), and this made my purpose seem more logical to him. He also was told that I would request a notarized and detailed document, to which he agreed, concerning anything he might find to have occurred within by whatever means were at my disposal.

Henson's method consisted of jamming a key into my own lock and applying special glue to both the broken-off portion and the shackle itself, etc., after I had installed the following target objects in the ML: a pile of seven different coins, a heavy serving spoon, a small piece of plywood containing a wood screw, and several other target objects. He was specifically asked to note the absence of any writing instrument.

The ML was then carefully removed to a special room in the Richards' basement. I placed a pen on the external platform of the ML. Two days later all seven coins had been moved onto assigned spots in two straight rows, the spoon was bent, the screw released, and other target objects disturbed. The pen had entered the ML and produced writing on prepared paper within, ostensibly by "direct writing." Two other nearby target objects, a penny and an X-ray packet, also had entered.

When the ML was returned to his shop, the reaction by Henson and his assistant was subdued. They appeared to maintain the casual opinion that magnetism, electricity, or a trick means of entry must have been used; but repeated scrutiny of the entire equipment revealed no fault. They required nearly half an hour to remove this Master Lock, due to the quantity of glue which had been injected along the broken-off key. (Sawing the shackle was not successful.)

A Second Attempt by the Locksmith. During the summer, Henson asked permission to make another attempt at security, without cost. Since he had no prior knowledge of the possible involvement of PK, and appeared to be of cautious mind, his security measures must not have seemed sufficient for his own satisfaction. In June I delivered the smaller aquarium tank. This one contained assigned places for two rows of four quarters each, instead of four assorted coins. Again I warned Henson to do the locking job well, and even offered to pay him if "I" failed.*

When next I visited his shop, he had cracked the glass. The cracks seemed innocuous, so I inserted a pile of quarters and several other target objects. When he had finished securing the lock, I removed it to the Richards' basement. A week later I returned it to Abel Lock & Key, with certain disturbances now evident, including the insertion of a balloon and an orderly array of six of the quarters. The other two were now on the front platform outside. But Mr. Henson then and there concluded that he should have purchased a new tank, and so preferred to discount the effects now evident.

I was quite willing for him to make another effort to prohibit trickery. He even installed a second steel band (crosswise the base), and "booby trapped" the tank. Target objects were installed, but this time I promised to enter eight quarters and also a heavy lock which he supplied. In four days a number of disturbances had been produced: both the lock and coins had been somehow entered in the ML.

Discussion. This confirmation of avowed and apparent departures from known physical laws was certainly warranted, what-

---

*The McDonnell Laboratory for Psychical Research was financially supporting the Rolla investigations at that time.

ever the quality of my own locks and seals. Until equal results had been produced under control of a stronger skeptic than myself, the possibility of erroneous judgment logically remained. Richards and I have been quite agreeable to visits by any qualified investigator; but only Drs. James McClenon and Peter Phillips were able to spend appreciable time at in-residence study.

Writing by the pen was an effect which I particularly desired to have confirmed, since this had occurred many times under seal. I regret that only one sequence of motion pictures was captured during tests under the locksmith's security. This was of a single levitating coin, which seemed to have been caught exiting through the glass front. Of the two expelled quarters, the other was already on the front platform, and they erratically moved closer together in the filmed sequence.

The most inexplicable feat was what appeared to be the interpenetration of matter-through-matter. A total of four entrances and two exits (counting the two and eight quarters as one item each) occurred under Henson's security. This occasionally has been reported in the literature, including by Hasted of Geller, not to mention the conspicuous capture, on camera, of several linkages and unlinkages of seamless rings at Rolla. (One pair of solid rings has remained permanently linked.)

Comments on J.T. Richards. The central party in nearly all of the Rolla disturbances has been Dr. Richards, yet Richards himself holds to the exceptional view that he is not personally to be so credited. This is clearly implied in his book SORRAT (1982, 289). That volume, being a journalistic one, does not deal very critically or analytically with given phenomena, however. Accordingly, I have one in preparation.

Comments by the Locksmith. Part of Mr. Henson's prepared document reads as follows:

> I ... find it difficult to believe that Mr. Cox did forcibly insert various large objects into my sealed tank, particularly the heavy lock.... It was simply far too well secured and tight.... The pen-writing, spoon-bending, screw-unscrewing, and entry of the pen, and [other objects are] totally inconceivable.... Thus arose my interest in ... later tests, with an additional steel band, a new tank ... and ["booby traps," etc.]. Yet these effects occurred exactly as described. [Signed] Ron. Henson

THE HAPPY PRINCESS: PSYCHOLOGICAL PROFILE OF A PSYCHIC

Joan Healy (Queens Children's Psychiatric Center)

This paper is part of a study of gifted psychics, designed to explore whether their developmental histories and psychological configurations show any common factors which may be useful in explaining why they provide the best channels for psychic ability. Psychological testing and a series of interviews were conducted with Mrs. J.M., a highly respected and gifted professional psychic.

The article's title comes from Oscar Wilde's "The Happy Prince," Mrs. M.'s favorite childhood fairy tale. The story's theme concerns a carefree young Prince, oblivious to the differences between his happy life and those of his subjects, who are poor and hungry. After his death, he is transformed into a golden, jeweled statue, standing where he can see the misery of his people, but unable to help them. A passing swallow is enlisted by the Prince to distribute his goldleaf covering and jewels, including his sapphire eyes, to the townspeople, who eventually notice how shabby the Prince looks and have him melted down. The Prince's leaden heart and his friend, now a dead bird, are thrown on the dust heap, but retrieved by an angel sent by God to bring to Heaven "the two most precious things in the city."

This story, and other responses, reflect themes which seem to be involved in the dynamics and behavior of Mrs. M., as well as some of the great psychics of the past, such as Mrs. Garrett and Mrs. Leonard. Issues include the abrupt shattering of childhood innocence, especially by a sudden awareness of death and grief, or by early unempathic handling of emotional development, especially parental discovery and disapproval of psychic abilities, as well as the premature development of a sense of responsibility for the welfare of others, especially involving a sense of betrayal and of having to sacrifice one's own needs.

As with the Prince, there seems to be a tendency for the psychic to blend emotional involvement with interpersonal distance (the Prince's bird; the psychic's guides), giving them the "detachment" they say they need to function psychically. This is exemplified by the Prince's anonymous gifts of his goldleaf "skin" and the jewels which symbolize his worth and beauty (as perceived by others), as well as by "The Elves and the Shoemaker," the favorite fairy tale of another extremely gifted psychic, who likes it because of its theme of "help and run."

The parallels of emotional experience which thread through "The Happy Prince" and the lives of Mrs. M. and other gifted psychics are borne out by test results. Findings include a very strong attraction to emotional stimuli and engagement, and an equally strong pull to the opposite pole of intellectual involvement.

This antithesis seems to be resolved by attempts to blend feeling and "logic," behaviorally, as well as through the dynamics indicated by the presence of color-shading blends on the Rorschach. Psychics may be drawn to the ambiguity of paranormal stimuli because of what seems almost to amount to a drive to resolve ambiguity, find the "right," "logical" meaning, and produce the subjective unity of thinking and feeling which seems to be one of the primary needs of the psychic personality. In a sense, it seems as if tenderness is dangerous unless there is logic to it, and this may be the core potential tragedy for the psychic, if it is pronounced and not balanced by the more "unrealistic" sense of trust characteristic of the hysteric. But this fear can also be a strength if it fosters the emotionally safer "cosmic connectedness" which may be the matrix of psychic ability.

"Mixed dominance" seems to pervade the personality of psychics, and perhaps all areas of their functioning, including sensory and other CNS functions. This seems to set the stage for the oxymoronic "detached merger" a psychic needs in order to produce evidential material. The dual high level of development of schizoid and hysteric personality components seems to allow the detachment necessary to observe and report information received during the emotional entrainment between the psychic and his or her sources of information. In mediumistic phenomena, especially, the emotional ties the "dead" appear to maintain with their lost loved ones seem to be the motivation for communication, if not its literal language or template. This study's findings indicate that it is the medium's ability to operate in both thinking and feeling modes, at the same time, blending traits of the more usual schizoid and hysteric personality types, which allows psychic ability to flourish. Hysterics are dolphins in the emotional ocean, blissfully at home when merged (in fantasy) and immersed in feeling; schizoids are submarines, attracted to the ocean, but needing a feeling-tight protection to allow them to avoid anxiety and "think" (especially when they're thinking about feeling, as they usually are). Psychics, especially mediums, seem to be mermaids, combining the best of worlds, able to function in either, but belonging totally to neither.

I am grateful to Dr. John Exner, a renowned Rorschach expert, who did a blind analysis of Mrs. M.'s Rorschach responses and their structural summary, finding her to be "obviously bright" (her IQ is 145), with "considerable resources readily available." The protocol showed "no marked evidence of psychopathology." There were suggestions of "a stringent effort to convey an intellectual image," together with a marked "emotional, intuitive-like style."

In general, Rorschach results corroborated findings of other investigators (notably the many studies by Schmeidler). Prominent features of Mrs. M.'s record were extreme productivity (73 responses); a large number of original responses; a high level of both color and movement percepts; much use of space, by itself or in conjunction with other determinants; and many nature and archetypal themes.

Psychics appear to share some of the abilities of very creative people, as well as some of the superficial signs of schizophrenia. The capacity of the great ones to safeguard and nurture their psychic ability in the face of intense opposition is a tribute to their basic mental stability. One of the findings of this study was that psychics can be both intellectually gifted and emotionally vibrant and healthy, as Mrs. M.'s test results indicate. Generous and caring, extremely outgoing, especially in their work, psychics are nevertheless not the sentimental romantics one might expect; they are intensely logical people, intuitive in a practical way, but more inclined to be superrealists than dreamers. Functioning as emotional seismographs, with their psychic ability, it appears they home in on the strong affective components in the holographic realm to which they have access, but once "there" switch into a mode of logical objectivity about the feelings they have when merged with clients or guides. In sharp contrast to multiple personality patients (with whom they also share some traits), they maintain well-defined ego boundaries. They also make a sharp distinction between daydreaming and psychic ability and don't relate the two to each other at all; this is crucial for investigators to understand, to avoid misinterpretation of test results.

Tests used in this study were found to vary widely in usefulness, with projective tests seeming to yield much clearer material, perhaps because of the tendency of objective tests to use means between opposite traits. This type of score may make the subject seem well-balanced, which Mrs. M. is, but the extremes tend to wash out, missing the intensity of opposite traits which seems to be one of the major keys to understanding the psychic personality. In general, it was found that the more projective the test, the more useful the information. Any kind of structured stimuli seems to bind them to "logic," and the best personality clues result when they can be lured away, without anxiety, from using "logic," as on Card 16 of the Thematic Apperception Test.

Other aspects discussed included the possibility that gifted psychics may have childhood problems with dyslexic-type disabilities, as Mrs. M. and Mrs. Garrett apparently did; this may be related to the general finding of "mixed dominant" functioning. The possible relationship of psychic ability to aspects of creativity was also considered, including similarities between the high level secondary thought processes involved in creativity and the synthesis of the various sensory (and extrasensory) modalities used by psychics in the symbolic retrieval of paranormal information. Some of the dynamics explored included the relationship between auras and ego boundaries, and the psychic's apparent extreme vulnerability to emotional pain, in herself and others, modified by an ability to "fence" it off in a "practical, logical" way. It was suggested that studies of laterality in gifted psychics might yield significant findings.

THOMASVILLE HAUNTING (RB)*

William G. Roll† (Psychical Research Foundation) and Barbara Brittain (West Georgia College)

In November 1982, the Psychical Research Foundation learned that sightings of an "apparition" was reportedly disrupting work at the San-Mor Furniture Factory in Thomasville, North Carolina. We made two visits to the factory, in December 1982 and April 1983.

Victor Couch, owner of San-Mor, reported he had seen the same apparition more than 50 times over seven years and that its description matched sightings by other employees. (Due to Couch's feeling that our activities would further disrupt work schedules we were unable to confer independently with these employees.) The sightings took place after working hours in the late afternoon and evening when the work areas were half lit. Appearing for 5- to 15-second intervals, a male figure about Couch's height was seen in profile, his face blurred and shadowed. He wore work pants and a checkered shirt. Couch said that several employees had seen him simultaneously, but that sometimes only one would see him and others not. The figure did not resemble anyone he knew.

In addition to the sightings, Couch and others, including his two brothers who work in the factory, reported that on about a dozen occasions loud sounds were heard, as of stacks of lumber falling. People also occasionally reported feelings of "a presence" and cold drafts. These incidents were intermittent with up to six months between events. The most recent sighting was two weeks before our visit. Couch was seated in his office after hours. The office has two windows facing the factory and he saw the figure walk past one window and then past the other toward the back of the room. There were further sightings between our first and second visits.

Couch was given the Wilson and Barber Inventory of Childhood Memories and Imaginings (ICMI) and produced a low score of 8 out of 48 which indicates a modest fantasy life. His eyesight is good. The recurrent experiences at the factory, sometimes seen simultaneously by two or more persons, the loud noises, the feeling of presences and drafts, are typical of hauntings and we decided to investigate the possibility of psi by employing two procedures: a psi scan by psychics and nonpsychics for active areas in the factory, and a psi session ("séance") by psychics to obtain information relating to the incidents and to the ghost. The nonpsychics were used as controls to test for any normal environmental factors which might facilitate illusory experience.

Two psi scans were conducted, one in December 1982 an-

---

*This research was made possible by a grant from Eugenia Porter Rayzor.

other in April 1983. In the first, Patricia Hayes, Kelly Powers, and Esterelke Kaplan of the Spring Lake psi development center near Durham took part. In the second, Debra Weiner, FRNM, and members of a class taught by W. G. R. at the Community Holistic Health Center in Chapel Hill participated. The Spring Lake group was designated psi-sensitive on the basis of experimental psi studies by the PRF; the Chapel Hill group was divided into four sensitives and three controls on the basis of personal statements regarding psi experiences. On a floor plan of the factory, psi sensitives and nonsensitives marked those areas they felt were active. These were later compared to floor plans marked by persons involved in the actual sightings. The result by the Spring Lake group, though not statistically significant, favored the target area. The Chapel Hill psi sensitives also favored this area and so did the controls.

In an attempt to obtain information relating to the incidents, a psi session was held with the Spring Lake sensitives. Couch and his daughter were also present. The sensitives collectively described the apparition as a person connected with the factory who had been handicapped, was an alcoholic, and had had family trouble. The person felt grateful to Couch and was looking after the factory. Couch said the description fit a person we shall call "Guy" who had died ten years earlier and whom Couch had befriended. Guy was a previous owner of the factory and had suffered a stroke which impaired his speech. He then became an alcoholic. What did not fit the description was the work clothes; Guy dressed more formally.

There were also three specific impressions worth mentioning. Kelly Powers received an impression of a sign that used to hang over a doorway. Couch said a "no admittance" sign which had hung over the machine room door had disappeared a year ago. Powers also evoked images of a license plate. Couch reported that four months earlier the license plate on his car which was parked at the factory had gone. Powers also mentioned a truck "that wobbles" and was in need of repair. Couch said this fit the description of his brother's truck.

The Spring Lake psychics scored an average of 32 on the ICMI, the Chapel Hill psychics 34, and the controls 13. The psychics clearly had a richer imaginative life than the controls.

In terms of the psi scans, the target area was probably more conducive to hallucinatory or imaginative experiences than other parts of the factory since it was farthest from the windows and near dark storage areas. This is consistent with the clustering of experiences in the late afternoon and evening and with the preference of the controls for this area. However, the apparition has also been seen under two 500-watt lights in the spray paint area.

Comparing our results with those of Maher and Schmeidler (JASPR, 1975, 342-351), whose controls failed to pick the target areas, it may be relevant that their controls were goats or disbelievers in ESP whereas ours were sheep. It seems possible that Maher and Schmeidler's sheep-goat difference could be explained either in terms of different responses to the same psi or sensory cues, and that the similar responses of our psychics and controls might also be due either to psi or sensory cues.

As to the psi session, it seems to us there was an above-chance correlation of events and the psychics' impressions. Interestingly, Couch recalls that sightings occurred when there were important business decisions to be made. We might speculate that Couch's need for advice was apparition-conducive and that the characteristics of the apparition were partially provided by Guy and partially by Couch and the other observers.

Part 4: Roundtables

THE POLTERGEIST AGENT: FACT OR FICTION?*

PSYCHOLOGICAL EVALUATIONS OF POLTERGEIST AGENTS:
A CRITIQUE

Carlos S. Alvarado (Division of Parapsychology, University of Virginia)

The generally accepted psychological theory of poltergeist behavior dictates that these phenomena are PK expressions of repressed conflicts, hostilities, and/or sexual problems. This theory is widely held and promoted by parapsychologists. It is likely, though, that this conceptual model is based on weak evidence and methodologically invalid research.

The psychodynamic model has been primarily based on clinical examinations of several poltergeist agents. The problems with this method is that it is very subjective and no hard data are usually presented in support of the clinician's views. The problem is complicated by the fact that most researchers using this approach are already biased toward the view that poltergeist agents are repressed or psychopathologically disturbed. The psychopathology we often associate with the poltergeist might therefore be the result of self-fulfilling prophecy.

Researchers have indeed attempted to demonstrate objectively that poltergeist agents are psychologically repressed or otherwise disturbed by the use of psychodiagnostic testing. However, most of the tests used to evaluate poltergeist agents are projective procedures (such as the Rorschach) which have questionable reliability. It is also unfortunate that, in many cases, the psychologists using these projective tests knew that they were dealing with poltergeist agents, which could well have biased them toward finding pathology when in fact it may not have objectively existed. Experimental research has shown that the expectations and previous knowledge of

---

*Organized and chaired by D. Scott Rogo (John F. Kennedy University)

the psychologist or psychiatrist evaluating a patient significantly influences his or her interpretations.

These problems lead to the conclusion that, at the present time, we have no right to accept the psychopathological model of the poltergeist agent without serious qualms.

THE PSYCHOPATHOLOGICAL AND PSYCHOPHYSIOLOGICAL THEORIES OF THE RSPK AGENT

William G. Roll (Psychical Research Foundation)

The validity of psychological and physiological approaches to poltergeist activity continues to foster debate. Criticisms have focused on three main issues: the validity and reliability of psychological/clinical testing of RSPK agents, the role of psychological conditions in RSPK activity, and the relationship of central nervous system (CNS) disturbances to RSPK (in particular, the connection with epilepsy).

Though I have been identified as a main proponent of the psychopathological theory, I will state again (Roll, The Poltergeist, 1972, 175) that "something else" besides repressed hostility must comprise the difference between those who express this unknown via PK and those who express themselves by normal means, and that this key difference so far eludes our psychological tests.

The question of what makes some angry people RSPK-prone and others not leads naturally to CNS considerations. Are there CNS anomalies that can be linked to poltergeist phenomena? The case that focused our attention on abnormal firings of neurons in the CNS came in 1975 (Solfvin and Roll, RIP 1975, 115-120) and involved an epileptic who displayed an inverse relationship between RSPK incidents and epileptic seizure. When the seizures came, they were followed by the only two periods during this time when no poltergeist incidents were reported.

To propose a direct, one-to-one relationship between epilepsy and RSPK is to misstate our intentions, however. It is crucial to remember that epilepsy is not a disease, but a collection of symptoms resulting from CNS disturbances. Thus the CNS theory is much broader and complex than is implied by critics. RSPK may in fact be the only "symptom" of a CNS disorder. It is at the same time logical to expect that epilepsy and poltergeist activity may sometimes be observed in the same person.

My survey of RSPK cases lent support to the CNS approach. Four agents had shown clinical or EEG symptoms suggestive of epilepsy, but about half of 92 agents surveyed had other medical or psychological problems, often serious: muscular contractions, convulsions, fainting fits, comas, mental retardation, violent alcoholism, schizophrenia, hysteria, etc. It is reasonable to look to CNS disturbances as a linking factor. It is also suggestive that RSPK, like epilepsy, is concentrated in ages before 15 and that abnormal EEGs are often found in children not manifesting epileptic symptoms. It is also interesting that many RSPK incidents, like epileptic symptoms, are observed under stressful conditions. People involved with poltergeist disturbances clearly suffer; certainly from their point of view RSPK is a pathology. But to me, it is a psychic or parapsychological pathology in which the relationship between a person and his or her environment is key; the phenomena do not depend simply on the mind or brain of the person alone. Thus, the question of why many hostile and repressed people are not RSPK agents, and why many RSPK agents do not display CNS anomalies, may be answered by the fact that social and environmental factors lend key ingredients to the recipe. The notion of "interaction" is supported by the use of Rorschach and TAT tests, which have shown how emotionally loaded images seem to be reflected in RSPK events. Field studies utilizing telemetry EEG units and neurophysiological examinations of the persons may provide the best test of the CNS theory for RSPK.

PATHOLOGY OF THE POLTERGEIST: NOTES ON A PROPOSED VALIDATION

D. Scott Rogo (John F. Kennedy University)

The crux of the current debate over whether there actually exists any such thing as a pathologically disturbed poltergeist agent rests with the nature of the tests hitherto used to isolate this syndrome. The poltergeist agent has been typified as a teenager repressing massive amounts of hostility and aggression by the use of denial and sublimation. The tests used to validate this model have been ones with low reliability such as the Rorschach and TAT. They can also be used to fulfill the researcher's expectations. Poltergeist researchers, however, seem unaware of Megargee's concept (Journal of Abnormal Psychology, 1967, 519-528) of the "overcontrolled hostile" type--a repressed individual who denies his or her hostility until it breaks out in the form of anti-social acts. The O-H type seems similar to our concept of the pathological poltergeist agent, and Megargee and his associates have developed a high reliability subscale of the MMPI that tests for the O-H type. Several independent studies have documented the validity of this test. The use of the O-H scale during poltergeist investigations may therefore provide researchers with a more objective tool by which to document the possible pathology of the poltergeist agent without relying on more subjective projective tests.

THE ROLE OF CONJURORS IN PSYCHICAL RESEARCH AND PARAPSYCHOLOGY*

This session consisted of a panel discussion by a group of magicians, associated with leading conjuring societies (including the Society of American Magicians, the International Brotherhood of Magicians, the Psychical Entertainers Association, and The Magic Circle), and presenting a wide diversity of viewpoints. The panel consisted of Loyd Auerbach, Robert E. Cassidy, Milbourne Christopher, Scott Gordon, Jack Malon, James Randi, Anthony Raven, and Marcello Truzzi (moderator and convener).

The moderator introduced the subject matter by giving a brief history of the relationship between magicians and psychical research. Three points were emphasized: 1) Not only have magicians and psi researchers cooperated well in the past, but the need for such cooperation has been well stated in the literature by leading researchers. 2) Magicians have endorsed as well as discredited past claims of psychical phenomena. 3) There are problems in defining a legitimate magician just as there are in defining who is a legitimate parapsychologist.

The panel then responded to questions from the moderator and from the audience. All the panelists agreed that only magicians with specialized knowledge about psychical research and the simulation of psychical phenomena should be consulted by parapsychologists. All agreed that most magicians are probably not competent in this specialty area. All agreed with James Randi when he stated that it was not necessary to involve a magician in all cases of psychical research. Several panelists, following comments by Robert Cassidy, indicated that only magicians with no public vested interest in the outcome should be used as consultants, and Cassidy pointed out that mentalists (conjurors who specialize in simulating psi phenomena) usually have a vested interest in public belief in psi. Milbourne Christopher and several other panelists stated that any magician consultant must agree to do so with the condition that no publicity be present about his or her role. In response to an audience question, Anthony Raven indicated his strong disapproval of any magician covertly entering a psi laboratory with the intention of fooling and ridiculing the experimenter to obtain

---

*Organized and chaired by Marcello Truzzi (Eastern Michigan University).

publicity, and he asked that parapsychologists should not judge all magicians by the actions of a few "bad apples." James Randi defended his recent "Project Alpha" in which his confederates fooled several prominent psi researchers. He pointed out that the operation was never intended to damage professional reputations and was called off (made public) before serious damage was done; and he stated that his desire has always been to improve legitimate psi research by making more parapsychologists aware of their need for the help magicians can give them.

During the course of the panel discussion, the panelists expressed their own views about the reality of psi and several indicated their personal view that psi was real. All indicated their support for the legitimacy of parapsychological investigation and expressed their desire to be of help to serious researchers.

At the close of the audience-panel discussion, Stanley Krippner had a newly passed motion of the PA Council read. It expressed a desire for cooperation between magicians and psi researchers and indicated that the major magical societies would be contacted with the aim of obtaining lists of qualified magicians endorsed by those societies as potential consultants for parapsychologists in different parts of the world.

NONLINEAR THINKING IN PARAPSYCHOLOGY*

NONLINEAR THINKING IN PARAPSYCHOLOGY
Daniel J. Benor (Philadelphia, Pa.)

Two problems complicate psi research experiments: 1) multifactorial influences which as yet cannot be adequately controlled, and some of which may as yet not be fully appreciated; and 2) psi-interactive effects, wherein participant expectations may affect the results.

Linear designs, persistently applied in large numbers of experiments over long periods of time, can help to isolate some of the first type of variables. For instance, some evidence has been found to support effects from such variables as moon phases and the hypothesized morphogenetic field in influencing experiments.

Linear designs may identify factors of the second type, such as subject belief systems (e.g., sheep/goat effect), experimenter effects, and experimenter-subject interactions. Linear design is limited in this type of problem, however, as the participants' expectations (include here readers of experimental reports, if retro-PK is a valid construct) may create the anticipated results.

New paradigms may be needed to make sense of psi phenomena. Tart suggests simultaneously-experienced, consensual validation of ASC experiences. The consensus format of psychic archaeology and police work may be applicable to such questions. I propose further in-depth psychological studies of psi-gifted individuals, especially healers, to extract further clues re the nature of psi realms, whose realities probably are more accurately described in our linear language by "and" rather than "either-or" thinking.

---

*Organized and chaired by Daniel J. Benor (Philadelphia, Pa.)

ACAUSAL WORLD VIEWS AND SHAMANIC HEALING MODELS

Stanley Krippner (Saybrook Institute)

Carl Jung's lifelong effort to understand synchronistic phenomena culminated in 1955 in his essay "Synchronicity: An Acausal Connecting Principle." Jung defined synchronicity as "a coincidence in time of two or more causally unrelated events which have the same or similar meaning" (p. 36). Jung's concept has been critically examined by Braude (ESP and Psychokinesis, 1979, 240-241) who concludes "so long as we must explain why events have occurred in a meaningful rather than a non-meaningful way, our explanations will be causal explanations" (pp. 240-241). Yet even if synchronicity is not a viable theoretical concept, it may have some application on the clinical level. Jung used apparently synchronistic events in the context of the psychotherapeutic session. Ponting, in an unpublished dissertation proposal, has teased out the factors that appear to comprise Jung's procedures: 1) The client is at a therapeutic impasse; 2) the client's impasse somehow involves a rigid world view; 3) the therapeutic solution appears to require something which will violate that world view; 4) a startling or dramatic gesture which brings about shock, confusion, or surprise is used by the therapist; 5) the ensuing temporary breakdown of the client's world view is utilized to produce a breakthrough in therapy as new possibilities become apparent.

This psychotherapeutic utilization of purported synchronistic events is rarely attempted in Western psychotherapy, possible exceptions being Ericksonian hypnosis, neurolinguistic programming, and other varieties of so-called paradoxical psychotherapy (Weeks and L'Abate, Paradoxical Psychotherapy, 1982). However, this approach is not uncommon in shamanism, as the world view of many native people does not hold that causality is the only, or even the principal, operating order by which events occur.

Shamans are individuals who voluntarily alter their consciousness in order to help and to heal members of their community who have conferred the shamanic role upon them. The shaman's approach to the sickness of his or her client is primarily psychotherapeutic (Rogers, S. L., The Shaman, 1982, 132). Shamanic methods may seem peculiar and irrational to Westerners but there can be little doubt as to their effectiveness. The data are sparse but indicate that cure rates of shamans and psychiatrists are about the same (American Journal of Orthopsychiatry, 1972, 69-76). Many shamanistic therapies subject the client either to the persistent monotony of drumming and chanting, or to a complex harangue of sounds, orders, demands, and dramatizations. Either procedure enhances the client's suggestibility, opening him or her up to new possibilities and alternative solutions.

Shock and surprise are typical shamanic ploys. The use of electric eels in shamanic healing goes back some 4,000 years.

Zulu shamans are known to treat epilepsy by throwing the client into a pool infested with crocodiles or pythons. A folk healer in Guatemala may spray his naked client with a chilling alcoholic liquid. These procedures are often beneficial (Rogers, op. cit., 148); they appear to break a cycle of psychophysiological inaction that has demoralized the client and led to a physical deterioration. Other methods used to break the cycle include participation in supernatural rituals, issuing forceful demands to the client, and subjugation to emotional excitement through psychodrama, being thrown into cold water, or being given mind-altering drugs (ibid., 149).

A typical nonrational approach is the use of an apparent synchronistic procedure, supported by the world view that all events are related even if not contiguous in time and space. I observed the Zulu shamans (or "sangomas") utilize the ritual of "throwing bones." These were goat bones, decorated to symbolize an "old man," "old woman," "young man," "young woman," and sometimes other figures. The sangoma would instruct the client to concentrate on his or her problem while both parties blew air into a skin bag containing the bones. The air supposedly provided a conduit for benevolent spirits who would assist the process. As the sangoma shook the bag and threw the bones to the ground, the client observed the resulting pattern. Sometimes the bones would represent a member of the family or community. Sometimes they would represent various aspects of the client, or the client at different stages of life. Ultimately, a meaning would be assigned to the configuration by the sangoma, in consultation with the client. In this way, new possibilities are opened up for the client in a manner which appears to be nonrational. However, one's rational faculties had led to nothing but an impasse and so a nonrational procedure was justified. One sangoma, Credo Mutwa, told me, "Throwing the bones is very much like the I Ching you use in the United States." Indeed, the one attempt to apply the causal paradigm of parapsychological experimentation to a supposedly acausal paradigm was undertaken by Rubin and Honorton (PA Proc., 1971, 6-7). Significant results were obtained for I Ching hexagrams, but only for those subjects who were favorably disposed to psi phenomena.

On several occasions, I have seen the intertribal medicine man Rolling Thunder utilize possible synchronistic events in psychotherapy. In one instance, he asked me to hypnotize a young Indian brave who was severely alcoholic. The session was preceded by 90 minutes of chanting and drumming around a campfire attended by four dozen members of the local community. Following my hypnosis and guided imagery session, Rolling Thunder asked if the group had heard the hooting of an owl. He commented that the owl was a symbol of death, hence this was the young man's last chance to stop drinking. However, the owl hooted nine times; nine was a lucky number, thus the prognosis was favorable. Indeed, the last we heard from the Indian brave, he was still abstaining from alcoholic beverages. But is an owl really a symbol of death? Is nine actually a lucky number? Did the owl hoot nine rather than eight or ten times? The important fact was simply that the shaman had used a purported synchronistic event in a psychotherapeutic manner.

In 1970, I visited Maria Sabina, the legendary Mazatec Indian shaman. I discovered that her healing mission dated back to an apparition of death during her sister's illness. Ingesting the sacred mind-altering mushrooms of Mexico's Oaxaca region, Sabina received guidance as to how to cure her sister. And before the arrival of Gordon Wasson, who was to be the first outsider admitted to a mushroom ceremony, Sabina reported a dream forecasting his arrival.

Just as synchronicity does not make sense in a world of causality, paradoxical psychotherapy "does not make sense within traditional views of therapy" (Weeks and L'Abate, op. cit., 239). Nevertheless, there is a pragmatic factor that may intrigue parapsychologists. For example, would ESP and PK testing with persons who accept the acausal world view yield high scores on parapsychological tests? Could the acausal world view be induced hypnotically among extremely suggestible subjects before a psi test is administered? These are questions that must await the efforts of ingenious researchers. But in the meantime, the world's shamans --and their Western counterparts, the paradoxical psychotherapists --are keeping Jung's concept of synchronicity alive and well in therapy sessions around the world.

RESEARCH MODELS FOR HUMAN SCIENCES

Lawrence LeShan (New York, N.Y.)

One of the reasons our results in parapsychology are so sporadic and confusing is that much of our fundamental methodology has been wrong. We have followed as the basic way of organizing our data the model of physical sciences instead of the model of the human sciences.

The idea that different kinds of models are needed in the human and physical sciences is not a new one. It was widely known in early twentieth-century Europe (e.g., Windelbad, Renan, Cassirer).

It has, however, been largely forgotten in the great rush (since 1910) of the human sciences in general (parapsychology did not really arrive until the 1930s) to ape the methods of the dramatically successful nineteenth-century physics and machine design. Since 1910 the social sciences have had (in Sigmund Koch's words) only one question, "What to evaluate in the physical sciences?" Results and progress in this have been about what one would expect.

The history of this concept is briefly traced and suggestions given as to how to adapt our research to human instead of machine studies, since it is humans who exhibit psi.

LINEAR RESEARCH FOR ANY KIND OF THINKING

Gertrude R. Schmeidler (City College of the City University of New York)

If a purpose of parapsychological research is to understand psi, and our speakers are right in asserting that simple linear designs are inadequate, what methods are appropriate? Benor argues that complex linear methods are required, but Krippner that psi itself is nonrational, nonlinear. Must research methods then also be nonlinear? I will argue for a firm yes and an equally firm no. First the yes.

Research with any species is ineffective unless the experimenter sets a task which the subjects will perform. An animal experiment is futile if a pigeon is supposed to respond to a light but instead responds to an apparatus click. A human experiment is futile if the experimenter supposes the subject is responding to a target picture but instead the subject responds to an adjacent nontarget. If indeed psi subjects do nonlinear thinking whether or not the instructions ask for it, then the effective parapsychologist must set nonlinear tasks to study psi.

But having set nonlinear tasks, how are the research results to be evaluated? Surely not in a global way, without constraints of time, space, or logic. This would be nonsense from one point of view, though it might be Higher Truth from another. In either case it does not merit the suffix "ology" of parapsychology. Linear thinking is requisite for research design and evaluation, whether or not a global, nonlinear task was set.

Part 5: Invited Addresses

ON THE REPRESENTATION OF PSYCHIC RESEARCH TO THE COMMUNITY OF ESTABLISHED SCIENCE*

Robert G. Jahn[†]

Introduction

Although I am grateful to the Council of the PA and to the Program Committee of this convention for their invitation to speak to you on this topic, I must confess some insecurity in accepting it and in fulfilling it. As you probably know, I am not a member of your organization, and I am a relative newcomer to psychic research. Beyond that, I suspect that my perspective on this field, and my purpose in it, are somewhat different from those of most of this audience, all of which may combine to make my remarks at best somewhat obscure, and at worst downright unpopular. (In that regard, I feel a little like the poor chap at the rostrum in the cartoon on page 128.) A few of you have graciously tried to reassure me that it is just this difference in orientation that will make my thoughts helpful, and it is with that hope and intention that I proceed.

Background

At the risk of prolonging the nominative portion of the message, it may be best to summarize at the outset the heritage and perspective from which the following opinions emerge. My professional background has been mainly at the interface between engineering and applied physics, practiced almost entirely in the academic sector. Major research interests have comprised topics in fluid mechanics, ionized gas physics, plasmadynamics, and advanced aerospace propulsion systems, and in these contexts, as well as

---

*Chaired by Stanley Krippner (Saybrook Institute)

[†]This is a slightly revised version of the paper given by Dean Jahn on August 9, 1983. The original is available as Technical Note PEAR 83004 August 1983 from Princeton Engineering Anomalies Research, School of Engineering/Applied Science, Princeton University, Princeton, NJ 08544.

"To begin with, I would like to express my sincere thanks and deep appreciation for the opportunity to meet with you. While there are still profound differences between us, I think the very fact of my presence here today is a major breakthrough."

Drawing by W. Miller; © 1983 The New Yorker Magazine, Inc. Used by permission.

in administrative roles in engineering education, I have interacted with numerous major research laboratories in industry and government; with various agencies, panels, and advisory groups; and with many individuals bearing significant scholarly and administrative responsibilities at the cutting edge of several sectors of "established science." The opinions and recommendations which comprise the body of this paper are largely synthesized from the feedback I have received when attempting either to represent our own psychic research efforts or to offer broader assessments of the field as a whole to such groups or individuals. (The cartoon is also quite appropriate to my role in this regard, albeit with a somewhat different audience before me.)

My own involvement in psychic research traces back some six years, when I was introduced to the topic via supervision of an undergraduate independent project. Although I had no professional or personal background or interest in the field up to that time, and although my initial attitude was quite skeptical, by the time this student had completed her program I had become persuaded that this was a legitimate and potentially important topic for a high technologist to study, and one that I would enjoy pursuing.

Thus, in mid-1979, the Princeton Engineering Anomalies Research project was organized for the purpose of scholarly assessment of selected problems in the field which seemed viable for systematic study and relevant to forefront engineering science. In its current complexion, this program employs Ms. Brenda Dunne as Laboratory Manager, Dr. Roger Nelson as Professional Research Staff, myself as Project Director and part-time researcher, various technical and administrative assistants as needed, and a few undergraduate and graduate students in informal roles.

At present, our attention is confined to three main areas: 1) a selection of experiments in low-level psychokinesis which seem to have relevance for contemporary engineering practice; 2) a program in precognitive remote perception with principal attention to analytical methods for quantitative evaluation of the degree of information acquisition; and 3) development of a theoretical model to help explicate and correlate portions of the experimental data and guide the design of future experiments. In all of this work we endeavor to employ the most efficient and accurate methods of instrumentation, data collection, processing, and interpretation, and the most incisive analytical techniques available. All of our data, most of which have been reported to this association in various technical papers, have been obtained using anonymous, uncompensated operators, none of whom claim any special talents in this capacity.

Thus, while our entrance into this field has been from the domain of "Established Science," we now feel very much a part of the psychic research community. As Judy Collins sings, we've looked at the topic "from both sides now," and the following remarks will attempt to blend these two perspectives.

The Problem

I suspect that there are very few people in this room who have not attempted, at one time or another, to share their ideas or their enthusiasm about this topic with a professional colleague or friend only to be met with some degree of recalcitrance ranging from a bland tolerance, a shuffling of the feet, or an averted gaze on one extreme, to outright scorn or hostility on the other. I also suspect that few of you have not at one time or another attempted to get financial support from some agency or foundation, to present a paper in a prestigious journal or at a professional meeting, or just to solicit some moral endorsement from your own organization, and have had that rejected for a variety of transparent reasons. I confess to you that in my earlier days I, too, was guilty of at least some of the milder forms of such recalcitrance, reflecting my initial skepticism and discomfort about this topic when I first began to look into it. But more recently, we too have drunk from the other side of that cup and shared our portion of rejection by the community of established science. Without reciting that litany in full, you might enjoy one curious example: we have had commentary on our program from no fewer than six Nobel laureates, two of whom categorically rejected the topic, two of whom encouraged us to push on, and two of whom were evasively equivocal. So much for unanimity of high scientific opinion.

Now some may reasonably counsel that the wisest course is simply to ignore such rejection; to follow our own best path without any effort to represent our work to the established science communities. Although this option has some attraction, ultimately I think it must be rejected as a viable alternative. The psychic research community needs the endorsement, the support, and indeed the participation of many components of established science if it is ever to fulfill its mission. It needs its insights, its tools and techniques, and the resources, political clout, and public endorsement that would follow that acceptance. Equally important, researchers in this field need, and are entitled to, respect from their colleagues in more traditional fields. There is nothing unreasonable about any of these needs, and we should continue to strive toward their fulfillment.

What then is the source of the problem? Does it arise primarily from the community of established science, or from the community of psychic research? Is it the fault of poor communication between them, or are there other factors that contribute to it? I believe that the answer is yes to all of the above and that we can benefit from examining each in some detail.

The Culpability of Established Science

Before undertaking much criticism of the science communities, I want to emphasize that based on my 30 or 35 years of scholarly involvement with them, I have acquired an immense respect for their character and accomplishments. In my view, there are no human enterprises that have deported themselves with greater efficiency, effectiveness, or morality than high science and high technology. The record of accomplishment, the beneficial influence on human affairs, and the lineage of good and great people that have characterized these fields are beyond any argument.

All of this notwithstanding, in the matter before us, and indeed in the case of almost every dialogue established science has had over the years with research into "anomalous" phenomena, it has tended to forget, or at least to exercise rather selectively, some of its own most precious high principles. I was asked to speak a few weeks ago on the topic "What Are the Criteria for Research in Unconventional Science?" My thesis then, and here, is that they are exactly the same as the criteria for research in conventional science, but now you really have to mean them. The vaunted principles on which established science has always rested are absolutely basic to the integrity of any professional inquiry: openness of mind and freedom of inquiry; rigor of experimentation and humility in the face of experimental data; informed deduction and informed criticism; and dispassionate fairness of judgment in all matters. Yet, in too many cases, facing possible threats to established paradigms and, let's be frank, possible threats to personal belief systems, established science has tended to erect some defense mechanisms that in my opinion exceed legitimate conservatism. In particular, it has tended to pound rather slavishly on the issue of replicability, refusing reasonable generic or statistical treatment of that criterion, while neglecting other equally cardinal caveats. In some cases it has resorted to uninformed criticism and allowed personal biases to replace legitimate intuitive insights. Worst of all, on occasion it has invoked categorical rejection and guilt by association to justify dismissal of all efforts, however disciplined, to address this topic.

Sadly, I think we are not about to change much of this. The history of established science testifies to the enduring and endemic character of this reaction, which is by no means restricted to the lightweights of the business. If one makes a survey of the number of breakthroughs of scientific insight, from the time of Aristotle to the present, that were at the time rejected on the basis of the prevailing scientific criteria, one finds that as often as not it has been the patriarchs who were most unreceptive to the new visions. It has been just those giants to science who, earlier in their own careers, with soaring insight and great courage, violated established tenets to lead their fields to new plateaus of understanding, who later led the recalcitrance of the establishment against the comparably sacrilegious visions of their successors, while still endorsing in general terms the importance of visionary thought. The list is depressingly long: Galileo, early champion of scientific methodology and revolutionary concepts in terrestrial and celestial mechanics against vicious dogmatic opposition, later rejected Kepler's elliptical orbits as "occult fantasy." Thomas Young, whose brilliant interference experiments established the wave character of light, refused to accept Fresnel's theoretical formulations of the very same processes. Ernst Mach, father of modern classical mechanics, snorted at relativity and atomic theory. Ernest Rutherford, who showed the world the nuclear atom, dismissed any practical significance for nuclear energy. Lavoisier and Ostwald disputed atomic theories of chemistry. D'Alembert opposed probability theory. Edison discounted alternating current. Lindbergh despaired of Goddard's rocketry. And Albert Einstein retained an enduring uneasiness about quantum theory despite his many crucial indirect contributions to that topic.

Thus, if history holds, we cannot reasonably expect much less intransigence to so controversial and threatening a topic as psychic phenomena. We may only hope for rare objective hearings before rare open minds, and it is therefore critically important that our case be cleanly and crisply prepared for such opportunities.

The Culpability of Psychic Research

Clearly this will be the least popular segment of this paper, but if I am to speak honestly I must next contend that the community of psychic research has not, so far, optimized its case for such presentation. In particular, it has fallen short in several aspects of its philosophical and pragmatic housekeeping, namely, in the quality, clarity, and emphasis of its research, especially the selection of its topics; in the modes and styles of representation of that research; in its reaction to criticism and skepticism; in its professional, administrative, and political structure and behavior; in clarifying and ordering its overall collective and individual purposes. Some of these shortfalls, unlike the posture of established science, are amenable to change, and these will be the major focus of the balance of this paper.

Recommendations

Lacking the space for extended logical development of the following suggestions, I shall simply submit them in frankly empirical and unsubstantiated form, as some combination of my own rationalization, experience, and intuition, humbly offered as starting points for possible further consideration in other forums and formats.

(1) My first recommendation would be that this community concentrate on clean, conservative experiments that are firmly rooted in ground familiar to established science, which then move out cautiously and systematically to demonstrate and to explore anomalies with respect to that familiar ground. Putting it in the negative, I do not believe that the science community is likely to be impressed by any "gee whiz" class of experiments or by any "gee whiz" attitudes on the part of the experimenters. This runs against the conservative grain of traditional science, and those

approached in this tone will most likely run and hide, or at least turn off their hearing aids. What are much more likely to persuade are experiments that resemble as far as possible the usual scientific investigations, i.e., that are characterized by the following:

(a) <u>A well-defined purpose and protocol, clearly stated in advance.</u> Experiments which meander empirically over a broad conceptual terrain and then extract anomalies <u>ex post facto</u> from the composite data are less persuasive than those which directly address a stated hypothesis.

(b) <u>Thorough exploration of one parameter at a time before attempting to trace cross-correlations.</u> In the present dialogue with established science, the issue is still the reality of the phenomena, rather than their details. The more monotonic the data base, the less controvertible.

(c) <u>As elegant and sophisticated instrumentation and data processing as the budget and abilities of the investigators will permit.</u> Established science is very proud of its instrumentation and its data processing, and much of its progress can be attributed to the elegance of its equipment. I believe this will be true for psychic research as well. There is great hope in the capability of modern instrumentation and data processing to extract valid signals from the noise of these elusive phenomena and there is little excuse, within budgetary limitations, for not invoking the most sophisticated gear that can now be put into place.

(d) <u>Attention to baseline stability against artifact.</u> There is nothing that will make anomalous data more credible than showing that the same equipment and protocols, operating under identical conditions save for the intention of the operator, maintain complete stability against any artifactual disturbances.

(e) <u>The use of bi-directional protocols whenever possible.</u> Demonstration of anomalous effects in both directions from a well-established baseline on stated intention greatly reduces the suspicion of artifact in the active trials.

(f) <u>Very large data bases.</u> The larger the data base, the more systematically one can study very small effects, rather than having to rely on a few anecdotal large ones. From my experience, the established science community is much more comfortable with the former than with the latter.

(g) <u>Theoretical models laid beside the experimental effort.</u> However empirical these models may be, they are necessary to begin the traditional dialogue between theory and experiment on which so much of established science relies.

(h) <u>More attention to results generated by "common" operators, i.e., people who make no claims of special gifts or of any special records of accomplishment.</u> I find my colleagues in established science are much less nervous about data generated by our students, our staff, or people with an academic interest in the project, than they are about data provided by "gifted" individuals. Ideally, of course, we would like to construct an experiment that is so reliable or whose data accumulation is so effective that even the skeptical established scientist can obtain his or her own effects. Once that is achieved, his or her interest is much more likely.

In summary, this composite first recommendation is essentially that the choice of the problems for research may need to be influenced by more than the usual criteria: the interest of the investigator, the importance of the task, the tractability of the task remain relevant, of course, but in addition the credibility with which the experiment can be represented may now be an important ingredient.

(2) My second recommendation, and surely a controversial one, is that topics also be selected for their eventual practical implications as well as for the basic insight they may provide. Clearly there are two motives for performing research: the accumulation of fundamental knowledge and the pragmatic applications of that knowledge. Perhaps here I show the bias of my own heritage, but I have found the potential applications to be the more powerful persuasion to get people from the other side of the street to listen. Our work on random event generators becomes more consequential to them when it is related to the accuracy of microprocessor controls in an aircraft cockpit or the data processing fidelity of a very large integrated circuit array. Our analytical recipes for processing remote perception data become more relevant to them when they understand their implications for various aspects of human factors engineering and the man-machine interface. Much of established science has always been reactive to its ultimate applications. Certainly "big" science in this country derives quite directly from very specific applications: high energy physics owes its paramount position to the nuclear weapons applications; the space program has pushed a variety of basic sciences far beyond the dimensions they would have achieved in isolation; and the present-day computer applications are driving much more basic research in solid-state physics and device physics than would ever be supported in their own right. From the funding standpoint, any of the major mission-oriented agencies has great power to drive basic knowledge in fields relevant to its concerns. The field of psychic research need not be an exception.

(3) My third recommendation has to do with the manner in which we treat certain of the cast of characters who appear in our drama. I'll have a bit more to say about the deportment of the psychic researchers themselves later, but let's for a moment talk

about some of the ancillary characters. First, there is the community of critics, which I would like to divide somewhat arbitrarily into two groups: the responsible critics and the irresponsible critics. One can be an irresponsible critic by being uninformed, by being biased, by being self-serving, or by being malevolent. To be a responsible critic requires that one be fully informed of the research data and the conditions under which they were obtained, and that one have a truly open mind to all reasonable interpretations of those data. Such a responsible critic can be immensely useful, and should be cherished by us. With him or her we may engage in constructive dialogues which may uncover errors in our logic or alternative interpretations of our data that for our closeness to the problem we have missed. The irresponsible critic, on the other hand, is a parasite and should be treated as such. In my opinion we would do well to avoid dialogue with such critics, and not squander energy or resources to feed their parasitic appetites.

There is another character in our drama whom I will call the zealot: the person, who, with great hue and cry, carries forward the banner of the task, sometimes to our advantage, but more frequently to our embarrassment. I suppose one could say that there are also good and bad zealots, where the bad zealot again is uninformed, biased, self-serving, malevolent or just plain exaggerative or paranoid. Clearly, one should also disengage from the bad zealot. He or she hurts the image of the field and the images of those who interact with him or her. Unfortunately, I am afraid we must also be cautious of the good zealot, not because he or she is incompetent or insincere, but simply because the established science community has such a low threshold of tolerance for the topic. If the data or logic comes at it in too shrill a voice, or with too much lapel-grabbing, it will be put off.

Next, we should consider our friends from the media and any other public commentators. Here it is important to remember that the media are not in the business of research publication; they are properly, and in most cases responsibly, in the business of entertainment and they will naturally select their sources, their topics, and their styles of presentation to fulfill that function. Hence, if we are going to interact with them, that interaction should be limited to conservative statements of what we are trying to do, why we are trying to do it, and how we are trying to do it. It is a mistake to expect the media to represent research results, or the implications of those results, with great precision. And it certainly is a mistake to expect them to adjudicate our quarrels with the critics and the skeptics. In short, we should not try our case in the public press.

The final characters I would like to mention are the operators or subjects who generate our data. Whether they are "gifted" or "common" operators, I think it is important that they not be clothed in mystery or closeted apologetically as we represent our case. Even though there is good reason to keep their data achievements anonymous, these people are nonetheless very important partners in our enterprise, and their aesthetic, impressionistic, and intuitive insights gathered from their operational experience provide invaluable guidelines for the design and interpretation of our experiments. They should be accepted on that basis throughout and represented that way to our professional colleagues. It is the essence of this field that our right hemispheric functions be put in good dialogue with the left, and that point must be acknowledged openly; it is too fundamental to be obscured.

(4) My fourth recommendation has to do with the administrative and political effectiveness of our professional organizations. This field is currently represented by several societies and organizations of disparate size, style and heritage, not one of which, in my opinion, really has adequate resources, staff, membership, professional cognizance, or political clout fully to advance the credibility of, and provide leverage for, the psychic research community. I submit that now might be the time to begin consideration of subsuming all of these groups into one strong organism that could speak with greater authority and strength for psychic research as a whole in the academic, industrial, government, and financial arenas. There is ample precedent for such mergers in the established science communities. For example, the Institute of Aeronautical Sciences merged with the American Rocket Society some twenty years ago to form the American Institute of Aeronautics and Astronautics, a powerful professional organization which has represented aerospace research and development with great effectiveness. Most of you are familiar with the effectiveness of the American Medical Association, the American Physical Society, or many of the major Engineering societies, each of which provides strong logistical support of the professional field it represents. Such a merger of the psychic research organizations would clearly require immense good will and deep sacrifice in many quarters of our field, but it could make a great difference in the credibility of our efforts to the established science community.

(5) My fifth, final, and least tangible recommendation is that somehow we try to sharpen the individual and the collective image and attitude of psychic researchers within our own community. All of my earlier recommendations notwithstanding, it seems clear to me that the ultimate credibility of this field must trace primarily to the stature and spirit of its principal investigators. If they shuffle along, whimpering about their poor circumstances, lack of respect, lack of funding, snarling and snapping at one another's heels, the field will inevitably be regarded as immature and suspect. If, on the other hand, they exude an attitude of quiet confidence, with congeniality and mutual reinforcement for one another, that will go a long way toward establishing confidence from without.

This field is not simply another insular splinter of science. If it is to succeed, it must blend many disciplines and many points of view, both technical and impressionistic. It is imperative, therefore, that we communicate with genuine respect and humility, indeed with affection, with one another, across both the technical subdivisions and the alternative intuitive approaches to our common work. I do not believe it is excessive to suggest that the very nature of the phenomena we seek to demonstrate and study require a form of mutual trust and respect between human consciousness and the environment in which it is immersed. Can we expect to prevail in our work if we cannot even trust and respect our fellow researchers as we proceed?

Summary

Where does all this put us? My critical remarks notwithstanding, I would not want to leave you with any sense that I regard this field as a failed or failing operation. To the contrary, I believe heartily that it is the best game in town. In its potentialities for our own scholarly satisfaction, and for its ultimate effect upon human society, it is the most exciting forefront research topic on line today. To be sure, it is a formidable task, and it is at present a lonely business. There are many detractors and, let's be honest, we are somewhat of a rag-tag army. But rag-tag armies have prevailed in the past. Think of Valley Forge; of the Russian resistance of Napoleon and much later of the Nazi armies; or of that marvelous description in Shakespeare's Henry the Fifth (Act IV, Sc. 3) of the agonies of the young king on the eve of a critical battle with the French on the plains of Agincourt. Desperately outnumbered, his troops deserting him right and left, no supplies or support appearing from any direction, even his own nobles were in bitter complaint. His cousin, Westmoreland, bemoaned,

> "O that we now had here
> But one ten thousand of those men in England
> That do no work to-day!"

(That's a familiar sort of complaint; in our case it is more often phrased: "O that we had but one ten thousandth of the financial support....") In any case, Henry's reply could be a model for our own attitude today:

> "No faith, my coz, wish not a man from England:
> God's peace! I would not lose so great an honour,
> As one man more, methinks, would share from me,
> For the best hope I have. O do not wish one more!
> Rather proclaim it, Westmoreland, through my host,
> That he which hath no stomach to this fight,
> Let him depart; his passport shall be made,
> And crowns for convoy put into his purse:
> We would not die in that man's company
> That fears his fellowship to die with us.
> This day is call'd the feast of Crispian:
> He that outlives this day, and comes safe home,
> Will stand a tip-toe when this day is nam'd,
> And rouse him at the name of Crispian....
> And Crispin Crispian shall ne'er go by,

> From this day to the ending of the world,
> But we in it shall be remembered, --
> We few, we happy few, we band of brothers;
> For he to-day that sheds his blood with me
> Shall be my brother;...
> And gentlemen in England now a-bed
> Shall think themselves accurs'd they were not here,
> And hold their manhoods cheap while any speaks
> That fought with us upon Saint Crispin's day."

I truly believe that if we, like them, trust in the nobility of our task, we shall, like them, ultimately prevail, and human society shall be much the better for it. And those of the community of established science who stayed safely home in their beds, rather than risk the intangibilities and insecurities of this field, shall not share the satisfaction of those of us who fought together this day on this cosmic plane.

DREAM, METAPHOR, AND PSI*

Montague Ullman†

Over the years I have tried in every way I know to capture psi in a dream and learn something of the possible interrelationship of the two. The net result was a series of close encounters with this elusive prey, ending with an ongoing approach I am engaged in and will later describe. Each encounter was of value in its own way, but none brought me as close to my goal as I would have wished. Despite this I remain convinced more than ever that dreams have something of importance to tell us about psi. I can't prove this statement, but at the same time, I don't discount the possibility that something credible underlies my continuing enthusiasm. I want to share the distillate of my experience with you in the hope that some of my enthusiasm is contagious enough to keep dream-related psi research alive.

Encounter Number One

Like many others I have had, on occasion, dreams that struck me as paranormal. Experiences of this kind deepened my belief in the reality of psychic phenomena, but did little in the way of advancing its scientific standing.

---

*Chaired by Robert Van de Castle (University of Virginia)

†Delivered August 11, 1983

Encounter Number Two

In the forties and fifties a number of psychiatrists, including myself, tried to track the appearance of psi in the course of psychoanalytic therapy. Psi effects did crop up, most frequently around dreams, and were meaningful in terms of the specific psychological constellation in existence at the time between patient and therapist. They were both analogous to and different from spontaneously occurring anecdotal reports of psi. In the latter instance objective external circumstances block a compelling communication. In the clinical situation internalized necessities block communication. Those necessities arise out of the defensive operations we have unconsciously adopted to protect vulnerable areas of our personality. These defensive measures generally take one of two forms, compulsive distancing or compulsive closeness. In both instances entrapping security measures block the kind of emotional interaction that sustains genuine contact. Defensive operations arise out of earlier unmet needs and will tend to arise, along with the possibility of a psi component, whenever current counterparts of these earlier and more visceral areas are touched upon. The current reminders of these earlier progenitors are situations that are experienced either in dependency terms, as in the parent-child constellation, or as problematic peer relations, most commonly in the form of male-female tensions.

Except for the continuing heroic efforts of a few, the psychoanalytic epoch has all but come to an end, having had very little, if any, impact on the development and direction of parapsychological research.

Encounter Number Three

Much has been written about the work of the Maimonides Dream Laboratory so there remains little to add. The investigations provided experimental evidence that linked psi and dreams, but produced little else of any heuristic importance.

Encounter Number Four

This last, and probably final, encounter evolved out of the preceding ones and was further stimulated by a change that my own professional career took about ten years ago. At that time I had the opportunity to devote myself to the development of a small group approach to dreams. This was not psi-oriented, but was designed both as a teaching instrument to familiarize professionals with the unique healing potential of the dream and as a way of structuring a small group process so as to make dreams generally accessible in a safe and effective way. Working with dreams in a small group setting has enriched and, in some ways, modified the view I had of dreams as a practicing psychoanalyst. For one thing, it has brought me closer to seeing the dream in its self-healing potential. It is available as an instrument by means of which a greater state of wholeness can obtain. Emerging as the product of a "larger self," it confronts the dreamer with an aspect of the self that has not heretofore been acknowledged or utilized. The dream does not yield its secret easily. Work has to be done in the waking state before this healing potential can be realized. The language is strange for someone who, upon awakening, immediately drops the figurative mode of the dream and resumes the discursive mode of the waking state, along with the habitual strategies of self-defense such a mode offers (denial, rationalization, etc.).

I would like to share a number of speculations that have come out of this work that may have a bearing on the relationship of dreaming to psi. They also provided the stimulus for initiating the psi-oriented dream group that has been held at the ASPR for several years.

The Metaphorical Transform

The most interesting feature of our dream life, to my way of thinking, is the way that significant information is encoded in highly personal and often ingeniously crafted metaphors. Our dream life becomes manifest to us figuratively through the use of the visual metaphor. This involves the selection and restructuring of socially available imagery so that it can serve as a metaphorical carrier of meaning. The visual metaphor of the dream serves this purpose through the selection of an image or sequence of images that have an implicit similarity to events in the life of the dreamer. Our dreams may be thought of as metaphors in motion.

In general, metaphor links two separate domains and achieves its expressive power by the implied similarities involved in the linkage. The oneiric or dream metaphor does this by linking imagery generated in an imaginative domain in a sleeping subject to specific constellations of events that took place in the recent and past life of the dreamer. We usually assume that the memory of these events and the feelings associated with them are the starting point of the dream image. In fact we don't know where and when the metaphorical process begins. What we do know is that the oneiric metaphor is immediately available to the dreamer and with effortless skill the succeeding images unfold, adding depth and range to the original statement. There is no laborious search for the proper image, no hunting through the files to select the most appropriate one. It is simply there when it is needed, or so it seems. Although most of the imagery emerges out of the recent and remote past of the dreamer, the existence of the telepathic and precognitive dream suggests that any event anywhere in time and place can, on occasion, be recruited into metaphorical service for the dreamer.

The ready availability of appropriate visual metaphors for the dreamer suggests the possibility that, not only do we experience events in our waking life, but that we also screen them unconsciously for their metaphorical value. The ones we end up with in our dreams are those with either the greater metaphorical valence or the most recent, or some combination of both. Perhaps the hypnagogic image has a bearing on this question. At one moment we are closer to the waking state and are aware of a succession of thoughts going through our mind. At the next instant we are closer to the sleeping state and there is the immediate appearance of the image metaphorically expressing the last thoughts we had. It seems to have come into being at the moment as a transformation of the waking event that stimulated that particular train of thought. The image then forms part of the visual metaphor repertoire of the dreamer that is available for use any time it may be needed.

Stated another way, there are two simultaneous ways of processing the passing streams of sensations to which we are subjected. One is the familiar waking mode, the end point of which is the sense of order and understanding we come to about the world. The second way is to extract from the happenings around us their metaphorical potential and to express the result in the form of imagery which becomes available when we surrender the waking mode. The first mode is structured in and therefore limited by time and space. The second is structured more as a field extending in time and space with the greatest concentration of force being around the limited space-time frame of the individual, but with no sharp boundaries between that frame and the frame of others, nor between past, present, and future frames. What we refer to as ESP would then be the manifestation of this force field as it manages to transcend the individual and reach into someone else's space-time or the future space-time of the same individual. A limited but suggestive analogy might be that of the magnetic field generated by an electrical current, the latter being the palpable structure of reality as we assume it to be, and the former what we might call the metaphorical psi field, being continuously generated by real events. Paranormal cognition is rarely, if ever, precisely on target. There is enough similarity to the real event to classify it as paranormal, but it is generally embedded in the idiosyncratic productions of the particular percipient. What I am suggesting is that what we all recognize as the elusive aspect of the psi event may simply represent the emergence of a metaphorical statement in which the psi factor is one among many in the creation of the metaphor. Its frustrating elusive character then becomes an interesting allusive one. If the connection to metaphor is valid the task of the investigator becomes somewhat more difficult. He or she has to use a double-barreled approach that will identify both psi and the metaphor.

A point worthy of note is how remarkably articulate we are in the figurative domain. We have the necessary visual metaphors immediately on hand. They are incredibly apt, ingeniously constructed, and remarkably comprehensive. We are less articulate when we rely on words alone to describe our state of being (unless we revert to a metaphorical mode as the poet does). Perhaps we should modify our analogy and view the metaphorical psi field as primary and the linguistic discursive mode as secondary. Metaphors, which often originate in dreams, do provide the rich and fertile soil of language. Metaphor is the initial way of grasping on to something felt and something in need of gaining expression. When a metaphor is newly created it is alive in contrast to the dead ones which have already passed into everyday speech. The live metaphor offers a creative jolt to the literalness of language. It makes use of our versatility with language, but is never quite reducible to the literalness of language. There remains something ineffably elusive about the metaphor whether it be of the poet or of the dreamer. The same is true when we deal with a metaphor that encapsulates a psi event. We know it is true, but we know it is not true in a literal sense, and cannot be reduced to a state of literalness.

The newly generated metaphor has a creative, living thrust. There are two processes that came together in its birth. There would have to be a selection process to ascertain what it is that has to be expressed, and then a choice has to be made of the most suitable vehicle. Both these processes have potential theoretical linkages to the operation of psi. A psi effect can be thought of as a kind of information scanning process and one that often uses imagery as the vehicle. There are shared end-points in each instance; namely, a heightened feeling response and a sense of an opening to larger vistas--a sense of moving into unexplained territory and going beyond the self. A powerful and original metaphor, when it first arrives on the scene, does seem to connect the creator and all those affected by it to a universe larger than the self. It propels us deeper into that universe in an ineffable and feeling way rather than in a rational and logical way. If science carried us into the future in discrete steps, the metaphor does it by setting off an unending set of ripples that may diminish in amplitude, but never quite fade out. Shakespeare offered us a supply that will last for an eternity.

Dreaming is the metaphor-creating state par excellence. It is also a state quite conducive to the spontaneous generation of psi. We have made very little of the possible relationship between the two. Is our capacity to zero in on just the right image to serve our metaphorical needs cut from the same cloth as our ability to paranormally apprehend an event that would otherwise be beyond our reach? I have suggested that to some extent a psi event is a psi event because of its metaphorical potential. Perhaps when a reality constellation is as good a metaphor for both subject and agent, a psi event occurs. Or, perhaps the psi connections are ever-present, but it takes a metaphorical spark to make them explicit.

In summary, what I am saying about the connection of the oneiric image and psi is that it has to be viewed as part of a more general metaphorical way of processing ongoing events. Our feelings are the starting point for this flow of imagery. It is our feelings which mobilize, on the basis of emotional rather than logical contiguity, the information we need either from our past or, paranormally, from external sources in the construction of the metaphorical image. In the course of dreaming those metaphorical images emerge which express, reflect, and shed light on our current predicament. The creation and deployment of the visual metaphor is a remarkably powerful way of revealing, at a feeling level, where we are in relation to these issues and the impact of recent events in our lives upon them. In our dreams we give visibility to the emotional components of the interpersonal fields of greatest importance to us. The potential for psi events is intrinsic to this field but hardly ever actualized, perhaps because of our underdeveloped sense of the reality of psi.

Species-Connectedness

In a tantalizing way dreams seem to originate in a source outside the self we are ordinarily familiar with while awake. From an early age our waking self organizes experience in space and time. The view taken by the self asleep and dreaming is quite different. For one thing it links events together not in space, time, and logical causality, but on the basis of emotional contiguity. It is as if our waking experiences leave emotional traces which are always available to our dreaming self but which can be manipulated in one way or another by our waking self (forgotten, repressed, denied, rationalized, etc.). This extended view of ourself in sleep has been the starting point of conjecture about the unconscious dimension of our existence. Labeling that source the Unconscious (Freud) or adding the notion of the Collective Unconscious (Jung) is to foreclose too quickly on an aspect of our existence that contains mysteries yet to be solved.

I was taught that dreams were very personal narcissistic indulgences. I now view them quite differently. I believe that the source that informs dreaming consciousness includes but goes beyond issues of personal motivation. I have come to feel that our dreams are fundamentally concerned with the assessment of damage to, repair of, and enhancement of our connections to others. The notion of species-connectedness seems to me to be the underlying motif of our dream life. There is a part of our being that is fundamentally concerned with the survival of the species and only incidentally with the problems of the individual. The sense of our own discreteness dominates the scene while awake and we view the world and ourselves from that position. This perspective changes radically when we are asleep and dreaming. We rearrange our recent waking experience into a different order of priorities. Our dreaming self is reactive to anything in our waking experience that tampers with the state of our connectedness to others, beginning with significant persons in our life, but extending outward to all others. We reorder these experiential residues around the issue of connectedness. In our dreams we get down to basics and, from a more global perspective, see ourselves in the closely linked mosaic that makes up the human species.

Our dreaming self seems to hold onto a notion that escapes

us in our waking moments--namely, that we are all members of a single species. Our historical fate has fragmented that unity, often in self-defeating ways, along every line of cleavage conceivable by our ingenuity and foibles, e.g., politically, religiously, economically, ethnically, etc. This fragmenting process continues macroscopically in the way we divide the nations of the world into forces of good and evil. It goes on microscopically in the way we hurt, corrode, or destroy our sense of connection with each other, by the countless ways in which we pursue individualistic goals at the expense of others. Whereas we may be perfectly capable of living a long life as an individual thriving on dishonesty (the reverse of the adage of "the good die young"), the likelihood is that we won't long survive as a species if unchecked dishonesty undermines our humanism. And, of course, there is ample evidence currently of the danger of that possibility. The part of our being that shapes our dreams seems very much concerned with this issue. Our dreams reflect back to us with ruthless honesty how our connections to significant others fared on the previous day. We seem to have a built-in way of monitoring the extent to which inner and outer events interfere with (or enhance) our own humanity. The dream can be looked upon as a kind of steering mechanism which, if attended to, can help us stay on a survival course. Considering the calculated neglect accorded dreams on our march toward civilization it may already be too late. At any rate, it is this more global concern, one that transcends the existence of the individual as a discrete entity, that suggestively parallels or may be more intrinsically related to the way that manifestations of psi seem to have a bearing on issues of connectedness.

The evidence for the dream's proclivity for species-connectedness is only suggestive at this point. There is much in Jung's emphasis on the connection of myth to dreams, his notion of archetypes and the collective unconscious that may have a bearing on this.

Nonreflective Consciousness

There is yet another aspect to the dreaming experience that bears mention. I refer to the nonreflective way in which we experience ourselves while dreaming. This is a point emphasized by Sartre (as set forth in Tolaas, in press) in his discussion of images and the same point is made by Rechtschaffen (1979), although he refers to it as the single-mindedness of the dream. While dreaming we do not reflect on what is happening to us. We accept everything unquestioningly, unreflectively, as a living experience. It is there for us in its actuality, not as a dream or a fantasy or a story we are telling ourselves. We have translated the complexities of our life into a series of seemingly real perceptual experiences. Perhaps this is the closest we come to the kind of direct experience of the world that lower animals have. Ordinarily we know the world through the categories of language. In experiencing the world only perceptually we may inadvertently experience more

of it than we usually do. Perhaps what we consider a limitation in
lower animals, their failure to reach our levels of abstraction, is
for us, under these circumstances, something of an enhancement.
And, since this experience is beyond our ordinary comprehension,
metaphor is the only vehicle we have for capturing something of its
essence. How might a psi effect be connected with it? If dreaming brings us into a different relationship to an inner reality, it
might also bring us into a different relationship to an outer reality.
We are filtering in what our categorical understanding awake filters
out. It is now reaching us indirectly through the metaphorical construct. To some extent this rippling outward transcendence of space
and time, this sense of being brought closer to a more mysterious
matrix, is an aspect of all creative metaphor. It is also, perhaps,
the essence of the aesthetic experience. Psi research may ultimately bring us closer to a point of convergence of the scientific
and aesthetic so that the satisfaction of greater knowledge will always be tempered by the awareness of greater mystery.

The ASPR Dream Group Project

The group work I was doing with dreams soon led to the
idea of adapting the process I was using in a way that would be
oriented to the occurrence of psi effects and still include an experiential arrangement to explore the contextual references of the
images when correspondences were noted. The project was initi-
ated with a small group of coexplorers a little over five years ago
at the ASPR. I hesitate to dignify what we are doing with the name
"experiment." It is more in the way of an experience that we are
having together out of which psi seems to crop up in its characteristically tantalizing and elusive way. There have been a number of
changes in the make-up of the group and in the approach in the
course of this time. An earlier report covers the work we did
through 1979 (Ullman, 1980). We will deal here with developments
since then. The group has become smaller in size. It now numbers four.*

Procedure

We have weekly meetings that last approximately one and a
half hours. Each member keeps a written record of his or her
dreams, which are then typed, copied, and distributed at each meeting. Time is set aside to review and compare the dreams of others
to his or her own dreams. From this point on, the process evolves
quite informally. A light and spontaneous atmosphere prevails in
our pursuit of a suggestive correspondence. We seek out any correspondences between the dreams of others and events in our own
lives and any correspondences between our dreams and paranormally

---

*The members of the current group are Barbara Shelp, Patrice
Keane, Nancy Sondow, and myself.

apprehended events in our own lives. Where manifest correspondences occur or simply intuitive guesses hint at a possible psi effect an experiential process is invoked to uncover further possible correspondences and to explore the dynamics of the particular relationships in which these effects are happening. In brief, this consists of an exploration of the emotional context that led to the dream and the shared free play of the collective imagination of the group to elaborate on the metaphorical possibilities of the imagery in an effort to help the dreamer arrive at the one that fits. As is characteristic of dream work, significant emotional patterns are often exposed and shared. The experiential dream process as here structured facilitates access to material of this kind in a safe and nonintrusive way. Many of the correspondences noted, though exposable to view in a small group setting, were too private for a larger public exposure.

The emotional set of the group and the challenging novelty of each dream heightens the expectancy level with regard to the possibility of psi occurring and prevents the process from ever lapsing into a stereotyped or dull operation. The procedure lacks any formal experimental design features. Our judgments of correspondences remain purely subjective. No blind or objective judging procedure has been introduced.

We are dispensing with the assumption that we can designate an agent, subject, and target in advance and are starting with what we know about psi, namely, the significance of an emotional field and the predilection for the dreaming state. We add to this the stimulation of the group setting and the challenge (and fun) of looking for psi effects not only in the manifest dream but also in ferreting them out from behind their metaphorical coloring.

We are replacing the controlled environment of the laboratory with an ongoing social context of people who are interested in and open to psi effects. As investigators we are simply orienting ourselves to an observational process geared to recognizing psi events wherever and whenever they turn up in the lives of the group members. There is no specification in advance of the kind of psi effect we are looking for. Our interest is not limited to effects that occur within the group, but extends to the outside context that involves the lives of each individual member. We are not setting aside specified laboratory time for the occurrence of psi but, to the best of our ability, we are prepared to look at events that occur during the nocturnal as well as the diurnal phases of our existence, and to do this seven days a week. In effect, we are allowing ourselves to be guided by the phenomena rather than setting more restrictive conditions for their appearance.

There are, of course, serious pitfalls in so personal an approach as well as in the methodology itself. A good deal of enthusiastic subjectivity undoubtedly colors our judgment. We amass more data than we can handle in the time available to us and we are often unable to deal adequately with the complexity of the data

that we are able to look at. Antecedent common chance factors that
may facilitate correspondences are not systematically ruled out. We
end up with consensual, subjective evaluations that lack quantitative
assessment as well as predictability. Our hope is that, what we
lose in control and quantitative certainty, will be offset by a better
understanding of the developmental aspects of psi sensitivity.

An unexpected development was the emergence of psi ability
in one person (B.S.). It became more and more apparent that most
of the effects we observed involved B.S. either in relation to events
in her life outside the group or in relation to what was occurring
between her and other members of the group. Prior to her experiences in the group, B.S., although interested in psychical research,
had not had any personal psi experiences. We began more and
more to focus on her dreams, singling them out for experiential exploration of how they touched her life paranormally or were linked
paranormally to the lives of the other participants. We were thus
in the privileged position of participating in and observing the evolution of this type of sensitivity in one of the members of the research team. To a lesser extent I think it occurred in each of us.

What had been noted earlier, namely, the way psi effects
seemed to ride along on specific dyadic motivational channels, continued to be observed in this recent period. The motivational patterning that seemed to channel psi between M.U. and B.S., for example, took various forms at different times. They included:
Father-Daughter, Doctor-Nurse (B.S. is a psychiatric nurse),
Nurse-Patient, Man-Woman.

Examples

In the first two examples that follow I wish to illustrate
some of the ways that I became more aware of psi occurring in
my dreams and related events in my life.

Dream: Saturday, August 29, 1981. I am close to someone who is a president. He and I are on very familiar
terms. Something about Arthur Twitchell, Tuesday night
and his going to the Psychiatric Institute at the Columbia
Medical Center. Some man told his wife that they had to
leave for the Island Tuesday night.

Life event: Friday, August 28, 1981. Arthur Twitchell,
then president of the ASPR, was hospitalized at the Columbia Presbyterian Medical Center early Friday morning, Aug.
28, 1981. He had been ill for several days before that. On
Saturday, Aug. 29, I learned that he had been taken to the

---

*The date given for the dream is the morning the dreamer awakens
with the dream, which may have occurred at any time during the
night.

hospital in acute congestive heart failure. The last contact I had with him was several weeks earlier at the Parapsychological Association convention in Syracuse. To my knowledge this is the first and only dream that I ever had of him. There was no opportunity to explore with Arthur the possible metaphorical overtones to the manifest correspondence. What I could and did do was to correlate what little I knew about his personal life with what I felt might be a related context from my own life. The word president is mentioned in the dream and, of course, earlier that year, Arthur had succeeded me as president of the ASPR. I thought, however, that the relevant context might have gone back to much earlier time. I was a psychiatric resident at the New York State Psychiatric Institute in 1942. The Institute is one component of the Columbia Presbyterian Medical Center. I was called into the military in November of 1942 and shortly thereafter served as a medical officer in a POW camp for German prisoners in Georgia for a brief period. During the war Arthur served in the Air Force. He was shot down over Germany and was a POW for several years. Although in no way objectively comparable to the time Arthur spent as a POW the year of my residency at the Psychiatric Institute was the most stressful one of my life.

The following dream of mine may have been no more than a coincidence. On the other hand, it may possibly have been precognitive.

Dream: Friday, March 12, 1982. My wife and others had left our house and had driven away. Sometime later I noticed they were all back and gathered in the driveway. Her cousin P.R. was also there as was a policeman who had driven up in a police car. They had been in some sort of accident.

Life Event: Friday, March 12, 1982. Friday night, about 11:00 p.m., while driving home from a talk in Ossining, I stopped at a stop sign before making a turn onto a major highway. I was struck suddenly from behind by a large car and catapulted onto the highway. Somewhat dazed, I got out of the car to investigate. There was minor damage to the rear bumper and I suffered a slight whiplash injury. The real danger was my exposure to oncoming cars which, fortunately, were going slow enough to stop in time before hitting me. It was the first accident I had had with a car in over twenty years. My wife had had an accident with her car last December. Her cousin P.R. very much reminded me of the woman who was the hostess for the evening. In the accident my wife had a police car run into her as she was making a turn.

Anyone who drives into New York will be apt to have dreams about cars. When they do crop up in my dreams they generally involve parking problems. This was the first dream depicting an accident. Cars are, of course, a source of rich metaphorical potential and in this age of dependency on cars, they often symbolize an aspect of the self. Certainly an aspect of my own narcissism may have been involved. I was driving a new car and this was the first marring of its appearance. My dream also confronts me with a bit of residual chauvinism. It made me aware how convinced I was that if anything happened to the car it would occur while my wife was driving.

Another vulnerable area of mine tapped by the car as metaphor is that of relationship to authority. The car is my own object, but it is an object which at every moment that it is in use brings me into a potential tension with the law. There are red lights and stop signs that tell you to stop; signs that tell you to yield; there is registration, licensing, and insurance; there is the constant possibility of accident; and finally, there is always the temptation to go a little above the speed limit. A number of other problems with cars play into aggressive undercurrents--problems with other drivers on the road, the difficulty in finding a parking space in New York, fear of being towed away as one inevitably has to take risks in parking, and finally, the real danger of having the car stolen or broken into.

None of the presumptively psi exchanges between Barbara Shelp and myself were directly on target. They were all tantalizingly suggestive, feeling truer to the participants than they are apt to strike an outside observer. I think this is so because, however slight the surface correspondences may seem, they set off resonating effects at deeper levels in the involved parties. Although that is hard to evaluate with any degree of objectivity, 'it is a definite felt reaction that has to be taken into account in judging whether the seeming coincidence is or is not meaningful. The following is an example:

> My dream: Thursday, January 7, 1982. Something about Groucho Marx and surprised to see him looking so young.
>
> Life events. The Marx Brothers have always been favorites of mine, particularly Groucho. I could think of no reason why he turned up in my dream that night. Here are Barbara's comments on Thursday, January 7, when we met to review our dreams.
>
>> On the evening of January 6th [the night I had the dream--M.U.] I was talking to my neighbor and telling him of a birthday party I had had four years ago. I had decided to give myself a birthday party and to invite whomever I wanted. At the time I invited them I also told each guest what I wanted each one to bring, something I felt was appropriate for that person to do or bring. I asked one young friend to write a poem, which he did. He also came in with a package. It was a framed picture of

Groucho Marx which was taken when he was much younger. This gift referred to a special incident that had occurred between us. There is a hole in the wall beside the door in my house which had originally housed an intercom. He had earlier noticed that unseemly sight and had brought the picture so that I could hang it over the wall to cover the hole. Last night I was telling my neighbor about it and having a good laugh over it. This morning (January 8th) I had noticed a thick layer of dust on the frame of Groucho's picture. I took it down. With the picture off I could hear what was said in my neighbor's living room.

This incident, including Groucho as a metaphor, was replete with possibilities for me, possibilities that I will just hint at, since they are too private to be explicit about. In his films Groucho usually had a way with women, or thought he did. The relationship of the location of the picture to an old and unused communication channel is also of interest. The link to a communication device has often been associated with the appearance of psi in a dream.

Dream of Barbara Shelp

The following account was prepared by Barbara Shelp. It is possibly precognitive and illustrates the value of working with a longitudinal recording of dreams:

On February 27, 1982, my daughter Eileen received a telephone call from a friend named Phil in Florida, whom I do not know, asking her to visit during her vacation. On March 1, 1982, I was looking through the record of my past dreams in preparation for a paper. My daughter, looking over my shoulder, took note of the following dream from several months before:

9/3/81 "Regisistra" Something about a training program for teaching; class; with a large bet riding on its success ... name Smetana

My daughter pointed out that the name Regisistra is the last name of her friend Phil and that she had discussed with him the fact that she would have to arrange her visit so that it would not conflict with a summer course she is registering for.

Notable about the above example is the space of time over which the series of dreams is spread, and that I had apparently picked up on a rather unusual name. I also had the correct pronunciation. None of the latter part of this would have been recognized if I had not gone back over my dreams and if my daughter had not happened to look over my shoulder.

Discussion

The approach I have described has something in common with the psychoanalytical way of observing psi, but it is also different. The psychoanalytic model enables us to witness the sporadic occurrence of psi and, at the same time, provides us with an in-depth view of the dynamics involved in the evolution of a special kind of human relationship. We are dealing with psi arising spontaneously in an emotional field but of a specially structured sort. It is a therapeutic rather than an investigative effort. Neither the patient nor the therapist come together for the purpose of generating psi effects. In contrast to that model in our group project the investigative interest remains dominant and all involved are both subject and agent, participant and researcher. We are exploring the psi potential of each other. In both instances the appearance of psi is unpredictable and spontaneous, occurring in an interpersonal field as yet too complex to specify with accuracy at any given moment and not controllable by the waking ego.

The laboratory model characteristically involves experimenter and subjects and introduces controls designed to identify variables and test hypotheses. The arena in which the psi effect is sought is specified in advance. The laboratory investigator is involved in a trade-off. He or she is seeking greater control over the conditions that make for the appearance of psi at the expense of the more cumbersome and uncontrollable factors involved in the pursuit of spontaneous cases.

Let me close with a number of questions addressed to a future generation of experimentalists:

1. Why limit the appearance of psi to a predetermined experimental moment, generally arbitrarily chosen by the experimenter? Why not include the entire diurnal cycle as the possible temporal field for the appearance of psi?

2. Why not explore further the range and depth of the scanning that goes into the production of dream imagery?

3. Why not exploit the feeling of communality and connectedness that is the inevitable outcome of dream work in a group?

4. Why not take advantage of the opportunity for varied dyadic arrangements that are possible in a mixed group?

5. Why not add a longitudinal temporal dimension to the tracking of psi, such as is possible in an ongoing long-range dream group?

6. Why not explore how psi sensitivity can develop in an individual over time, given the support, encouragement, and enthusiasm generated in a group situation?

Summary

The group approach I have described has the advantage of working with spontaneously generated psi effects and then using the dynamics of the dream to gain access into the nature of the emotional currents favorable to or presaging the appearance of a psi event. It not only adds a longitudinal dimension to a psi research project but also, by using the full diurnal cycle, casts a wider net.

It embodies the elements of spontaneity and play and provides for an opportunity to note and explore the appearance of psi in naturally occurring emotional contexts that are ongoing, changing, and developing. Since the psi effect is not specified in advance the technique is open to any manifestation of the information gathering aspects of psi and does so in terms of unconscious as well as conscious manifestations. As both investigators and subjects we are the source and explorers of what we produce.

I have also shared a number of theoretical speculations that have arisen in connection with group dream work. These have focused on the role of metaphor, the concern of the dream with the survival of the species, and the yet to be explored aspects of unreflective consciousness.

References

Rechtschaffen, A. The single-mindedness and isolation of dreams. Sleep, 1979, 1, 97-109.

Tolaas, J. Transformatory framework: Pictorial to verbal. In B. Wolman and M. Ullman (Eds.), Handbook of Altered States of Consciousness. New York: Van Nostrand Reinhold, in press.

Ullman, M. Psi communication through dream sharing. In B. Shapin and L. Coly (Eds.), Communication and Parapsychology. New York: Parapsychology Foundation, 1980.

Part 6:   Presidential Address

A SYSTEMS APPROACH TO PSI RESEARCH BASED ON JUNGIAN TYPOLOGY*

Stanley Krippner[†]

    The psychological system of Carl Jung is one of the few which not only accords a place to both cognition and affect, but attempts to integrate them--or at least define the barriers to integration. Ian Mitroff and R.H. Kilman (1978) in their provocative book Methodological Approaches to Social Science contend that Jungian personality types provide an appropriate framework for a comprehensive typology of social scientists based on two dimensions of Jung's system. The first dimension is a person's preference for the kinds of information sought from the world. The second dimension is an individual's choice of decision-making process characteristically brought to bear upon the preferred type of input data, whether those data are from the world external to the individual (as would be typical of extraverts) or from the internal world (as would be true of introverts). This address will attempt to relate this system to psi research.

A Jungian Typology

    According to Jung (1921/1971), people can assimilate data from their inner or outer world either by sensation or intuition, but not by both processes at the same time. As Jung describes them, sensation and intuition are antithetical psychological processes; therefore, individuals tend to develop a noticeable preference for one mode of information input over the other.

    The sensation category consists of individuals who typically perceive information by means of the senses. They are most comfortable when attending to the details of any situation, and prefer basic facts with regard to problems. Sensation types are realists who take a hard, objective stand. They are practical and are

---

*Chaired by John Beloff (University of Edinburgh)

[†]Delivered August 10, 1983

oriented to what is feasible in the immediate present, not with vague hopes for the future.

In contrast, intuitive individuals take in data by means of their imagination. Intuition involves an awareness of the whole configuration, whether it pertains to inner or outer phenomena. Unlike sensing types--who prefer to divide a situation into its parts, gather hard information, and comprehend details--intuitive types prefer to perceive the whole or "gestalt." They prefer to focus on the hypothetical possibilities in any situation rather than on the actual facts. These people take a broad, long-range view of an issue, concentrating on "what might be" rather than "what is." As a result, they often create novel situations which allow them to innovate. The sensation type cannot see the woods for the trees; the intuitive cannot see the trees for the woods (Maduro & Wheelwright, 1977).

Sensation and intuition are nonrational functions, not because they are contrary to reason but because they are outside the province of reason and therefore not bound by it. Thinking and feeling, however, are two functions used in an assessing or judging capacity; they are termed rational functions and are antithetical to one another.

Jung describes the thinking individual as one whose every important action proceeds from intellectually considered motives. Thinking is the process of reaching a decision based on impersonal, formal, or theoretical modes of reasoning. It seeks to explain inner or outer phenomena in technical, logical, or theoretical terms independent of human purposes, needs, and concerns. Thinking classifies, clarifies, and categorizes. It is always concerned with content; it is not concerned with moral, ethical, or aesthetic values.

Feeling, in contrast, is the process of reaching a decision based on value judgments that may be unique to the particular individual. It imparts to the content a definite value, asking whether it is good or bad, pleasing or unpleasing, moral or immoral, likable or unlikable to a particular individual. The feeling function judges by an evaluation of the time, the place, and the person. Given two or more inner or outer phenomena, feeling seeks to find what is unique about each of them.

Whether one takes in data by sensation or intuition, one may come to some conclusions about the data by thinking or feeling. Thus, there would be four basic personality types: sensing-thinking, sensing-feeling, intuition-feeling, and intuition-thinking. This typology does not imply that a person is fixed for life in a single type. Jung's concept of personality is dynamic, not static. An individual may behave as one type in one kind of situation or phase of life and as a different type in another. In addition, a person's opposite type may be in an unconscious, formulative state of development which may achieve salience later in life.

Social Scientists

Mitroff and Kilman (1978, 30-31) have devised descriptive names for each of the four Jungian types as they apply to social scientists. The sensing-thinking type is the Analytical Scientist; the intuition-thinking type is the Conceptual Theorist. The Conceptual Humanist is the intuition-feeling type and the Particular Humanist is the sensing-feeling type.

The Analytical Scientist's outlook is representative of a world view which embodies a belief in the value-free nature of science. The Analytical Scientist's key characteristics are precision, accuracy, reliability, exactness, skepticism, and impersonality. The preferred mode of inquiry is controlled investigation as embodied in the classical concept of the experiment. The preferred logic is strict Aristotelian logic--nondialectical and indeterminate.

J. B. Rhine (e.g., 1938) serves as an example of the Analytical Scientist. Moving to Durham, North Carolina, in 1927, he soon became director of the newly formed parapsychology laboratory at Duke University. Rhine's work at the laboratory represented the substantiation of a quantitative, statistical approach in the search for qualitative evidence of a paranormal character (Beloff, 1977, 17). It was hoped that this move would not only enhance the general credibility of the evidence, but would also demonstrate that psychic ability was distributed normally and was not just the gift of rare sensitives. The idea of using probability theory was by no means a novel one, but Rhine (1934/1964) replaced the playing card pack with the specially designed ESP cards. In 1937 the Journal of Parapsychology was launched, its contents mirroring Rhine's (1977) dictum that the success attained by parapsychologists resulted from adhering to problems that are logically possible to solve with the methods available. He stated, "only through this discipline can we make parapsychology a firm science" (p. 36).

Whereas the Analytical Scientist works best within a single, well-defined, self-consistent explanation, the Conceptual Theorist prefers to construct bridges between paradigms, believing that nature must be treated holistically and conceptually. The Conceptual Theorist values the creation of novel conceptual possibilities, schemata, and hypotheses which allow us to revise, rethink, and challenge entrenched assumptions. Like the Analytical Scientist, the Conceptual Theorist is typically unbiased and impersonal. But in addition, he or she is speculative, holistic, and imaginative, and is frequently a generalist. The ultimate aim of science is seen as a construction of the broadest possible conceptual schemes. The preferred mode of inquiry is the treatment of innovative concepts from multiple perspectives, whereas the preferred logic is dialectical and indeterminate.

Evan Harris Walker (e.g., 1975) has contributed to parapsychology as a Conceptual Theorist. Former faculty member at the University of Miami's Institute of Atmospheric and Space Physics,

Walker has been a research physicist at the Ballistic Research Laboratories of the U.S. Army Aberdeen Research and Development Center since 1967. His theory arises from the Copenhagen interpretation of quantum mechanics and the physical characteristics required of any hidden variable reinterpretation of that theory (Walker, 1974). For Walker, interactions between the consciousness of the observer and the physical world do not occur in the form of force or energy, but through what might be called an "information field" processed by what he has called the "will" (Villoldo and Krippner, 1981). This theory has already stimulated several research studies and has been called "the most testable to come out of modern physics" (Rao, 1978, 257).

Conceptual Humanism is one of two methodologies based on feeling. Scientific knowledge is seen as a value-constituted activity; its ultimate aim is to promote human development on the widest possible scale. The Conceptual Humanist can be described as interested rather than disinterested, personal instead of impersonal, and free to admit and know his or her biases. Dialectical behavioral logic is the preferred mode of logic, whereas the preferred mode of inquiry is conceptual. Maximum cooperation between the investigator and subject would be urged so that both might better know themselves and one another.

Lawrence LeShan (e.g., 1974a) would be an example of a Conceptual Humanist. LeShan was chief of the Department of Psychology at New York's Trafalgar Hospital and Institute for Applied Biology before his appointment as chief investigator on a research project investigating the psychosomatic aspects of neoplastic disease for the Ayer Foundation. In 1964, the same foundation sponsored a research project on psi phenomena, headed by LeShan, who directed his investigations toward the study of paranormal healing (1974b) and "alternate realities" (1976). In constructing a theory of psi phenomena, LeShan drew from his work with such "psychic sensitives" as Eileen Garrett, attaining the maximum cooperation with one's subjects typical of Conceptual Humanists. These "sensitives," he feels, are able to enter "clairvoyant reality," a world view also described by mystics and physicists, often in language that is remarkably similar (LeShan, 1969).

LeShan (1974a) has taken the position that the exploration of psi is incomplete without the parallel exploration of mystical understanding. He also insists that parapsychological data do not contradict the basic "laws" of science, but do necessitate a redefining of reality (LeShan and Margenau, 1982, p. 210). A number of hypotheses have been generated by LeShan, e.g., psi occurrences are more frequent in egalitarian than in authoritarian groups; psi occurrences are more frequent between people who like each other than between people who do not (ibid., p. 219). These hypotheses and LeShan's other inquiries reflect the emphasis on human development characteristic of Conceptual Humanists.

Of the four world views adhered to by the investigators

described, that held by the Particular Humanist represents the greatest challenge to contemporary ideas regarding science. Particular Humanists hold that the ultimate aim of science should be to help a specific person know himself or herself uniquely. Science does not necessarily occupy a privileged position; it may be subordinate to literature, art, music, and mysticism, often seen as older and wiser ways of knowing. The Particular Humanist can be described as biased, poetic, and committed to the postulates of an action-oriented science. The logic of the unique and singular is stressed and the case study is the preferred mode of inquiry.

In some ways, Louisa (pronounced Lou-EYE-sah) E. Rhine (e.g., 1981) represents the position of a Particular Humanist. Her collection of spontaneous cases exceeded 15,000 reports; in one analysis, 64% involved imagery compared with 29% which were intuitive in nature, and 7% which were undetermined (Rhine, 1953). Other analyses suggested that imagery was present in more of the purported precognition cases than in clairvoyant and/or telepathy reports; also, the information was presented in a relatively complete form in 78% of the imagery cases compared with 55% of the intuitive cases (1962).

Rhine (1977) noted that case studies "can give tentative hints on which the slower methods of experimentation can capitalize" (p. 78). An example was Rhine's (1962) finding that 65% of her cases occurred while people were dreaming; this observation was one factor which led to the experimental investigations of dreams and related states of consciousness. Admittedly, case material could be fabricated or distorted by exaggeration or memory lapses; yet the various percentages Rhine compiled remained steady over time, a result hardly to be expected if the cases had been the result of deceit (Dean, 1974, 161).

L.E. Rhine (1977), however, stated that case studies possessed inherent weakness and depended upon experimental investigations to provide the strongest evidence for psi. Indeed, she conducted laboratory research and wrote experimental articles about both ESP (e.g., Rhine, 1937) and PK (e.g., Rhine, 1951). She would serve as another example of the Analytical Scientist, demonstrating the errors one could make in categorizing people on superficial grounds such as the type of research they typically perform.

One might suggest that Ian Stevenson (e.g., 1974) is a better example of a Particular Humanist. Like L.E. Rhine, he collected cases of spontaneous ESP claiming that they helped to illuminate knowledge of psi processes (Stevenson, 1970). He asserted that laboratory tests often inhibit ESP because of the controls utilized (p. 9) and pointed out that experiments may be flawed; "judgments about whether or not extrasensory perception did occur in a particular experiment depend upon a complex assessment of all sorts of factors, including how much confidence to place in the competence and integrity of both subjects and investigators" (p. 10). This assessment of probabilities, Stevenson observed, is exactly what is needed when judging spontaneous cases. "They too rest on the integrity, accuracy of memory, and attention to detail of percipients, witnesses, and investigators" (ibid.).

For many years Stevenson chaired the Psychiatry Department in the University of Virginia Medical School. When he left that position, he accepted an endowed professorship at the same institution that enabled him to study reincarnation-type phenomena more intensely. Stevenson (1966) has investigated possible reincarnation cases in several countries, reporting an interval between the birth of an individual and the supposed previous death that typically varies from five to ten years. In Asia (where most of the cases were collected), the person lived no more than 100 miles from his or her supposed previous home. Sometimes an individual has been taken to that location and allegedly has recognized various places and even, on occasion, specific people. In one case, a woman is said to have given descriptions to her supposed former husband of their life together, correctly stating the location of a box in which she had hidden some money before she died (Stevenson, 1960). In another case, xenoglossy (the speaking of a foreign language to which a person has had no apparent exposure) was reported following a carefully executed case study (Stevenson, 1974). This type of research has not been taken into the laboratory by Stevenson, who stresses the evidential value of case reports, analyzing them from a variety of positions.

Even Ian Stevenson, however, does not fulfill many of the key requirements of a Particular Humanist. He gives the scientific approach a privileged position and takes a cautious stand in regard to the implications of his data, unlike the typical Particular Humanist who is action-oriented, poetic, and admittedly biased. An excellent example of a Particular Humanist would be Hans Bender (e.g., 1958/1959), the founder and director of the Institute for Border Areas of Psychology and Psychohygiene in Freiburg, West Germany. Bender's case studies have involved a wide range of alleged psi phenomena including precognitive dreaming (1966) and poltergeist activity (1979). A psychologist by training, who received an MD degree while he was in his 70s, he has worked diligently to establish parapsychology in his country. Further, Bender has successfully demonstrated a relentless investigative drive which has resulted in the founding of a journal, The Journal of Parapsychology and Border Areas of Psychology, and the publication of detailed descriptive works in the field (e.g., Bender, 1968, 1972). He seems to place art, philosophy, and mysticism on an equal basis with science as regards the obtaining of knowledge. Finally, he takes an interest in his subjects and the effect that his investigations will have upon their personal development.

Benefits to Parapsychology

Parapsychology might benefit from awareness of this typology for several reasons:

1) In evaluating research, one can make better judgments if one can identify the approach used. The reader might also be wary when one type of scientist, say the Particular Humanist, suddenly begins writing in the style of another type, say the Conceptual Theorist. It is not impossible for a scientist to master more than one approach, but the parapsychological literature is filled with instances of poor theory and inadequate research resulting from competent investigators who simply strayed too far afield from their area and mode of expertise.

2) Historians of parapsychology might observe how the typology of prominent researchers influenced the direction taken by the field. There are fads and fancies in parapsychology just as there are in other sciences. However, it may be the case that significant research emphases occur when the representative of a given typology coincides with a research approach which happens to be in vogue at that time. Particular humanists would have been in the forefront of research activity early in the century only to be superseded by analytical scientists in the 1930s and 1940s as laboratory experimentation found favor.

3) In working with students interested in parapsychology, a teacher can obtain clues as to each student's optimal type. When writing essays, does a student gravitate toward analysis or conceptualization, toward particulars or abstraction? Is an experimental approach preferred or does the student relish descriptive studies? When answering questions, does a student use specific examples or make generalizations? There is no need to force a premature closure on any one approach for a student. In addition, there are some problem-solving strategies which need to be acquired by all future parapsychologists. Further, it is possible that a number of exceptional students will be able to attain eminence using more than one style. Nevertheless, an awareness of the possible types can enrich the contributions made by teachers to the budding psi researchers in their classes.

4) I have often taken the position that criticism needs to be an integral part of parapsychology. The scientific enterprise, at its best, is self-correcting and the corrective mechanisms have operated most effectively when they have allowed for a dialogue which sharpens and focuses the dialectical process. Some critics are Analytical Scientists who analyze experimental data, attempting to identify methodological shortcomings and offering suggestions for improvement. Some critics are Conceptual Theorists who have traditionally taken a skeptical position on the existence of psi in terms of their own understanding of the nature of reality, especially as revealed by physics, chemistry, and psychoneurology. Other critics are Conceptual Humanists who point out the role that belief systems and personality traits play in the evaluation of parapsychological data. A Conceptual Humanist might also discuss the proclivity of so-called gifted subjects in psi research studies to use trickery to enhance their reputations, or the propensity of overly enthusiastic experimenters to disregard data that are not in accord with their

biases or attitudes. The Particular Humanist may investigate specific case reports, pointing out how a purported psi event might be explained by leakage, faulty memory, deliberate falsification, or fraud. As an action-oriented investigator, the Particular Humanist often makes a personal visitation to determine whether previous reports stand up under careful scrutiny. It is apparent that critics enter the parapsychological arena with different types of expertise; a Particular Humanist might be out of his or her league analyzing an experimental series, just as a Conceptual Theorist might prove to be naive and unqualified in criticizing a case study.

5) In determining the direction of their own contributions, parapsychologists might take stock of their own personal type. In selecting a research question and the mode of investigation, one must take care that one is following the best approach not only for the topic but for the investigator. If a Conceptual Humanist were to naively embark upon an experimental study, there might be unforeseen difficulties (especially if the tasks involved were attempted without a consultant). If a Particular Humanist were to forge into the arena of abstract theory, a waste of time and talent might result. A function of graduate education should be to expose individuals to all four lines of investigation in the social sciences--but without elevating one approach above the others or insisting that all students be competent in each mode of inquiry. The outstanding contributions in parapsychological theory and research have been made by people quite familiar with ways to make maximum use of their own investigative strengths. Perhaps a project for the future would involve bringing together researchers of different types to coordinate their efforts on a single problem. For this to succeed, a systems model of social science is needed that would utilize all four approaches in psi research.

A Systems Model of Science

Just as the personality breaks down into two components, the perceiving component served by sensation or intuition, and the conceptual component served by thinking or feeling, so science itself may be considered as consisting of two components. The heuristic component is that concerned with hypothesis testing, theory in itself, and the acquisition of knowledge. The hermeneutic component is that concerned with hypothesis formation, application of theory, and the interpretation of knowledge. It is the contention of Mitroff and Kilman (1978) that a complete science cannot occur unless both components are present in a dynamic balance.

In broad terms, the heuristics of science are accomplished by the thinking personality types: the Analytical Scientist and the Conceptual Theorist. Hermeneutics in science is most readily accomplished by the feeling types: the Conceptual and Particular Humanists. A balanced science can only be one whose frontiers are guided by considerations of the purposes and goals of discovery. It is especially urgent now, in the light of advances in brain research, biology, and quantum physics, that the interpretive, guiding, hermeneutic aspect of human knowledge be integrated within the institutional structure of parapsychology.

Science might well be viewed as a human institution, not as a value-free quest for ideal knowledge. Kuhn (1970) has shown that the actual structure of science lies within its community nature, and that scientific revolutions are often engendered by shifts in a paradigm. Paradigms characterize communities of human beings in communication. The scientific community is one such communicating organization that has an especially important place in our society today. It is precisely this community aspect of science that needs to be considered and reconsidered in the light of the possible evolution of human institutions, human values, and human consciousness.

Jung resisted the temptation to systematize his work. However, Mitroff and Kilman (1978, 116-121) have proposed a systems model of science in which each of the four types of social scientists would play an important role. In their model, one can start or end an inquiry at any one of four different points, each of which is a potential candidate for explication by all four research traditions. However, none of the four can be entirely explained by any of the four traditions acting in isolation (see Fig. 1).

The recognition of a Problem Situation can lead to a Conceptual Model which defines that problem in the most basic terms. The choice of a Conceptual Model is tantamount to the choice of a

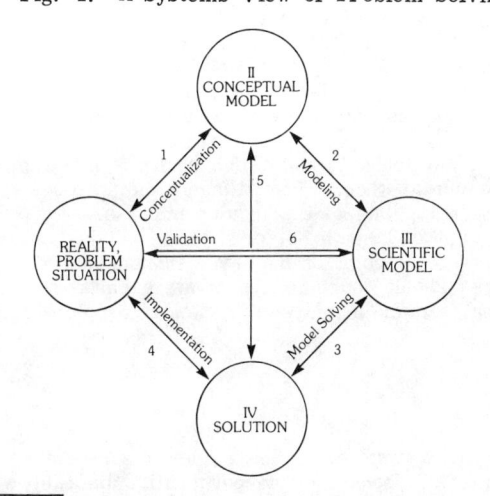

Fig. 1: A Systems View of Problem Solving*

*Reprinted with permission from I.I. Mitroff and R.H. Kilman, Methodological Approaches to Social Science. San Francisco: Jossey-Bass, 1978, p. 117.

world view; for example, the Conceptual Model specifies whether the problem is one of physics, anthropology, or psychology.

Once a Conceptual Model has been chosen, a precise Scientific Model can be formed and a Solution derived from it. For example, if the Scientific Model is mathematical, then the Solution will be formally derived; if the Scientific Model is empirical, then the Solution will be an empirically testable hypothesis. The four points of the model, therefore, are the Problem Situation, the Conceptual Model, the Scientific Model, and the Solution. And if the Solution is finally fed back to the initial Problem Situation for the purpose of taking action on it to remove the problem, it reaches the point of Implementation which constitutes the action-taking phase of problem solving.

Different psychological types, of course, are better suited for some of the phases of the model than for others. The Conceptual Modeling phase is the domain of the Conceptual Theorist and the Conceptual Humanist. But while the Conceptual Theorist stresses the analytical, impersonal features of reality, the Conceptual Humanist emphasizes the personal, human features. Both, however, are concerned with posing significant semantic questions, whether or not they can be asked or answered with the precision of the Analytical Scientist.

Thus the Analytical Scientist is best suited for the Scientific Modeling and Solution phases of inquiry. Here precision and lack of ambiguity are appropriate criteria, but the Analytical Scientists go too far if they insist that these procedures are appropriate at other points of the model.

The Particular Humanist is well suited to the implementation phases of research. Working with individuals, organizations, interpersonal relationships, and issues of timing are important here; the Particular Humanist is extremely sensitive to these issues.

It makes no sense to ask which phase is most important for all presuppose one another. The different methodological types are attuned to different points of the inquiry process. But sometimes one type will want to take the favored phase out of context and make it the privileged focal point of inquiry. Instead of fighting each other, the types should learn to appreciate each other as they all have something to offer if a systems view of problem solving is adopted.

An Example

As an illustration, we might review the recent literature on individuals suffering from multiple-personality disorder who report psi experiences when a particular personality emerges (e.g., Hawksworth, 1977; Keyes, 1981; Pittillo and Sizemore, 1977). We could state that as our Problem Situation and initiate investigation of this

alleged phenomenon by sending a questionnaire to study purported
psi experiences. Our decision to use the questionnaire would define the Conceptual Model as that of psychology. The Analytical
Scientist would give the proposed set of items to as large a population of multiple personality cases as possible in order to ascertain whether the items are each individually and jointly discriminat-
ing enough. The Analytical Scientist would also be concerned with
test-retest reliability of the items. For scales in the questionnaire
to be valid enough for the Analytical Scientist to accept them, they
would have to adhere to some rather precise and vigorous methodological standards. In this fashion, the Scientific Model would
emerge and the investigation could proceed.

One of the major differences between the Analytical Scientist
and the Conceptual Theorist is that the Analytical Scientist uses a
questionnaire to test already formulated hypotheses but the Conceptual Theorist uses it to develop new ideas. The Conceptual Humanist might use the questionnaire scales as a projective technique, allowing multiple personality cases to verbalize their reactions to the
collection of questionnaire items. The Particular Humanist might
use the questionnaire as an opportunity to elicit personal stories
about multiple personality cases reporting psi experiences. Thus
the same questionnaire could serve different purposes for the different approaches, each of them making a contribution to the solution of the problem. If the problem outcome was supportive of the
psi hypothesis, the data could be applied in psychotherapy with multiple personality disorders, fulfilling the Application phase of the
system.

A new problem analysis and scientific model could then be
proposed. A group of mentally healthy, highly hypnotically suscep-
tible subjects could be given suggestion that they were gifted "psychic sensitives," either historical or imaginary. The Analytical
Scientist could design a series of psi tasks for them to attempt in
their new roles. In other words, the multiple personality syndrome
could be experimentally induced. This would offer no undue risks
because previous research (Kampman, 1976; Raikov, 1976) has demonstrated that absence of psychopathology is associated with the ability of hypnotic subjects to take on an imaginary identity. Part of
the experimental design, of course, would involve giving similar instructions to nonhypnotized role-playing subjects as well as to low-
susceptibility subjects who would serve as controls. Should robust
psi scores emerge from a series of experiments of this nature, the
Particular Humanist could make individual case studies of the most
outstanding subjects. The Conceptual Humanist could attempt to relate those findings to personal identity theory. The Conceptual Theorist could propose biochemical and psychoneurological mechanisms
that may be involved, perhaps relating the ideas to data already obtained from multiple personality cases using electroencephalographic
and nucleo-magnetic resonance technology.

A similar procedure could also be applied to a number of
other problems in parapsychology, utilizing a systems approach

which is both holistic and scientific--and which would incorporate criticism. This systems approach might even bring psi research into the mainstream of scientific inquiry in a way that builds upon rather than negates a century of investigation. It would also reward discipline and excellence for each of the four psychological types, honoring the various research styles but coordinating them in a way that would advance knowledge in a field which urgently needs both theory and data, both hypotheses and solutions.

References

Beloff, J. Historical overview. In B. B. Wolman (Ed.), Handbook of Parapsychology. New York: Van Nostrand Reinhold, 1977.

Bender, H. [Mediumistic psychoses: A contribution to the pathology of spiritualistic practices.] Zeitschrift für Parapsychologie und Grenzgebiete der Psychologie, 1958/1959, 2, 173-201.

Bender, H. The Gothenhafen case of correspondence between dreams and future events: A study of motivation. International Journal of Neuropsychiatry, 1966, 2, 398-407.

Bender, H. [The Rosenheim case--an example of spontaneous psychokinesis.] Zeitschrift für Parapsychologie und Grenzgebiete der Psychologie, 1968, 11, 104-112.

Bender, H. The phenomenon of Friedrich Jurgenson. Journal of Paraphysics, 1972, 6, 65-75.

Bender, H. Modern poltergeist research. In J. Beloff (Ed.), New Directions in Parapsychology. London: Paul Elek, 1974.

Dean, E. D. Precognition and retrocognition. In E. D. Mitchell et al. (J. White, Ed.), Psychic Exploration: A Challenge for Science. New York: Putnam's, 1974.

Hawksworth, H. The Five of Me: The Autobiography of a Multiple Personality. Chicago: Henry Regnery, 1977.

Jung, C. G. Psychological Types. (Collected works, Vol. 6.) Princeton, N.J.: Princeton University Press, 1971. (Originally published 1921.)

Kahn, S. D. Ave atque vale: Gardner Murphy. Journal of the American Society for Psychical Research, 1980, 74, 37-52.

Kampman, R. Hypnotically induced multiple personality: An experimental study. International Journal of Clinical and Experimental Hypnosis, 1976, 24, 215-227.

Keyes, D. The Minds of Billy Milligan. New York: Random House, 1981.

LeShan, L. Physicists and mystics: Similarity in world view. Journal of Transpersonal Psychology, 1969, 1(2), 1-20.

LeShan, L. Psychic phenomena and mystical experience. In E. D. Mitchell et al. (J. White, Ed.), Psychic Exploration: A Challenge for Science. New York: Putnam's, 1974, pp. 571-576. (a)

LeShan, L. The Medium, the Mystic, and the Physicist: Toward a General Theory of the Paranormal. New York: Viking Press, 1974. (b)

LeShan, L. Alternative Realities: The Search for the Full Human Being. New York: M. Evans, 1976.

LeShan, L., and Margenau, H. Einstein's Space and Van Gogh's Sky: Physical Reality and Beyond. New York: Macmillan, 1982.

Maduro, R. J., and Wheelwright, J. B. Analytical psychology. In R. J. Corsini (Ed.), Current Personality Theories. Itasca, IL: F. E. Peacock, 1977.

May, R. The Courage to Create. New York: W. W. Norton, 1975.

Mitroff, I. I., and Kilman, R. H. Methodological Approaches to Social Science. San Francisco: Jossey-Bass, 1978.

Pittillo, E. S., and Sizemore, C. C. I'm Eve. New York: Jove, 1977.

Raikov, V. L. The possibility of creativity in the active stage of hypnosis. International Journal of Clinical and Experimental Hypnosis, 1976, 24, 258-268.

Rao, K. R. Theories of psi. In S. Krippner (Ed.), Advances in Parapsychological Research: 2. New York: Plenum Press, 1978.

Rhine, J. B. Experiments bearing on the precognitive hypothesis. Journal of Parapsychology, 1938, 2, 38-54.

Rhine, J. B. Extrasensory perception. Boston: Bruce Humphries, 1973. (Originally published, 1934.)

Rhine, J. B. History of experimental studies. In B. B. Wolman (Ed.), Handbook of Parapsychology. New York: Van Nostrand Reinhold, 1977.

Rhine, L. E. Some stimulus variations in extrasensory perception with child subjects. Journal of Parapsychology, 1937, 1, 102-113.

Rhine, L. E. Placement PK tests with three types of objects. Journal of Parapsychology, 1951, 15, 132-138.

Rhine, L. E. Subjective forms of spontaneous psi experiences. Journal of Parapsychology, 1953, 17, 77-114.

Rhine, L. E. Psychological process in ESP experiences, Part I. Waking experiences. Journal of Parapsychology, 1962, 26, 88-111.

Rhine, L. E. Research methods with spontaneous cases. In B. B. Wolman (Ed.), Handbook of Parapsychology. New York: Van Nostrand Reinhold, 1977.

Rhine, L. E. The Invisible Picture. Jefferson, N. C.: McFarland, 1981.

Stevenson, I. The evidence for survival from claimed memories of former incarnations, Part I. Journal of the American Society for Psychical Research, 1960, 54, 51-71.

Stevenson, I. Twenty cases suggestive of reincarnation. Proceedings of the American Society for Psychical Research, 1966, 26, 1-362.

Stevenson, I. Telepathic Impressions: A Review and Report of Thirty-five New Cases. Charlottesville: University Press of Virginia, 1970.

Stevenson, I. Xenoglossy: A review and Report of a Case. Proceedings of the American Society for Psychical Research, 1974, 31, 1-368.

Stevenson, I. Cases of the Reincarnation Type. Vol. I: Ten Cases in India. Charlottesville: University Press of Virginia, 1975.

Stevenson, I. Cases of the Reincarnation Type. Vol. 3: Twelve Cases in Lebanon and Turkey. Charlottesville: University Press of Virginia, 1980.

Villoldo, A., and Krippner, S. Quantum theory and "psychic healing." Humanistic Psychology Institute Review, 1981, 3(1), 41-56.

Walker, E. H. Consciousness and quantum theory. In E. D. Mitchell et al. (J. White, Ed.), Psychic Exploration: A Challenge for Science. New York: Putnam's, 1974.

Walker, E. H. Foundations of paraphysical and parapsychological phenomena. In L. Oteri (Ed.), Quantum Physics and Parapsychology. New York: Parapsychology Foundation, 1975.

RIP 1982 ERRATA

Corrections are listed in the order in which they appear in RIP 1982 (Scarecrow, 1983).

On pages 110-111: P. J. Kejariwal, the senior author of the brief by Kejariwal, A. Chattopadhya, and J. K. Choudhury, "Some Observations on the Phantom Leaf Effect," has submitted the following statement re their paper:

> I would like to bring to the notice of RIP readers an irregularity in our report on the "phantom leaf effect": On a subsequent follow-up of the work we found that the phenomenon seemed to depend on one particular operator who was our research assistant. He disappeared without notice when the occasion arose to demonstrate the effect to foreign visiting scientists and we now suspect that he was producing a spurious effect. At all events, I have since failed to obtain the effect and would suggest, therefore, that our report will need to be reassessed. The effect we got might be explained by electrostatic forces which allow the leaf to oscillate in the air gap in our apparatus and the oscillating corona discharge would then fill the gap of the cut portion which, to visual observation, would appear as a phantom effect. I now no longer believe that the phenomenon exists but I would still be interested to hear from anyone who thinks he or she has a proof of its existence.
>
> Prakesh Kejariwal
>
> Sitaram Chartia Institute of Scientific Research
> 55 Gariahat Road
> Calcutta - 700 019, India

On pages 224-225: Richard Loosemore should be listed as delivering the Cambridge University Society for Psychical Research brief, "Transmission of Emotion by Psi under Hypnosis as Measured by Galvanic Skin Response," not Bernard Carr.

On page 291: The last two lines of the second paragraph of

"Psychical Research and Parapsychology: Notes on the Development of Two Disciplines," by I. Grattan-Guinness, should read:

> of its members, Rudolph Carnap, published in 1928 as his an outline of the Circle's ideas on "the logical structure of the world."

On page 303: The second citation for Bertrand Russell was published in 1946. "New ed." should be deleted.

NAME INDEX

Ackles, L. 78-80
Alvarado, C. S. 117-18
Anderson, M. 102-103
Angelini, R. F. 35-38
Ashraf, I. 81
Assailly, A. 12
Atkinson, G. 35
Auerbach, L. 120

Barker, P. 32-33, 78, 93-94
Barnes, A. 4
Barrett, W. 5
Batcheldor, K. 1, 102
Beloff, J. 39-42, 153, 155, 164
Bender, H. 158, 164
Benor, D. J. 122, 126
Berendson, J. 14
Berger, A. S. 104-107
Bergson, H. 10
Bierman, D. J. 14
Bjerre, P. 5
Blackmore, S. J. 42-44, 57-61
Braud, L. W. 3, 78-80, 92
Braud, W. G. 1-3, 6, 14-18, 92
Braude, S. viii, 123
Brittain, B. 114-16
Broughton, R. viii-xi, 2-4
Budzynki, T. xi

Cassidy, R. E. 120
Cassirer, E. 125
Chevako, R. J. 80-81
Child, I. 85, 94
Christopher, M. 120
Collins, H. M. 45-46
Collymore, J. L. 30-31

Couch, V. 114-16
Cox, W. E. 107-10

D'Alembert, J. 132
Dean, D. 81-83, 157, 164
DeDiana, I. P. F. 2
Descartes, R. 42
Dicara, L. V. 47-48
Dierkens, J. 2, 6
Drab, K. 43
Duke, D. M. 78
Dunne, B. J. 86-89, 129
Dunne, J. W. 75
Dworkin, B. R. 47-48

Eastman, M. 43
Edge, H. viii
Edison, T. 132
Einstein, A. 132
Eleveld, A. 26-27
Exner, J. 112

Flew, A. 41
Fresnel, A. J. 132
Freud, S. 143

Galileo 131
Gallup, G. 67
Garrett, E. 111, 113, 156
Geller, U. 110
Giesler, P. V. 83-84
Girard, J.-P. 2, 6
Goddard, R. H. 132
Goodrum, S. 11
Gordon, S. 120
Grad, B. 81-83
Gregory, A. 6

Gregory, E. 101
Grimson, R. C. 72-74

Haraldsson, E. 57, 62-66
Hasted, J. 110
Hawksworth, H. 162, 164
Hayes, P. 115
Healy, J. 111-13
Hemlich, J. 22
Henson, R. 108-10
Hill, S. 2
Honegger, B. 42-44
Honorton, C. viii, 32-33, 102, 124
Hooks, C. 10
Hooks, I. 10
Houtkooper, J. M. 2
Hovelmann, G. H. 44-47
Huegel 11
Hurst, L. A. 9

Ille, G. 82
Irwin, H. 4, 57
Isaacs, J. 1

Jahn, R. xi, 86-89, 127-38
Jung, C. G. 41, 123, 125, 143-44, 153-54, 161, 164

Kahn, S. D. 164
Kampman, R. 163-64
Kanthamani, B. K. 6
Kaplan, E. 115
Keane, P. 145
Kelly, E. F. 94
Kennedy, J. E. 53
Kepler, J. 131
Keyes, D. 162, 164
Kilman, R. H. 153, 155, 160-61, 165
Knipe, L. F. xi, 61-62
Koch, S. 125
Koenen, C. 14
Koestler, A. 41
Kohr, R. L. 57
Kramer, U. 28-30
Krippner, S. xi, 121, 123-27, 153-66
Kuhn, T. 44-46, 161

Kuipers, C. 14
Kulagina, N. 2, 5-6
Kyles, W. 78-80

L'Abate, L. 123, 125
Lavoisier, A.-L. 132
Leaf, W. 5
Leary, P. 22, 24
Leibniz, G. W. 42
Leonard, G. O. 111
LeShan, L. 125-26, 156, 165
Levi, A. 85
Lindbergh, C. A. 132
Louman, J. 14
Louwerens, N. G. 102

McBeath, M. K. 47-48
McClenon, J. 110
McCormick, D. xi, 68
Mach, E. 132
Maduro, R. J. 154, 165
Maher, M. 3, 18-21, 115-16
Maissan, F. 14
Malon, J. 120
Manning, M. 2
Margenau, H. 156
Marx, G. 149-50
May, R. 165
Megargee, E. I. 119
Miller, N. E. 47-48
Milton, J. 85-86
Mitroff, I. 153, 155, 160-61, 165
Monroe, R. 59
Montagno, E. de A. 4-7, 10-13
Morris, R. viii, 33-35, 97
Mulders, C. 104
Muldoon, S. 59
Mutwas, C. 124
Myers, F. W. H. 2, 104

Na, H. 95
Nash, C. B. 21-25
Neidhart, J. G. 107
Nelson, G. 7
Nelson, R. D. 86-89, 129
Neppe, V. M. 7-10
Neylon, A. 85
Nybergh, N. K. 61-62

Name Index

Orme, J. E. 75-76
Osis, K. viii, 60, 68-71
Ostwald, W. 132

Palladino, E. 2
Palmer, J. viii, 6, 25-30, 57-58, 60
Parise, F. 2, 5
Penfield, W. 4
Petrellis, L. 22, 24
Phillips, P. 110
Pinch, T. J. 45-46
Pittillo, E. S. 162, 165
Popper, K. 44, 46
Powers, K. 115
Pratt, J. G. 5

Radin, D. I. 30-31
Raikov, V. L. 163, 165
Randi, J. 120-21
Rao, K. R. 6, 53, 156, 165
Raphael, A. 37
Raven, A. 120
Rayzor, E. P. 114
Rechtschaffer, A. 144, 152
Renan, E. 125
Rhine, J. B. 107, 155, 165
Rhine, L. E. 4-5, 157, 165-66
Richards, J. T. 107-10
Robinson, D. viii
Rogers, S. L. 123-24
Rogo, D. S. 85, 117, 119
Roll, W. G. 1, 4-7, 10-13, 72-74, 114-16, 118-19
Rolling Thunder 124
Rubin, L. 124
Rudolph, L. 33-35, 97
Ruiz, J. G. 89-93
Russo, G. 22-24
Rutherford, E. 132

Sabina, M. 125
Saltmarsh, H. F. 4
Sargent, C. 55, 98-99
Sartre, J.-P. 144
Schechter, E. I. 32-33, 49-52, 93-94
Schlitz, M. 14-18
Schmeidler, G. R. xi, 3, 6, 94-96, 98-100, 112, 115-16, 126
Schmidt, H. 33-35, 83, 96-98
Schneider, R. 2, 6
Schouten, S. A. 4-6
Serios, T. 2
Shakespeare, W. 137, 142
Sheldrake, R. 48
Shelp, B. 145, 147, 149-50
Silvio M. 2
Sizemore, C. C. 162, 165
Solfvin, G. 6, 118
Sondow, N. 75-78, 145
Stahla, R. 101
Stanford, B. 37
Stanford, R. G. 4, 35-38, 53, 55, 85
Stevenson, I. 105, 107, 157-58, 166
Streber, K. 98-100
Swets, J. A. 37

Taddonio, J. L. 53
Tart, C. T. 76, 122
Tedder, W. 100-101
Tellegen, A. 35
Thalbourne, M. xi, 40, 62-67
Thouless, R. 104-107
Tolaas, J. 144, 152
Tornatore, R. P. 102-103
Tribbe, F. C. viii, 104-107
Truzzi, M. 120
Twitchell, A. 147-48
Tyrrell, G. N. M. 85

Ullman, M. xi, 6, 138-52

Van de Castle, R. 138
Van der Velden, I. 26
Varvoglis, M. P. 32-33, 93-94
Villoldo, A. 156, 166

Walker, E. H. 155-56, 166
Wasson, G. 125
Watkins, A. M. 5
Watkins, G. K. 2, 5
Watson, G. 91
Weeks, G. R. 123, 125

Weiner, D. H. 52-56, 115
Wheelwright, J. B. 154, 165
White, R. A. vii-ix, 5, 103
Williams, L. 66-67
Williams, W. B. 72-73
Windelbad, P. 125

Winkelman, M. 84
Wolman, B. B. 87

Young, T. 131

SUBJECT INDEX

Aberdeen Research and Development Center (U.S. Army)   156
absorption   32, 35-38, 70; see also attention; concentration
Advances in Parapsychological Research   6
Adventures in Immortality   67
age differences   43-44, 60, 63, 65, 84
agent   6
   experimenters as   16
   -percipient relationship   6, 25, 28, 71, 156
   role of   85-86
aggression   6
altered states of consciousness   8, 12, 43, 76, 78, 122-23; see also dissociation
American Institute of Aeronautics and Astronautics   136
American Journal of Orthopsychiatry   123
American Medical Association   136
American Physical Society   136
American Rocket Society   136
American Society for Psychical Research   61, 68, 70, 140, 145, 147-48
amygdala   6
Anabiosis   43
anger   6
anomalies   31-32, 41
anxiety   15, 54
apparitions   57, 68-71, 114-16, 125; see also hallucinations
   duration of   69
   interpretation of   70-71
   time lag in   71
applications   134; see also criminal investigation and psi; PK--on equipment
archetypes   144
arousal   1-2, 6, 15
astral projection   42; see also out-of-body experiences
astrology   42, 64
attention   1, 4, 6, 28, 35; see also absorption; concentration
attitudes   20, 129-36; see also belief; sheep-goat differences; surveys
   changes of   71
   toward experiment   103
   toward experimenter   78
   toward Ganzfeld   37-38
   toward psi   28, 32, 62, 102, 124, 159
   toward targets   80, 100

auras 113
automatisms 2
autonomic activity see nervous system
awakenings, false 43-44
Ayer Foundation 156

behavioral response 19
belief 13, 62-66, 159; see also attitudes; sheep-goat differences
    in psi 32, 58-60, 63-65, 78, 120-21
    in survival 59-60, 62-67, 69-71, 107
benefit rule see motivation
bias 50, 57; see also random event generators--bias
biochemistry and behavior 90, 93; see also physiological factors
biofeedback 47-48
biomedicine 30-31
birth, type of 43-44
body image 57-58, 60
boredom 86
brain 4-7; see also hemispheric differences; reticular formation;
    temporal lobe
  stem 10-13
  waves 2, 18-21
Brazil 83
Buddhism 67

Caesarean section 43-44
caffeine 2
causality 123-25, 143
Christianity 67
circadian rhythm 6-7
City College, CUNY 18, 75, 94, 98, 126
clairvoyance 14, 17, 19-21, 85-86, 100-101, 157; see also remote
    viewing
cognitive factors 3-5, 15, 18-21, 35, 37-38; see also arousal; attention; boredom; concentration; hallucinations; imagery; intention
coincidences 42, 75, 148-49; see also synchronicity
Columbia Medical Center 147-48
communication
  model of ESP 39-40
  with deceased 7, 112
competitiveness 32
concentration 86, 101; see also absorption; attention
conditioning, operant 47
confidence 54
conformance behavior model 53
connectedness 143-44, 151
consciousness 4-6, 40-41, 78, 87, 89, 144-45, 152, 156, 161; see
    also altered states of consciousness; dreams; unconscious processes
  and apparitions 68, 71

during out-of-body experiences 59
control 41
    of dreams 43-44
    of nervous system 16-17
creativity 113
criminal investigation and psi 72-74
critics 33-35, 132, 135, 159-60; see also methodology--criticism of; skeptics
cross-correspondences 4
curare 47-48

decline effect 28, 31, 47-48, 54-55
defense mechanisms 139-40
defensiveness 64
déjà vu 9-10, 75
demographic variables 57-58, 60, 63-66, 78, 102; see also age differences; sex differences
depersonalization 8
differential effect 17, 24, 28; see also preferential effect
"direct" writing see writing, "direct"
displacement effect 85-86
dissociation 6; see also multiple personality; schizophrenia
divination 42
dreams 4-6, 58, 138-52, 157
    control of 43-44
    falling 43-44
    flying 58, 60
    lucid 42-44, 57-58, 60
    precognitive 75-77, 125, 140, 158
    recall of 32, 57, 59-60, 63-64
drugs 89, 124; see also curare
dualism 39, 41
Duke University 155
duration of experimental session 23, 37-38
dyslexia 113

Edinburgh University 39, 85, 153
education see demographic variables; schooling
electrodermal activity 14-18
emotions 1, 5-7, 15, 19-20, 78, 100, 111-13, 119, 142-43, 146, 151-52
energy and ESP 39
engineering 129
epilepsy 4, 6, 8-9, 12, 118-19, 124; see also temporal lobe
ESP 1, 3-7, 25, 38-40, 141; see also clairvoyance; precognition; telepathy
    calling, speed of 94-96
    form of 4
    research 31
    selectivity of 40
    signal transmission model of 3

subject matter of 6, 40
  super- 70-71
ESP and Psychokinesis 123
European Journal of Parapsychology 2, 4-6, 98
Evidence of Personal Survival from Cross-Correspondences 4
expectation 26, 51-52, 117, 119
experimenter
  as agent 16
  effect 18, 29, 31, 52-53, 122
  -subject relationship 78, 97, 103, 122, 156, 158
  successful 33
extinction, belief in 66-67
Extrasensory Perception After Sixty Years 54
extraversion 1, 6, 32-33, 78, 94, 153

false awakenings 43-44
fantasy 13, 70, 102-103, 112, 114
feedback 14, 16, 18, 28, 32-34, 37, 54, 80, 86-87, 89, 97, 101
feeling 154, 160
fields 31, 40, 122, 141, 143, 151, 156
Flewism 41
formative causation 48
Foundations of Physics 97
fraud 9, 34-35, 47-48, 70, 108-109, 159-60
free-response 14, 25, 28
FRNM see Institute for Parapsychology

Gallup Poll 62
Ganzfeld 1, 14, 35-38, 78-80, 85-86
  pink noise vs. silence in 35-38
genetic factors 9, 40
groups, sitter see sitter groups

hallucinations 8-9, 57-58, 60, 71; see also apparitions
Handbook of Parapsychology 6, 87
healing 11, 64, 83, 123-25, 139-40, 156; see also shock and healing
  experiments 17, 81-83
heart rate 2, 47
hemispheric differences 2-4, 7, 18-21; see also laterality
  and psychological factors 18-19
hemispheric interactions 4
Henry the Fifth 137
hidden variables 156
Hinduism 67
hippocampi 4-5
holography 10
hormones 11-12
Human Personality and Its Survival of Bodily Death 104
hypnosis 6, 25-26, 49-52, 123-25, 163
hypothalamus 5, 12

Subject Index

I Ching 124
Iceland 57, 63, 65
imagery 5, 15, 57-60, 70, 140-43, 151, 157
   hypnagogic 43-44
   vs. verbal responses 4
India 63
individual differences 42
   in PK output 89
infrared 81-83
instinct 5
Institute for Applied Biology 156
Institute for Border Areas of Psychology and Psychohygiene 158
Institute for Parapsychology 1, 52
Institute of Aeronautical Sciences 136
Institute of Atmospheric and Space Physics 155
instrumentation 133
intelligence 66-67
intention 42, 133; see also volition
International Brotherhood of Magicians 120
International Journal of Neuropsychiatry 4
International Journal of Parapsychology 12, 81
introversion 80, 153
intuition 4, 41, 153-54, 157, 160

J. B. Rhine Address xi
Japan 63
John E. Fetzer Foundation 86
John F. Kennedy University 83, 89, 117, 119
Journal of Abnormal Psychology 35, 119
Journal of the American Society for Psychical Research 1, 3-6, 8,
   10, 15, 43, 53, 57, 85, 92, 96, 105, 115
Journal of Parapsychology 4-6, 34, 53, 94, 97, 102-104, 155
Journal of Parapsychology and Border Areas of Psychology 158
Journal of Religion and Psychical Research 104
Journal of the Society for Psychical Research 2-3, 55, 57
judging 14, 25
   by subject 80

lability 17
language 142, 144
   and hemispheres 18-19
   foreign, knowledge of 4
laterality 113
learning 11, 47-48
Learning Tests for Survival 104
levitation 107, 110
limbic system 5-6

McDonnell Foundation 86
McDonnell Laboratory for Psychical Research 109

McGill University 81
magic 42
Magic Circle, The 120
magicians xi, 108, 120-21
Maimonides Dream Laboratory 139
majority vote technique 72
Marburg University 44
media 135
meditation 1, 8
mediums 4, 7, 10-13, 64, 68, 112, 156; see also psychics; séances; shamans
  physical 1, 6
  trance 7
memory 4-6, 11-12
  and precognitive dreams 75-77
MENSA 66
metabolic type 89-93
metal-bending 1-2, 11-12
metaphors 140-43, 145, 148-50, 152
metaphysics 39, 41-42; see also philosophy
Methodological Approaches to Social Sciences 153
methodology ix, 7, 49-52, 76, 105-207, 122, 125-26, 132-34, 136, 151-52, 155-64; see also judging; majority vote technique; process-oriented research; signal detection theory
  criticism of 7, 25, 50, 125
mind-brain relationship 9, 39-42; see also psychosomatic medicine
Mind Science Foundation 1, 14, 33, 96
mini-lab 107-10
mood 78, 80, 86, 91
morphogenetic fields 122
motivation 15, 28, 53-56, 73, 86, 112, 143, 147; see also purpose
motor activity 5
movement of objects 5
multiple personality 113, 162-63; see also dissociation; schizophrenia
mysticism 57-60, 63-64, 156-58
myth 144

near-death experiences (NDEs) 68, 71
need 15, 18, 53, 116
nervous system 1-13, 15-17, 118-19; see also physiological factors
  self-control of 16-17
nervousness 15

observational theory 40-41, 53
Ohrstrom Foundation 86
On the Threshold of the Unseen 5
operant conditioning see conditioning, operant
out-of-body experiences (OBEs) 42-44, 57-61
  characteristics of 59
  circumstances for 59

duration of 59
 ESP in 57, 59
 incidence of 57-58
 multiple 57, 59
 theories of 57, 60

Paradoxical Psychotherapy 123, 125
paragnost see mediums; psychics; shamans
Parapsychologica 7
Parapsychological Association viii, 62
 conventions vii-ix, xi, 81, 93, 148
 Council of 121, 127
Parapsychological Journal of South Africa 9
parapsychology 39
 funding and 134
 history of 159
 organizations professing interest in 61-62
 science and 44-47, 130-38, 156
 societies in 136
Parapsychology Foundation 83
Parapsychology Information Network 100
Parapsychology Review 6
perception 31, 41, 70
 subliminal 1
percipient-agent relationship 6, 25, 28, 71, 156
personality factors 9, 153-64; see also extraversion; introversion; psychological factors; religiosity
 and belief in survival 63-66
Personality Strength and Psycho-Chemical Energy 91
personality tests; see also psychological tests
 Betts' Questionnaire upon Mental Imagery 68
 Cattell Sixteen Personality Factor Questionnaire (16PF) 64-65
 Messer's Matching Familiar Figures Test (MFFT) 95-96
 MMPI 119
 Myers-Briggs Type Indicator Extraversion/Introversion 32-33, 94
 Rotter's Internal-External Locus of Control Scale 65
 Tellegen's Differential Personality Questionnaire 32, 68
 Thurston's Closure Speed Test 68
"Philip" group 1
philosophy 44-47, 158
photography 108, 110
physicalism 39-41
physics 39-41, 134, 156
physiological factors 1-19, 31, 89-93, 118-19; see also energy and ESP; heart rate; hormones; metabolic type; mind-brain relationship; motor activity; nervous system; pulse; respiration; water retention
physiological responses 47-48
piezoelectric sensors 1
PK 1-7, 28-29, 34, 41, 83, 96-98; see also levitation; metal-bending; movement of objects; poltergeists; release-of-effort

effect; sitter groups
  games 32-33
  macro- 5-6, 87, 89, 107-10
  micro- 1, 87, 129
  on biological targets 14-18, 21-25
  on equipment 17
  precognition and 76
  retro- 122
Poltergeist, The 5, 118
poltergeists 1, 5-6, 117-19, 158
  Lessing case 5
  Olive Hill case 5
  Peter (case of) 6
position effects see decline effect; displacement effect; psi-missing
precognition 64-65, 70-71, 75-77, 100-101, 125, 129, 140, 148, 150, 157-58
  time lag and 75-77, 150
preferential effect 17, 86; see also differential effect
Presidential Address xi, 153-66
"primary process" ideation 1
Princeton Engineering Anomalies Research 86, 127, 129
probability 155
Proceedings IEEE 87
Proceedings of the Parapsychological Association 6, 124; see also Research in Parapsychology
Proceedings of the Society for Psychical Research 2, 5, 43, 85, 104
process-oriented research 94
Program Committee xiii-ix, xi, 127
psi 7, 34, 41-42, 146; see also theories
  assumptions about 55
  biochemical changes and 89-93
  definition of 41
  distribution of 155
  dreams and 138-52
  existence of 33, 35, 39, 121
  integration of 7, 9
  limits of 52-55
  nonintentional 52-56
  schooling and 84
  sensitivity, development of 147, 151
  source of 52-56
Psi and States of Awareness 2, 6
"Psi Ball" 93-94
psi-conducive conditions 1-2, 5-6, 28, 38, 49-52, 78, 89-93, 100-101, 125, 142; see also Ganzfeld; hypnosis
psi-hitting 78, 80, 96, 99
psi-mediated instrumental response (PMIR) model 53
psi-missing 28, 38, 54-55, 85, 92-93, 99
Psychical Entertainers Association 120
Psychical Research Foundation 1, 4, 10, 72, 114-15, 118
psychics 9, 10, 105, 108, 111-14; see also mediums
  and criminal investigations 72-74

Subject Index

psychoanalysis 139, 151
Psychoenergetic Systems 102
psychological factors 2, 4, 6, 12, 18-19, 32, 42, 93-94, 100, 102, 111-13, 117-19, 122; see also absorption; aggression; anger; anxiety; arousal; belief; competitiveness; confidence; defense mechanisms; defensiveness; emotions; expectation; mood; motivation; need; nervousness; personality factors; resistance; stress
psychological tests 113, 117-19; see also personality tests
   Defense Mechanism Test 64
   Rorschach Test 5, 112, 117, 119
   Tellegen Absorption Scale 35-36
   Thematic Apperception Test 113, 119
   Wilson and Barber ICMI Scale 13, 114-15
psychology, cognitive 3
Psychology of Déjà Vu, The 10
psychometry 11
psychopathology 112, 117-19, 163; see also dissociation; multiple personality; schizophrenia
Psychophysical Research Laboratories 32, 49, 86, 93, 102
psychosomatic medicine 156
psychotherapy 123-25, 151, 163
publication vii-viii
pulse 2
purpose 42, 68, 71; see also motivation

qualitative factors 75
quantum theory 40-41, 156
Queens Children's Psychiatric Center 111

random event generators (REGs) 28, 32, 34-35, 52-53, 80-81, 87, 89, 93-94, 100, 134
   bias 29, 88, 94, 100
Random Mechanical Cascade 86-89
randomization 50
reason 154; see also thinking
reincarnation 66-67, 158
relaxation 1, 5-6, 15, 28-29, 36-38, 78-79, 92, 102; see also stress; tension
release-of-effort effect 28-30
religiosity 63-65
religious experiences see mysticism
remote viewing 14, 129, 134; see also clairvoyance
repeatability 3, 47-48, 51-52, 131
Research in Parapsychology (RIP) 3, 5-6, 25-26, 32-33, 35, 42, 57, 68, 78, 81, 87, 93, 104, 107, 118; see also Proceedings of the Parapsychological Association
   policies concerning vii-ix
Research Letter 85
resistance 102
resonance 40

respiration 2
resurrection 66-67
reticular formation 5-6
Rhine Address see J. B. Rhine Address
Rorschach testing see psychological tests--Rorschach Test
RSPK see poltergeists

St. John's University 35-37
St. Joseph's University 21-22
Saybrook Institute 102, 123, 127
schizophrenia 112-13; see also dissociation; multiple personality
Schmidt REG 83; see also random event generators
schooling 84
science 44-45, 131-34, 155-58, 160-61
Science 37
séances 114-16
sensation 153-54, 160
sensitives see mediums; psychics
sensory cues 16, 25, 27-28, 49, 78-79, 116
SERPA 11
sex differences 3, 19, 43-44, 63, 65, 67, 98-100; see also demographic variables
Shaman, The 123
shamans 83, 123-25
sheep-goat differences 64-65, 115-16, 122; see also attitudes; belief
shock and healing 123-24
signal detection theory 35, 37
signal processing 80-81
signal transmission model 3
sitter groups 1; see also "Philip" group; SORRAT
skeptics 42, 110; see also attitudes; belief; critics; sheep-goat differences
Society for Psychical Research 93, 104
Society of American Magicians 120
sociocultural factors 9
SORRAT 107
SORRAT 110
sounds 5, 107, 114
South African Society for Psychical Research 7
speed of ESP calling 94-96
Spökerier 5
spontaneous cases 7, 139, 151-52, 157-58, 160; see also apparitions; hallucinations; near-death experiences; out-of-body experiences; poltergeists
  vs. experimental work 151-52, 157-58
strain gauges 1
stress 5, 11-12, 15, 43, 119; see also tension
subjects 135-36; see also agents; mediums; percipients
  animals as 47, 97-98
  children as 102-03
  non-psychic 22, 25, 129, 134
  numbers of 50-51

Subject Index   183

   psi experiments as   8-10
   psychic vs. non-psychic   72-73
   selection of   15, 57-58, 60, 76, 100
subliminal perception   1
sugar, effects of   30-31
suggestibility   123
suggestion   83
superposition effect   96
surveys   5-6, 43-44, 57-67, 76
survival   7, 70-71; see also near-death experiences; reincarnation
   belief about   59-60, 62-67, 69-71, 107
   selective   66-67
   tests   104-107
Survival Research Foundation   104
synchronicity   41-42, 123-25; see also coincidences
Syracuse University   33, 80

targets; see also randomization
   attitude toward   80, 100
   biological   14-18, 21-25
   deity statue as   83-84
   distance from   100
   E. coli as   21-25
   encodability   35-36
   mice as   2
   multiple vs. single   94-95
   names as   98-100
   plants as   17
   pre-recorded   96-97
   qualities   78
   selection   78
telepathy   17, 40, 59-60, 71, 140, 157
temporal lobe   4-5, 7-10
tension   2, 6, 15; see also stress
Texas Southern University   78
theories   3, 40-41, 44-47, 89, 129, 133, 156; see also communication--model of ESP; conformance behavior model; morphogenetic fields; observational theory; physicalism; psi-mediated instrumental response model; quantum theory; signal transmission model; volitional model
Theta   104
thinking   154, 160; see also "primary process" ideation
time   76-77
   of day, and PK tests   89
time lag; see also release-of-effort effect
   in apparition case   71
   in precognitive dreams   75-77, 150
Trafalgar Hospital (New York)   156
trials, number of   50-51

ultraviolet   81

Umbanda 83-84
unconscious processes 19, 143-44, 154
United States 63, 65
University of
 Amsterdam 14
 Bristol 42, 57
 Edinburgh 39, 85, 153
 Iceland 62, 64-65
 Miami 155
 North Carolina 72
 Utrecht 25, 28
 Virginia 117, 138, 158

values 154-56, 161
visualization 15; see also imagery
volition 88-89; see also intention
volitional model 53

Washington University 47, 62, 66
water retention 11-12
West Georgia College 114
word association 36-38
writing, "direct" 109-10

xenoglossy 158